"GET ME SECURITY.

"*This is Bradley Snell. We've had a report of some missing records. I'd like you to contact Dr. Chinsky and start an investigation.*"

As the executive talked, Chinsky slowly, silently, turned around. Snell's long, erect back was to him, the executive's head gently undulated to the rhythm of his words. His long right arm holding the phone gestured emphasis to the unseen audience. Chinsky saw all of this, but his eyes fixed on the phone and the hand that held it. He blinked his eyes clear once, then again to make sure what he saw was actually there.

Snell's slender, patrician fingers cupped the instrument and his manicured thumb held the phone's plunger down. *Snell*, Chinsky realized, *was speaking into an empty phone. . . .*

THE CURE

Frank T. Wydra

A DELL BOOK

Published by
Dell Publishing
a division of
Bantam Doubleday Dell Publishing Group, Inc.
666 Fifth Avenue
New York, New York 10103

This is a work of fiction. Names, characters, places, and incidents are either the product of the author's imagination or are used fictitiously. Any resemblance to actual events, locales, or persons, living or dead, is entirely coincidental.

ISBN: 0-440-21158-1

Printed in the United States of America

Published simultaneously in Canada

November 1992

10 9 8 7 6 5 4 3 2 1

OPM

For Karen Branch Wydra

ACKNOWLEDGMENTS

While this is a novel, thus entirely fictional, the author is grateful to the following people for advice, counsel, information, and support: Bob Brennan, Dr. Richard Gauss, Charlie Keller, Esq., Jill Lamar, Jane Raitt, Ron Rivers, Bob Silverstein, Sandra White, Denise Wydra (my good right arm), Sandi Wydra, Tom Wydra, Sheri Wydra (my cheerleader) and, of course, Roget Hyman and Earl Sweet. Any errors of fact are, of course, my responsibility.

CHAPTER
1

THE RENTED BUICK crept through the posh suburb's back streets. Duke Van Allen flicked off the headlights and killed the engine. Noiselessly the car coasted for a hundred yards, then stopped, snug against the green of a curbless lawn. Across the street and fifty yards ahead, the faint silhouette of a two-story Georgian house nestled against the blackness of the sky. Duke pushed the buttons, and the car's door windows slid into their frames. The cool night air felt fresh.

No light showed from the windows of the house. He didn't expect any; it was four thirty in the morning, and all of Bloomfield Hills was sleeping. From his vantage point he could see what he believed to be the bedroom windows and all three garage doors. If by chance some restless phantom were awake, exploring the road from those windows, it would have been difficult to see the car, so unobtrusively did it meld into its background. He loosened his tie, slouched into the seat, and began his vigil.

After a while even the plush velour of the car seat felt hard. Duke shifted his bulk, easing the pressure on his right buttock. About five forty-five the sky began to lighten. There was no apparent activity in the house, but the world was waking. A jogger moving at a steady, labored pace came around the curve. Duke scrunched down to make himself less visible. It was unnecessary; the jogger paid no attention to the car.

■

David Rathbone rubbed his eyes. The night had been fitful, as unfulfilled dreams pranced on the stage of his mind. He was tired, yet fully awake, as alive as he'd been for two decades. Sleep could wait; it was time to rise, to greet this day with a gusto he thought he'd abandoned.

Today was his day.

Get up, get up, he silently shouted to himself.

God, how long since he had felt like this?

Not since Deoncol. How long ago was that? Twenty years? At least. But even that wasn't like this. Still, those were good days. Two years out of his internship, working with a team of brilliant researchers—Kadlec, Grimm, Duval, and the then chief, Simon—they had developed Hemorect, an adrenocorticosteroid anorectal cream, not earthshaking, but for its time, important. The compound became a cash cow for Croft, his employer. From there, he never looked back. The team of researchers split up; Grimm and he were given their own teams to lead. Kadlec and Duval, both more comfortable as players than leaders, continued to work with Simon. Rathbone's new team blazed forward, developing Dynacin, Leuklux, and finally, Deoncol, the tremendously successful antineoplastic that slowed the reckless rampage of certain cancers. Within five years Simon retired with honor, and he, Rathbone, became chief of research at Croft. Funny, no matter how successful he became, the old days always seemed better. Time, like a necromantic lens, obscured the pain, the frustration, the ignominy of frequent failure and magnified those things he chose to remember: the triumphs.

He sighed and tossed the covers back. No time to reminisce; there was a day to start. His day.

He reached over and gave Anne a pat on her behind, their signal that the bathroom would be free in half an hour.

■

At five o'clock a battered Pontiac wove its way from one circular drive to another. A newspaper flew out the side window, neatly landing near the door of each house. The driver was good at his job; he never came to a stop and most of the papers landed reasonably close to the front doors. At five thirty-five the front door of the two-story Georgian opened and a dark-haired man in a robe picked up the paper. The man surveyed the street, breathing in the dewy morning air as if drinking in the tranquility of the green suburban landscape, then he turned and went inside.

Duke's watch was almost over.

■

The confined space of the shower was an echo chamber adding resonance to Rathbone's deep baritone. At fifty-five he was in good shape: an almost-flat stomach, good muscle tone, and blood pressure of 110 over 72. With a full, thick head of only slightly graying hair, high cheekbones, and a pencil-straight nose, he was TV handsome. Today he hummed "The Impossible Dream," sounding surprisingly like a contented cat.

In the thin air of his soaring thoughts he knew that professionally, medically, and scientifically this work would be the Everest of his career. Perhaps the Everest of his generation's work. Not that he sought professional honor—a lifetime of accomplishment had left him jaded. Engraved brass placards linking his name and that of the American Medical Association, World Research Association, and a dozen other prestigious organizations covered his office wall. One served testimony that the president of the United States had appointed him head of a national commission on medical research. Princeton and Michigan had awarded him honorary doctorates. More recognition was just another jewel on an already studded crown; nice, but adding little sparkle.

Yet there were degrees of recognition.

The accolades of his peers were satisfying, the esteem of his profession, fulfilling. But recognition by the common man presages immortality.

And today that was within his reach. How many men were given that opportunity? One in a generation? Maybe less. Pasteur. Lister. Not many. In his own lifetime, Salk, DeBakey—a self-satisfied smile split his face, aborting the hum—and now him?

He snorted and water splashed from his upper lip. Why? Because of the press? No, that was too generous. Sure, the media had adopted the virus as its own; had broadcast chilling statistics on its swath, had alarmed the people to lurking devastation, had trumpeted every advance of medicine and research, dramatizing the injustice, human suffering, and egalitarian nature of the disease. But the media had not created the virus, only popularized it, and set the stage for the entrance of its conqueror.

He would have more than his fifteen minutes of celebrity.

The Nobel prize was certain, a footnote in history books inevitable. Immortality was within his grasp. Heady thoughts, indeed. He turned the water off and briskly ran the rough pile of the towel over his body as the shower fog dissipated.

■

Duke reached over to the backseat for a black molded plastic case a little longer than and about as thick as a briefcase. Setting it firmly on the front seat, he opened it. Inside was a custom-made .44 Magnum rifle. The barrel, stock, silencer, and scope were each housed in their own sculpted compartments. With care bordering on affection, Duke picked up the barrel, screwed it into the stock, and fitted the silencer to the muzzle. He snapped the scope to the fitting on the barrel. It was sighted in to a minute of angle at one hundred yards. Finally, and again with care, he moved the case to the floorboard and laid the rifle on the seat next to him.

■

Anne popped bran muffins into the microwave while Rathbone sipped his decaf and tried to read the *Free Press*. His concentration wouldn't stay fixed.

He hadn't told Anne. He hadn't told anyone other than Snell, but even so he probably wouldn't have told Anne. They never discussed his work. She was his delight, his social being, his other self. Without her, he would have become a laboratory recluse. But early in their marriage, he learned that things scientific glazed her eyes. She was simply not interested. Her world was that of society, with its intrigues and alliances. He missed the opportunity to tell her of his little triumphs. He had learned to live with her scientific indifference. This, though, was important enough to break the pattern.

"I've got something interesting going on at the lab," he said.

"That's nice," she said. "Speaking of the lab, would you remind Brad that we're getting together tonight. He's such a workaholic, he forgets all his social responsibilities. I've already mentioned it to Joyce, but unless you keep reminding them they'll show up late, and I hate when they do that." Brad Snell, the head of Croft, was Rathbone's boss. More than that, they were close friends. "Everyone," Anne rambled on, "has to wait on them. They don't seem to have any sense of responsibility. I don't mind them being late for cocktails, but dinner—"

"Sure," he interrupted, "I'll see him this morning." So much for sharing.

■

At six thirty, one of the garage doors began to rise.

Time, Duke thought, to go to work. He moved deliberately: starting his engine, raising the windows, and shifting into drive. Foot on the brake, he was ready to move at will. A blue Mercedes 560 SEL sedan backed out of the garage. Rathbone, behind the wheel, didn't seem to notice the Buick as he eased the two hundred and thirty-eight horsepower Mercedes onto the quiet, tree-lined lane. As Duke predicted, Rathbone turned north, heading toward Croft. Duke relaxed the pressure of his foot on the brake and took up position five hundred feet behind the Mercedes.

Rathbone turned onto Telegraph Road and floored the gas pedal. The Mercedes lunged forward and the speedometer jumped to sixty-five, then he eased off. This car was always a joy to drive, one of Rathbone's secret pleasures. The fine German craftsmanship gave him the reassuring feel of well-made laboratory equipment. His confidence in the machine allowed him to relax and think as he drove.

Financially, the cure would be a bonanza; medically, a windfall. In both cases it was an elixir of immense value. A minimum of one—perhaps two—million lives would be saved. My god, a quarter of a million people in the U.S. alone had contracted the disease. A scourge eradicated in one stroke. Pain, suffering, anxiety, trauma, unanticipated death, all banished—at least for a little while. Billions of dollars that would otherwise have been spent on research and ineffective treatment liberated for use elsewhere. And for Croft, thus him, enormous profit. Base metal into gold. He had trod the boardroom carpet long enough to think as much like a businessman as a medical doctor. In his head, he tried calculating the economic impact of the cure. The numbers were too large.

My God, he thought, *I did it! And not as part of a team. Alone!*

Sure, Croft deserved credit for the resources, but it was a high risk, solitary effort that had made it happen. It was a gamble, but it had paid off. It could have failed. What then? Ruin? Probably. Certainly the end of his career. But even then, only if word of the experiment became public. All the more reason for having kept it secret. But it didn't fail—he didn't fail.

He closed his eyes for a second to clear the consequences of failure from his mind. That didn't matter anymore. He *had* done it. He had succeeded. That was the only relevant fact. From here it was all downhill. God, he was tired. Three years of hidden early morning work, late night laboratory trysts, and stolen weekends were taking their toll. The wry thought that he wasn't thirty anymore crossed his mind. But now, standing here on the threshold of immortality, he knew it had been worth the effort. The keen thrill of triumph jolted his veins; this, the electric feel of success, was what life was all about. How few people ever felt it, how few knew its rapture. Still, he was tired; the years of sleeplessness were taking their toll.

■

Lone Pine Road jogged and curved, but the pace of the Mercedes was steady. It was easy to follow. The traffic was light, and Rathbone took all the expected turns. Duke had studied maps of the lake-studded terrain and concluded that this was the easiest route, the one most likely to be followed by Rathbone. Late yesterday Duke had driven this road, and two or three alternates, to get a feel for the terrain. It had been a useful exercise. Some of the turns, while logical on a map, were less so on the ground. He kept a car or two between himself and the Mercedes, making it hard for Rathbone to spot him. Every once in a while he'd reach over and feel the Magnum. Its cool black bulk reassured him.

■

It's time for a news conference, Rathbone thought as he crossed Union Lake Road. But it won't happen unless someone sets the wheels in motion. That's how things were in large corporations. Big business was quick to talk, slow to act, cautious. He wondered if Snell had alerted public relations. Probably not.

Snell was neurotic about keeping the cure a secret. With good cause, Rathbone mused. The vultures in the business of pharmaceuticals would rip the heart from their firstborn to gain information about a competitor's technical advances. It's a wonder, he silently chuckled, remembering the old joke, that they call it ethical drugs.

The thought set his mind racing off on a tangent. The lack of ethics when it came to stealing research bordered on the criminal. Headhunters regularly mined the drug companies to find disaffected employees. A hiring bonus was cheaper than research if the new employee would share his ex-master's secrets. Everyone signed confidentiality agreements, but they were impossible to enforce, and the raiding persisted. Unless a compound was filed with the Food and Drug Administration and the Patent Office, there was no real protection from corporate thievery.

Maybe that's why he hadn't told Chinsky about the work. Luke Chinsky was his associate chief and most trusted subordinate. Ironically, Chinsky didn't trust anyone; the man, brilliant as he was, was a loner, paranoid of betrayal. Christ! This was going to reinforce every suspicion the young doctor ever had about Rathbone. Too bad, it couldn't be helped. It had been difficult developing protocols, conducting the trials, keeping records, administering to patients without the competent services of his principal assistant. But it had been the right decision. Chinsky was too volatile, always demanding his own way, threatening to quit if he didn't get it. He was a perfect target for the rapacious headhunters. One day a recruiter would make a call when Chinsky was in the middle of a rage and he would be gone—and half of Croft's secrets with him. No. That was unfair. Chinsky would not steal from Croft, but there was no way he could fail to draw on his experience. And that experience was a mother lode of proprietary information.

He smiled. After the filing today, there would be little need to maintain total secrecy. Some would still be necessary, but at least he could bring Luke Chinsky and some of the other researchers into the picture. Keeping his key subordinates outside the curtain of information while he did his preliminary tests was, he admitted, the biggest strain. Was he being truthful? How much of his paranoia was caused by security and how much by the thrill of the lone chase? He had drafted the company's security policy. He could have voided it. He was the one who insisted on strict compartmentalization of each area of inquiry. He could have breached the barriers. But to do so would have meant sharing glory. And in his soul he knew that this triumph must remain unshared, his alone.

There was also the possibility—though he hated to admit it—that he had concealed his work from Chinsky solely out of pride. Chinsky was too smart, too analytical, too disciplined. Once into the bowels of the project, there was a better than even chance that he would make the crucial connection and with it garner a share of the glory. It was a risk he could not take. Nor had there been any reason to. He knew he could do it, and he had done it! He was Salk, Pasteur, working alone—brilliant, insightful, successful—perhaps the last of the great discoverers. There was no room here for collaboration. He had been right to do it this way—actually Chinsky's way—to work alone, not trusting anyone.

And then there was the other reason. It, too, was his fault; not that he thought of it as a fault. It was more a matter of sidestepping clumsy bureaucratic procedure; procedure imposed upon legitimate researchers by overcautious government regulators. True, he had broken the spirit of their strict protocols, but he was justified by the enormous value of his findings. His theory was correct from the start. He knew. He took the risk. No risk, no reward. No pain, no gain. A smug smile erupted at the cliches. Because of his independent action, his risk taking, he now had proof that the cure worked. The safe road would have been to announce his early work, publish it in one of the journals. But there was risk there too. Had the human trials failed, it would have tarnished the luster of his career. Now he was assured that the public tests would succeed. The sooner the *authorized* clinical trials started, the better.

Yes, he thought emphatically, it's time for a press release, today. It's time to get Snell off his duff. He would see to it. As if to emphasize the point he gunned the Mercedes; the machine's g-force threw him back into the seat as it accelerated. There was no time to waste!

■

The sudden acceleration of the Mercedes took Duke unaware. Reflexively his foot jammed the accelerator, but all he succeeded in doing was to climb up the back of the Ford separating him from Rathbone. What was the son of a bitch doing? Was Rathbone onto him? The oncoming traffic was heavy, making it impossible to pass the Ford. "Shit!" he bellowed. It was falling apart! Fucking Rathbone was racing away. Recklessly, Duke cut his wheel to the right. A cloud of dust exploded into the air as his tires churned the loose gravel of the shoulder. He pumped the gas and shot past the Ford, then cut his wheel to the left and vaulted the Buick back onto the asphalt. The Mercedes was out of sight. At the top of a rise he saw it again, now more than a half mile away. Too far! He kept the gas pedal to the floor, and the distance between the cars quickly narrowed. Too quickly. The Mercedes, no longer racing, had slowed. Careful, he cautioned himself, careful; everything depends on surprise. Five hundred feet behind the Mercedes, Duke eased off the gas and held his position.

A mile from the Croft headquarters, Duke gunned the Buick and moved in front of Rathbone. Once ahead he pulled away, losing sight of his target. Duke stretched the distance between the cars until he reached the green glade bordering the Croft parking lot. He was more comfortable now. Had Rathbone been onto him, the pass would not have occurred. The Mercedes had more than enough horsepower to lose him at will.

At this hour the white lines on the black asphalt of the lot were still visible, forming neat stalls waiting to be filled. He positioned the Buick horizontally straddling three empty spots. Duke followed his routine and lowered all the windows. The front passenger window was aligned with, and a hundred yards behind, a little blue rectangle with white lettering that read:

DR. RATHBONE
CHIEF OF RESEARCH

Over the years, Duke had learned that there are times when victims are relatively still. Sitting ducks. Parking a car was one of those special times. Seven seconds after Duke parked, the elegant bulk of the Mercedes cruised into the lot.

■

Rathbone pulled recklessly into his space. The Mercedes angled across the neat white stripes, the left front fender almost covered one hash mark while the right rear fender crossed the opposing stripe. The angle was as jaunty as his spirit. He felt good, invigorated. The Monday blahs were gone. He had a mission. He would show these kids how an old-time research chief could make things happen, by God. This was going to be an exciting, eventful day!

■

The odd angle at which Rathbone parked changed the line of sight, making a clean hit more difficult.

Without warning the Mercedes backed out of its space, freezing Duke with indecision. What was happening? Was the man finally onto it? Should he get out? The reverse momentum of the Mercedes stopped and the car pulled forward again, this time perfectly positioned between the white stripes. Duke smiled. The doctor was just being tidy.

Within two seconds after Rathbone parked, the back of his silver-tipped head was quartered in the cross hairs of Duke's telescopic sight. The nine-inch-long silencer, a full two inches in diameter, complemented the natural balance of the rifle, slightly pulling its nose toward the earth. The assassin braced one elbow on the seat back, the other on the steering wheel to steady the weapon. The hood of a cobra tattooed on his right hand, perpendicular to the weapon, told him that the weapon was leveled. Despite its awkward weight, the Magnum was rock steady. Rathbone leaned back to unbuckle his seat belt as Duke squeezed off the first round. The flat, hard crack was followed by the tinkle of shattering glass. The bullet entered just behind Rathbone's right ear and pushed its way through bits of chalky skull bone and spongelike cerebrum. Not quite spent, it came out through the socket of his left eye. Carrying microscopic bits of skin, hair, brain, eye, and bone, the bullet embedded itself in the windshield. Around it a red-gray splatter formed a halo for the dull lead.

Duke lowered the barrel a fraction of an inch to compensate for the slump of the body and resighted the cross hairs. His index finger gently squeezed the trigger. Again, the slight crack of glass and a small thump. This second round met more resistance and lodged in the corpus. This bullet wasn't really necessary, but Duke liked to do things well. Insurance, he called it. That's what they paid him for.

As Rathbone's body pressed into the wheel of his fine German car, his chest found the horn. A nasal electronic blare radiated from under the hood. The raucous, abrasive sound irritated a lone pedestrian who was within hearing but out of sight. Characteristically, the walker did not bother to come over and see if there was a problem. Just as Duke expected. You could count on city people to mind their own business. They didn't want to get involved.

In the Buick the assassin——methodically, with practiced motion—unscrewed the components from the Magnum and wiped clean the smooth black cylinders with a soft yellow cloth. He replaced each piece in its special compartment in the fitted case. The cloth went into a plastic bag, then into the case. Snapping the polyethylene box shut, he swung it over the seat back and gently lowered it to rest on the floor. The engine of the rented Buick was still running. Calmly, Duke shifted into gear and drove away.

■

A half hour later he turned into the driveway of the Townsend Hotel in Birmingham. The green-uniformed doorman took the keys to the car; Duke carried his own case. Time to worry about the money later. Now he'd report to Spangler.

CHAPTER
2

NINE O'CLOCK was early for Brenda Byrne to be in the newsroom. Last night she'd filed a late story from the ballpark. Once home, she couldn't sleep; the body dragged, but the mind raced. The sportswriter in her knew that, in battles like these, the brain always won the early rounds. The body inevitably won the fight, usually by a knockout. Knowing from experience that she wouldn't get rest, she got out of bed at six, showered, read a little, and then went to work. It would make a long day, but she could rest tonight. The Tigers always took Monday off. Besides, she liked to mingle with the newspeople, and who knew, something might turn up.

Brenda checked the West Coast scores on the wire service computer. The Jays had lost again. Two in a row. A streak. Maybe Maskera was right.

Delbert Maskera's two-run homer in the ninth had won the game. It was always nice when the hometown boys won; the story was easier to write. No alibis needed, thank you, just restrained gushing about the heroes. After the game she fought her way to the locker room, pushed past the TV crew, and interviewed Maskera while he pulled his socks off. The big outfielder thought the team had a chance at the pennant if they stayed within five games during the Milwaukee-Chicago road trip. She thought he was full of crap. The way Toronto was playing, the Tigers didn't have a chance unless they came out of the trip no more than two games back. It was almost impossible. What the hell, she figured—she put his prediction in the story. That way she could always pin him later if he was wrong. And if right, she could take part of the credit. "You read it right here back in August. . . ." Brenda inserted other notes from the interview in appropriate places in the story she had already written. Then she zapped the whole piece in, using the modem built into her Tandy P.C. The morning edition went to press at 1:00 A.M. Her deadline was midnight, and she made it by twenty minutes.

The morning newsroom was as quiet as the late night newsroom, only the character of the quiet was different. The atmosphere was tense, expectant—not relaxed. Now everyone was gearing up for the day, rather than tapering off. The stillness was, in part, caused by the distance to the deadline. In a business measured in minutes, hours seemed interminable. The afternoon deadline was, after all, a half day away. Almost a lifetime. Page editors worked out story assignments with reporters. Feature writers hobnobbed with cronies, talking about the day's contacts. Everybody was looking for an angle that would change the ordinary to magic. As morning wore on, the pace would pick up, and by press time the atmosphere of the newsroom would be frenzied, reaching a climax as the computers dumped the paper to the presses. From there, like ebbing tide, the room would slide down from its high to the evening quiet Brenda was used to. Then another cycle would start. The essential difference between the two quiets, she mused, was fatigue: absent in the morning, overpowering at night.

Brenda walked over to the news service computer, an index to the action of the world. Tension in the Middle East was tightening again. Congress and the president were at loggerheads over the budget. The navy had caught another spy. Same old stuff.

"Hey, Brenda, whatcha doin' tonight?" a voice behind her drawled. "You're sure lookin' fine this morning." Brenda's head turned first. The rest of her followed. "Ooowee," the voice continued, "this side looks even better. Whaddaya say, wanna boogie later?"

"Watch out, Billy," she said, smiling. "I'll slap you with sexual harassment. Better yet, I'll tell Carol."

"She'd never believe you. She thinks I'm a saint." Nearby reporters at their tiny desks had one ear cocked to catch the repartee. It was normal newsroom banter. More than one of the young bucks had silently framed the words Billy had spoken. Brenda was generally acknowledged as one good-looking woman. Her outstanding figure compensated for an ordinary face, but her thick mane of deep red hair gave her a presence more beautiful women lacked.

"Maybe she knows you couldn't be anything but a saint," Brenda retorted. A few grins broke across the mostly young faces. The women were particularly glad to see Brenda giving as good as she got. They would have preferred it, though, if she were a bit more dowdy. By now, Brenda was standing next to the sitting Billy; his feet were propped on his desk. She suppressed an urge to kick out the back legs of the chair. Instead she asked sweetly, "What's happening in the world of crime?" Paunchy, balding Billy covered the police beat. He was wired to the police computer, and all the police reports were dumped on his desk. Although she'd never admit it to Billy, she envied him his job. She was a good sportswriter, but she wanted to be a good hard-news reporter.

"Same old stuff. A couple of kids shot another kid. Twelve years old. Somebody ought to do something about it." He squinted his eyes in his puffy face. "That's the thirty-seventh kid to pack it in this year. We've got to get the guns off the street." Handguns were Billy's private crusade. He lived too close to the action not to be affected by it. Brenda nodded her head in understanding. "Even a guy up at Croft caught it this morning."

Brenda was instantly alert. A month ago Croft wouldn't have made a dent in her veneer of disinterest. Luke Chinsky had changed that. She had met him at a cocktail party. Both came with a friend of the same sex and neither knew the host. Strangers in the crowd, they wound up talking to each other. At the time it had surprised her. She was usually aloof to men—they were all on the prowl. Not that prowling bothered Brenda. It was just that she liked to control the action and was put off by macho types trying to make her. Chinsky had a different quality. The first impression he gave was that he could take her or leave her, yet he was such an interesting conversationalist that she stayed from moment to moment and eventually found they had spent the evening together. "What happened?" she asked Billy.

"Police report came in a couple minutes ago. A guy was shot in the head, in his car, in the parking lot. I'm going over to check it out. Want to come along? I'll show you how real reporters work."

Brenda's jaw tightened at the dig, but she kept her mouth shut. However unceremoniously, Billy was offering her a ride to the crime scene. It was the closest to real news she had been since she joined the paper and it was certainly better than a ballpark. She could get her licks in later; now she needed to close the offer. "You're on," she said before he could change his mind. "Do you have any more details? Is there a printout?" She was already prowling around his desk trying to get a better look at the printer output.

"Yeah." He picked the dispatch up from his desk. "The guy's name was Rathbone. A doctor. Somebody shot him right through the window of his car. He was dead when the police got there."

Rathbone! Brenda was stunned. She and Chinsky had just talked about him. Rathbone was Chinsky's boss. Luke admired him, but felt he hogged too much credit for the lab's accomplishments. Hearing his name from Billy unnerved her. "My God," she said out loud. Apprehension shrouded her like a thick, black cloak.

Billy was staring at her. "Hey, Brenda girl, what's wrong? You're white as a ghost. You all right?"

She closed her eyes, then opened them. She pressed her palms together, fighting to maintain composure. "I knew him," she said. "No," she corrected herself, "I didn't know him, but I knew *of* him." She stretched the "of" out, giving it emphasis.

"Hey, I'm sorry, I didn't know," said Billy. He started assembling his things. A couple of pencils went into the right hand pocket of a jacket hanging over the back of his chair. He slid a five-by-seven-inch notebook into the other pocket and slung the fully equipped jacket over one shoulder. "I guess you don't want to go." It was more question than statement.

"Yes, I do," she said urgently. "I need a minute, though. Is it all right if I make a phone call first?"

"Sure. Make your call, but make it quick. I'll wait for you by the elevator." As he walked away, Brenda grabbed the desk phone and dialed Chinsky's apartment. The phone rang four times, then was answered by his machine.

"*Hi. This is—*" Luke's voice began.

"Damn!" she swore before the beep. She wasn't sure why the call was so important. It could be their budding relationship, or the need to be the first to contact him about the tragedy. Or—driven by callous habit—to touch base with a potential source? Whatever the motive, the gesture was blocked by the deep baritone voice of the machine. "*And I'll get back to you as soon as I can.*" Beep.

"Luke, this is Brenda." She always felt stupid talking to an answering machine. It was as though she were being manipulated by a robot, responding like a trained seal. "Give me a call. I'm going out for a while, but I'll be back at the paper by noon."

"Let's go, kid." Billy's yell snapped her attention

back to the opportunity he was giving her. Down the corridor she could see him holding the elevator door open with his foot. Frustrated at not reaching Chinsky, she slammed the handset in the cradle and ran to catch up with Billy.

Three floors down, Billy snaked his car out of the *Free Press* garage and into the desolate streets of downtown Detroit.

He drove fast. In his mind, fifteen miles over the posted speed limit was a reasonable pace. He picked up the Lodge just north of Michigan Avenue. It wasn't the fast driving that bothered her. Instead, it was his habit of looking at you while he talked; Billy talked incessantly. She didn't hear much of what he had to say. She was absorbed by watching the road and thinking of Chinsky.

After their first meeting, Brenda ran a sheet on Chinsky and the company he worked for, Croft Pharmaceuticals, Inc. There was not much of a file on him: routine promotional announcements and a two-year-old short personality piece in the "Up and Coming" section of the *News*. A publication search gave her the names of fifteen technical papers on which he was either the principal collaborator or authored solo. The file on Croft was a lot bigger. They were a major employer and the largest drug company in town. Every time some pharmaceutical controversy arose, reporters interviewed the PR guy or a researcher to get the industry perspective. A giant in the industry, the company, its executives, and researchers were well respected. Bradley Snell was featured in a score of articles, mostly in the business section. Brenda had

culled the file and copied a dozen recent pieces. She
had read them while covering a dull local tennis tour-
nament. It was a toss-up as to whether there was less
action on the court or at Croft.

Slipping over to the Reuther Freeway, Billy made it
to Orchard Lake Drive and Twelve Mile Road before
he was forced to use surface streets. Watching the
road from the corner of his left eye, he peppered her
with questions: "What did this guy, Rathbone, do?"

"He was chief of research, I think."

"How did you get to know him?"

"I didn't. A friend of mine does, did."

"What does the friend do?"

"Damn it, Billy, watch the road. He's a researcher."

"How good a friend is he?"

"Good enough. Why, what does it matter?"

"He might be a lead."

"Yeah," she admitted, "he might."

It didn't take long to get to Croft. Brenda thought
it took forever.

She sighed with relief as the long, sleek profile of
the Croft headquarters building came into view. Its
smoked-glass skin reflected the shimmering majesty
of the blue morning sky and the tops of the trees
surrounding it. The entire first level of the building
was hidden by a series of low-lying long berms. It was
as if the building grew, monumentlike, from the fer-
tile suburban soil.

Plastic yellow ribbons with POLICE BARRIER, DO NOT
CROSS printed in bold black letters cordoned off the
parking lot. A small crowd of curious locals milled
about at the edge of the lot. Billy parked in the street,

next to a fire hydrant. Without waiting for Brenda, he got out of the car and headed toward the activity in the parking lot. Lifting the flimsy police barrier, he walked in as if it didn't apply to him. Brenda followed him and self-consciously slipped under the official barrier. Billy waved to an officer who was moving in his direction. The officer recognized him and waved him on. Just like getting into the locker room, thought Brenda. Same rules, different sport.

The scene was a microcosm of the city's service substructure; police, emergency medical, ambulance, and fire vehicles surrounded the killing ground. The fifty or so specialists who crawled the site were there for one purpose: gathering data. Squares within the cordoned area were marked off with thin white tape. A plastic number identified each square. People— bent over, crouching, kneeling—scraped, picked, and minutely scanned the black asphalt surface. Nearby, forensic lab technicians picked up samples from the asphalt surface with tweezers, methodically placing them in clear Ziploc bags, while recording the find in a book and tagging the bag. Brenda bent over to watch them work. It looked like they were collecting debris. Brenda squinted to get a better look but couldn't make out any difference between the samples retrieved and those left behind.

"Why all the squares and numbers?" she asked Billy.

He gave her a disdainful look indicating what he thought of her amateur question. "That marks the area. If any of this stuff is ever used in evidence, they have to establish a trail that leads from its source to the courtroom. The numbers identify the plot of ground the sample comes from and distinguishes that plot from all others. That way, when the prosecutor asks 'where did you find this?' the tech can say, 'at the site, square 12, fifty feet southeast of subject vehicle.' It's a pain in the ass, but that's the only way the courts will accept it."

"I don't know," she argued, "it seems reasonable to me. Otherwise evidence could be manufactured or mixed up."

He gave her that look again. "Shit, Brenda. Grow up. When you've seen as many killers, dopesters, rapists, and hoods walk as I have—because some judge doesn't like the way the evidence came in—you'll understand."

"Forget I mentioned it, sport," she said. *Watch the lip, girl,* she told herself. No time to get into a tiff with Billy. The S.O.B. let her come on the scene, but he could keep her off. Work it right and he might give her a chance to work with him on this story in some capacity; she'd sharpen his pencils if she had to. Fat chance. Jake Salley, the news editor, knew how much she wanted in on hard news reporting, but every time she talked to him about it he put her off. She suspected Salley was secretly intimidated by her boss, Gus Donovan. Donovan was fond of reminding anyone who would listen—around the office, in a bar, and at his frequent long lunches—that the *Free Press* fielded the best sports department in the country, and more importantly, that a good sports section sold newspapers. It would take a major issue before Salley would tangle with the sports czar. As far as she could see, her career was not that issue.

Brenda's pseudoattention wandered back to the data collectors. Half the people toted cameras with oversized lenses. Just now, the focus of their attention was the blue Mercedes. An E.M.S. truck and an ambulance were parked about fifty feet from the vehicle. The attendants were moving Rathbone's body out of the car. It was limp, like a boneless rag doll. The attendants' struggle to get a grip had worked the doll's suit coat up until it gathered under the armpits, revealing the tail of a white shirt. Below the shirt was a dark, wet stain where the body had released its excrement. Brenda, not prepared for this, gagged. She had come to report, not confront the reaper up close and personal. For the first time, the reality of the death grabbed her stomach and gave it a brutal twist. Rathbone was more than a name. He was a person, now a person no more. Mesmerized, she wanted to look away, but couldn't. Swallowing hard, fighting to retain her composure, her eyes involuntarily closed and opened. On the ground, a white sheet framed the bulk of a black rubber body bag. Expertly, the attendants maneuvered the flaccid body into the bag and zipped it shut. Brenda could feel the grip of each zipper tooth as it slowly, inexorably sealed the body from the outside world of the living. Was there a soul in there being sealed with the body? If so, she was the only one who gave it a thought; the callous skin of experience had numbed those around her to this tragedy of death. The police photographers, their work done, stood smoking cigarettes.

Officials, mostly men, stood around in groups of two or three talking, staring, passing the time. This ritual of investigation was new to Brenda, but not to them. Brenda followed as Billy went over to one group. "Hi, Cal. What happened?" Billy asked. A tall black man turned to acknowledge the question.

"Hi, Billy. Took you a while to get here. Most of your competition's come and gone," Cal said. He had a loose jaw that seemed to be attached with rubber bands. It kept moving even when his mouth was shut.

"Won't do them any good," said Billy. "We all have the same deadlines. This way I get you all to myself." Billy jerked his thumb toward Brenda. "Cal, this is Brenda Byrne, one of our reporters. Brenda, this is Sergeant Calvin Washington of homicide."

"Good to meet you, Miss Byrne. I read your column. You giving up sports?"

"No, I'm just hanging out with Billy this morning. And I'd prefer Brenda," she said, flashing a wide smile.

"Brenda it is. And I'm glad you're sticking with sports. It'd be a shame if you took up with lowlifes like Billy here," he gave a thin-lipped smile to show it was a joke. She noticed there was no reciprocal offer for her to call him 'Cal.' She'd call him that anyway. Cal turned to Billy and said, "How you been, Billy?"

"Not bad. What's the story?"

"A guy by the name of Rathbone caught it while he was sitting in his car. Two shots to the head. Seems to have come from over there." Sergeant Washington pointed across the parking lot to where a dozen techs lingered. The gesture was not precise, but gave the general impression that the killing had not occurred at close range. "From the angle of the hit, I'd say the bullet came from another car, probably parked in the area the lab boys are sweeping. Nobody heard shots. Probably a rifle with a scope and silencer."

Brenda looked at the two closely spaced holes in the back window of the nearby Mercedes. They looked like little spider webs with a center waiting for flies. All four doors of the car were open.

"Who was Rathbone?" Billy asked, already knowing the answer.

"Caucasian male, aged fifty-five, in good shape. Doctor at this place. Head of research. A pretty big muckity muck."

"Any theories?"

"None for publication."

"How about off the record?"

Washington considered the proposition before answering. "Could be a crazy out on a binge. But I don't think so. Crazies don't use silencers. And they usually don't stop at one. They're out for attention. In a place like this, a crazy would take out six, ten people. And then he'd wait around till we came after him. It's a better bet that the doc was dealing in something. Either that or someone in the family took him out."

"Oh?" Brenda prompted.

"Yeah. Most homicides—fifty-five, sixty percent—are committed by members of the same family. After that you can usually start looking for a drug connection." Brenda knew the statistics were for her information. They would be second nature to Billy, like batting averages were to her. "Maybe this guy was mixed up in drugs. He's a doctor, he works for a drug company, he drives a fancy car; it has all the marks." He looked stern and put a long, bony finger in the direction of Billy's face. "That's not for publication, at least not from me. Understood?"

Washington's hard eyes flashed from Billy to Brenda and back. A muscle along his jawbone pulsed. Washington didn't look like he took crap from anybody. Billy nodded to show he understood. Brenda nodded too.

She decided not to call him Cal.

"I don't want the establishment on my back because I'm de-fame-ing the reputation of some bigshot white doctor." Sergeant Washington scrunched up his mouth and clenched his teeth a couple of times, staring over their heads. Washington's mobile jaw rocked back and forth. An irreverent image of a cow chewing cud formed in Brenda's mind. The chin motion stopped for a moment as he said, "Everything else is pretty much as you see it. That's all I can tell you for now. And since you have no questions"—he made it clear they weren't to ask any—"I've got to get back to work."

"Mind if we look around?" Billy asked.

"Nah. Just don't mess with anything and don't bother the technicians. You know the rules. And Billy, spell my name right. Remember, I've two citations. Check my bio. You keep leaving out the important stuff." Washington grinned, but Brenda had no doubt that Billy's continued access to information was proportionate to the favorable press he gave the department's Sergeant Washingtons.

Brenda's problem now was how to get to Chinsky. With his insider's knowledge he could feed her background on both the company and Rathbone. This could be her break into hard news. It would give her that most elusive element of winning: an edge over the competition. She always searched for it on her sports beat and usually found it. Chinsky was her ticket to a piece of this story.

No building entrances were visible from where they stood. It seemed a strange place to put a parking lot. Usually, they were adjacent to entryways. "Sergeant," she asked as Washington started to turn away, "where are the building entrances?"

"Around the other side. There are two employee entrances on this side. You can't see them from here. They're in wells on the other side of the berm. But stay out of the building. I don't want reporters in there until my people have finished up." He turned and walked away, not needing confirmation that his order would be obeyed. Brenda didn't care. She was going to talk to Chinsky regardless of what Washington wanted.

"Billy, I'm going to wander around a bit. Do you mind?" she asked.

"No, go ahead. But there's not much here. I'll be leaving in ten or fifteen minutes."

"Don't wait if I'm not back."

"Where are you going?"

"To try and find a source."

"Hey girl, cool it. This ain't your story."

"You're right, I'm just here for the ride. But if I can get an inside lead, will you take it?"

"What's in it for you?"

"Let's see if I can get the lead."

"Brenda—"

"What have you got to lose?"

"That's the problem. With you, I don't know. But one thing I'm sure of is that it's more than I'm willing to part with."

"That's what I like about you, Billy. You really know how to bird-dog a story."

"Stay out of it."

"Roger. But if I'm not back, take off. I'll get a cab."

She walked back to the cordon. At the police checkpoint the blueshirts were looking over the identification of those who wanted in. Apparently, only employees were being given access.

Fifty yards from the small knot of people she walked around the berm, then toward the entrance. No one stopped her. The cops assigned to the detail were too busy checking ID's to notice.

She walked through the entrance of the sleek glass building behind an employee who used a card to open the door. No alarm rang. She was in. Now to find Luke Chinsky.

CHAPTER
3

THE PHONE RANG. Chinsky, reaching for it, brushed his forearm against the full styrofoam cup of freshly poured coffee and toppled it. The rich Colombian aroma wafted into the air as the brown liquid pooled over a thick undergrowth of lab notes.

"Shit!" Chinsky erupted, pulling his arm back, trying to right the cup and at the same time salvage some as yet unflooded papers. His effort only widened the reach of the pool.

The phone rang again. The wetness of the coffee pulled the dehydrated blue ink from the paper and turned the liquid a murky gray color. To stop the tide of destruction he blotted the surging coffee with the forearm of his lab coat. The phone rang again.

"Hold on, for Christ's sake," he shouted without picking up the receiver.

On the fourth ring he had won the battle and snatched up the handset. "What do you want?" he asked angrily.

"Dr. Chinsky, please," a smooth, refined female voice answered.

"This is Chinsky. What do you want?"

"Dr. Chinsky, this is Alice Murcheson, Mr. Snell's

secretary. You have a unique way of answering the phone."

"Aw, shit," he said again. "Sorry, but I just spilled coffee all over my lab notes. I'm afraid this isn't starting out to be a good morning."

"Yes, it's been a tragic morning," she agreed. "Still, though, it's important that we keep our poise."

He wasn't sure if she was talking about him or herself. "What can I do for you?" he asked. It was more than curiosity. In his ten years at Croft this was his first call from the president's office. Most executive communication came to him through Rathbone.

"Mr. Snell would like to see you. Can you come to his office?"

"Sure," he said, looking at his blue-brown-gray-stained sleeve. "When?"

"Right now, if you have time."

"How about in half an hour?"

"Mr. Snell has appointments. Right now would be better."

"Okay, okay," he said, nodding his head in resignation. "I'll be right up."

"Thank you," she said politely as she hung up.

Chinsky peeled off his wet lab coat and searched the closet for another. Out of luck. The closet was empty. Well, he would just have to cut the best corporate figure he could in his plaid western-styled shirt, blue corduroy jeans, and well-worn running shoes. Not, he speculated, the standard uniform for an audience with the president of the company. Too bad. Nothing he could do about it now.

The morning—the week—was not starting well. It had nowhere to go but up, right?

As soon as he walked into Snell's office, Chinsky knew he would have been better off in a soiled lab coat. He had this feeling of being different from the corporate chieftain. His comfortable corduroys and sneakers, symbols of independence from the establishment, looked shabby rather than defiant when contrasted with Snell's crisp dark-gray pinstripe suit and glossy Italian leather shoes. And it wasn't just the clothes. The two men came from different breeding stock. Physical opposites, Chinsky was chunky, barrel chested; Snell reedlike. Chinsky either had to stand six feet away or tip his head back a notch to look into Snell's eyes. The president was a head and a half taller than Chinsky. But the main difference was not in dress or physical characteristics. It was demeanor.

Snell exuded command. There was no deference to social convention, no humility, just raw power waiting to be applied. Chinsky was comfortable exercising power over facts, data, information, process, the tools of the intellect. Snell's power seemed more primitive. Chinsky's sense of foreboding increased.

"Good morning, Dr. Chinsky," Snell said, extending his hand. "On second thought, it's not such a good morning, is it? I assume you've heard of Dr. Rathbone's tragedy?"

Chinsky nodded as they shook hands. If Snell was put off by the way he looked, he didn't show it. The urbane Snell, motioning Chinsky to a chair, continued his monologue. "It's because of Dr. Rathbone that I've asked you up." Snell paused. Chinsky had no response, so he made none.

"I don't know if you were aware of it, but David Rathbone and I were quite good friends as well as business associates. I can tell you this has devastated Anne, his wife. Joyce, my wife, is with her now, trying to comfort her." Snell looked out the plate glass window, his back to Chinsky, and sighed. "I'm not sure that's a doable task." He shook his head and was quiet a second. Chinsky still had not said a word. After a moment Snell turned around to face him.

"The only reason I brought up our friendship," Snell's voice was firmer now, more businesslike, "is that David told me of some conversations you and he have had."

Chinsky raised his eyebrows. Reflexively, his hand went to his beard and he grunted. His most recent conversations with Rathbone had been somewhat unpleasant. Yet, he had thought those exchanges confidential, the discourse between superior and subordinate.

"David often came to me for counsel when he was," Snell paused, searching for the right word, "troubled." The executive gave a small nod as if to confirm his choice. Then, in what seemed to be an afterthought, he continued, "Especially in personnel matters. He told me you felt you were being deprived of responsibility and recognition. Is that right?"

It was true enough. "In part," Chinsky said a bit defensively. "The main thrust was that I felt as though I ought to be allowed to work more independently. That was the agreement we had when I was hired. The projects I'm on are interesting, but I feel I could make more progress if I pursued them alone, rather than as part of a team. And I told that to Dr. Rathbone."

"He said you had quite an argument."

Chinsky shrugged. "I wouldn't call it an argument. He had his viewpoint; I had mine." Chinsky felt a bit awkward talking about the dead man. It was almost as if he were being disloyal.

"You know he held you in high regard," Snell said —more statement than question—and with an abrupt change of tone. "He felt you were one of his best researchers and potentially his best team leader. What troubled him was he felt you were being un-fairly critical, and from his point of view, he had lim-ited options with which to satisfy you." Snell paused for the vote of confidence to be tabulated. "David always believed in treating all the people who worked for him in the same manner. He felt as if you were asking for, well, special treatment."

"That's not true!" Chinsky's voice rose slightly. Snell might be the boss, but Chinsky showed no def-erence when it came to defending his point of view. It had gotten him into trouble before. At the same time it had allowed him to question the unquestion-able, a trait that often made him successful while others stumbled on convention. "I felt, I still feel, there is an opportunity to make use of our relation-ship with the university in conducting clinical trials." Croft had recently entered into an affiliation agree-ment with Wayne State University Clinic and Hospi-tals to share basic research. Both sides were feeling their way along in the tentative relationship. Rathbone had been handling the discussions for Croft. To Chinsky, progress seemed slow. "I wanted his authorization to pursue discussions with them."

"In any case," Snell said soothingly, "I'm just telling you of David's concerns. He wanted to encourage you along the lines you suggested, yet was apprehensive about the effect giving you extra responsibility would have on the other team leaders."

Chinsky was chagrined. He had thought Rathbone totally against his suggestion. At least, it had seemed that way from the heat of their discussion.

"You know, Luke—may I call you Luke?" Snell paused long enough for Chinsky to acquiesce by a nod of the head, then continued. "Luke, David's death is going to leave a major void in our organization. He was one of the most respected laboratory chiefs in the world. The board will certainly want us to conduct a national search for his replacement. But in the meantime, our day-to-day work has to go on." He had Chinsky's full attention. "Since you've asked for more responsibility and since you've worked closely with Dr. Rathbone over the past few years, I'd like you to pick up some of his projects."

Chinsky was dumbfounded. Snell was asking him to fill in as acting chief? There were a half-dozen people more senior than he. Why him? "Are you asking me to fill in as acting chief?" he asked.

"I wouldn't want to use that title, but yes, in part. I'd like you to pick up the clinical side of David's work. There are a few administrative responsibilities

I'll ask others to handle, but I'd like you to take on most of the load."

Chinsky's mind raced. The pieces didn't fit together. Sure, he had led a work team. And, given the nature of their projects, it was a successful team. Very successful. But it was also common knowledge in the corridors of Croft that his group was the most tempestuous. Guerrilla war raged between the members of the group and Chinsky did little to negotiate peace. Usually the issue was allocation of resources; not something he chose to be bothered with unless it involved one of his personal projects. The only reason he had agreed to lead the team in the first place was that it gave him more independence in pursuing his own projects. He would be the first to admit that the skills he had were in managing data, not people. Now Snell was asking him to take responsibility for all of Rathbone's clinical projects—which meant responsibility for all the people doing that research as well. But it also meant more independence. "Mr. Snell, I'm flattered, but why me? There are others who are more senior."

"That's true. But let's not forget you've been here ten years. You're not exactly the new kid on the block." Snell flashed his smile. "And as I told you, from my discussions with David before his death, he felt you showed the most promise of any of his people. I've trusted his judgment in the past, and I'm inclined to trust it now. One thing you'll learn about me is that I always do what's best for the company. I have two priorities: the company and our customers. Given our business, you could say that we need to serve society, to do the right thing. I'd like you to keep those priorities in front of you. Serve the company by serving society. How about it, do we have a deal?"

Chinsky reflected before commenting. Taking the job would limit the amount of time he had for personal research. On the other hand, it would allow him to explore new directions unfettered. As much as he distrusted research by committee, he would be in a position to choose the path of inquiry. "I'm not sure what to say, other than yes. I'm flattered, honored, and of course, I'll do it. Are there things that need immediate attention? Are there any projects Dr. Rathbone was working on that I'm not familiar with or that have high priority?"

"No. Nothing out of the ordinary. You'll probably want to go through his files to determine the major thrust of his efforts. After you've had a chance to do that, draw up a list and we'll assign priorities. I may be assigning some projects to others once things settle down, but I'll let you know about them as I sort things out. In the meantime I'll have Alice set up a meeting with the team leaders to brief them on your new role. You can check with her if you need anything."

Snell stood up to signal that the meeting was at an end. He reached out his hand to Chinsky. As he did so he said, "I hesitate to mention it, seeing as how we pride ourselves on informality, but in your new role you may want to consider wearing a lab coat and suit. From time to time we take visitors out to lunch."

Chinsky flushed. "Of course," he said, taking

Snell's hand and shaking it decisively. "Normally I don't dress like this, but I gave my valet the week off."

Snell didn't seem to know how to respond.

"But seriously," Chinsky went on, "thank you for the opportunity. You can count on me."

"I'm sure you'll do your best, Luke," Snell said as he ushered him out the door.

■

Sergeant Washington didn't impress Snell. The policeman dressed almost as badly as Chinsky. Snell always said you could judge a man by the quality of his shoes. Washington's shoes were poor imitations of woven Italian loafers. And they were brown. And scuffed. His cheap poplin suit was rumpled; he probably slept in it, Snell thought. The color was a shade of blue that Snell associated with K mart. Washington's tie—one of the few shades of red that could clash with the suit—was loose at the neck, as was the collar of his shirt. His partner, whose name Snell instantly forgot, looked like he had the same tailor. Putting his feelings aside, he extended a hand to the policemen.

"Good morning, Sergeant. I hope my people have been giving you the cooperation you need." Snell was at his corporate best: officious, yet solicitous. He pitched his voice so that the grief he projected was unmistakable. "This is a tragic event, one we're unused to. I can't emphasize enough how important it is for you to find Dr. Rathbone's killer." Snell was unctuous. "He was a great man. A key part of the

Croft team. I can't believe this has happened. Do you have any idea who might have done this, and why?"

"No, we don't, Mr. Snell," Washington answered. "We're hoping you'd be able to help us." Snell perceived Washington as cocky. Not by what he said, but how he said it. There was little respect for authority. Snell hated cocky—which he interpreted as arrogant —public servants.

"Why don't you talk to me about Dr. Rathbone?" the detective asked. His partner turned on a tape recorder and took out his notepad.

"What would you like to know?"

"Just general stuff, like what he did here, what his personality was like, the people who liked or disliked him. Anything at all. Anything you can tell me will be useful." Washington looked him squarely in the eye. It was disconcerting.

Snell decided to be quick, to the point, but not brusque. No sense letting this small-time cop think he was hiding something. He could tell the detective was the type who would keep gnawing on meat until it was mush. "Well, that's not an easy task," he said obliquely. "Dr. Rathbone was a dear friend and Croft's chief of research. We went back a long time. I brought him in over twenty years ago. He started as a researcher, a very capable one, and quickly moved up. He is, was, considered one of the outstanding research chiefs in the world. Did you know he had presidential citations?" Snell asked. The unblinking Washington shook his head and Snell continued, "This is such a tragedy. I can't think of why anyone would wish to harm him." He paused, thoughtfully.

"Unless it was one of our competitors. Even then, they'd be more likely to pirate him away than kill him. I just don't understand why anyone would do a thing like this."

"Any enemies that you know of?"

"David?" Surprise accenting the name. "No." Snell snorted depreciatingly. "David didn't have any enemies. He was well liked—and well respected."

"Even outside the company?"

"None that I know of. He was just an all-around nice guy."

"Who were his friends?"

"Well, Joyce—my wife—and I were. We socialized with the Rathbones quite often."

"Any others?"

"Why, certainly," Snell said with feigned impatience. "The Rathbones counted most of the officers of the company as their friends."

"Can we get a list of the officers?"

"Certainly. I'll see that one is delivered to you."

"Did Dr. Rathbone behave differently over the past several months?"

"What do you mean?"

"Was he nervous? His work habits change? Anything like that?"

"No, Dr. Rathbone was one of the most consistent men I know."

"How about drugs? Was he on drugs?"

"Of course not!" Snell erupted. Then, with indignation, "What kind of question is that?"

"Sorry, I have to ask. Did he drink?"

"No more than any of us. A cocktail before dinner.

I've seen him high, but never drunk. What has this to do with his murder?"

"It's important that we know about his habits. Did he gamble, see women?"

"I'm sure I wouldn't know," Snell said icily.

Washington continued without notice, as if he were going through a mental checklist. "Did he live within his means?"

"He was well paid. He also had royalties from his patents and books. The Rathbones could afford most anything they desired."

"Any vices?" Washington stared through Snell.

"Other than a mean game of golf and a passion for work, I don't think so."

"He ever mention difficulty with his wife?"

"No. Of course not! We didn't discuss personal issues."

"Does that mean you suspected he was having difficulties?"

"Absolutely not! I think this questioning is improper."

"I thought you and he were friends. Would he tell you, as a friend, if he was having problems?"

"We didn't discuss personal issues," Snell said emphatically and in a tone that with most of his subordinates would have ended the discussion and sent them retreating, tail between legs. Washington ignored it.

"You and Rathbone ever argue?"

"Of course we did. There are always disagreements in business."

"You ever threaten him?"

"No. That's absurd! What are you getting at?"

"He ever threaten you?"

"Sergeant, what is the meaning of this line of questioning?"

"I need to know. Did he threaten you?"

"No."

"He argue with other people in the company?"

"Not that I'm aware of."

"Who is Dr. Chinsky? Dr. Luke Chinsky?" The unanticipated question caught Snell off balance.

"Why, he's a researcher. A bright, young fellow—one of our team leaders—who works, worked, for Dr. Rathbone." Washington continued to stare at Snell. When the policeman wasn't talking, his jaw moved rhythmically. His partner, the scribe, diligently copied the words although the recorder captured them electronically. A random thought passed through Snell's mind: this redundancy was typical of waste in the bureaucracy. Snell talked into the silence created by Washington. "I had a meeting with Dr. Chinsky just before you came in. I've asked him to take over some of Dr. Rathbone's responsibilities. We think very highly of Dr. Chinsky."

"You know if he and Dr. Rathbone ever argued?"

Snell looked hard at Washington before answering. How much did this cop know? "I'm sure they had technical disagreements. Both are brilliant, outspoken men who hold strong opinions."

"I'm not talking about professional disagreements here, Mr. Snell," Washington said with the practiced courtesy of a trained interrogator. "No." He shook his head. "I'm asking about loud shouting matches."

Snell grinned to ease the emerging tension. "Well,

I said they were both outspoken. It wouldn't surprise me if they raised their voices in the heat of debate."

"You said you've given Dr. Chinsky new responsibilities. Chinsky know he was next in line for Dr. Rathbone's job?"

"First of all, Dr. Chinsky was not and is not first in line for Dr. Rathbone's job. In all likelihood we will conduct a national search for a replacement. I said that I had asked Dr. Chinsky to assume some of David's responsibilities, to cover in the interim. He's agreed to do that. And second, I'm sure my request to him came as a complete surprise."

"Dr. Rathbone working on any special projects?"

"The only kind of projects Dr. Rathbone, or anyone in this company, work on," Snell said with practiced indignation, "are those that are special. That's our business."

"You know what I mean, Mr. Snell. Was he working on any projects that would create interest or animosity, anything that would make him a target for murder?"

Snell hesitated, thinking, then shook his head emphatically. "No. No, in that respect his projects were quite routine. As far as murder goes, I mean. All of his projects would create interest; one of our responsibilities is to serve society. In my opinion, we do that quite well. So well that some of David's projects might even create animosity—envy would be a better word—but I can't imagine a project that would . . ." He let the sentence trail off.

"What were the projects that would create envy?"

"I'm afraid that's proprietary information."

"Mr. Snell," Washington said patiently, "Dr. Rathbone's head is all over his windshield. Now, I'm trying to find out why. What you say you put aside these little corporate niceties?" He stared at Snell, his jaw moving rhythmically.

"Don't bully me, Inspector," Snell shot back. He had had enough of this man's insolence. "David Rathbone was my friend. I feel his death more than you ever will. I don't need your theatrics. When I say the projects are proprietary, I mean it. I'm not going to have our projects sprawled all over some police report that every reporter and competitor can read."

"Our reports are confidential while the investigation is active."

"That may be, but at some point this case will be inactive and your records will be fair game. If you want an answer to that question, get a court order; and if you do, my lawyers will fight it for the next ten years."

Washington looked thoughtfully at Snell. Snell unflinchingly answered his gaze. Washington let out a little puff of air as if to indicate contempt for Snell's threat, then switched his line of questioning.

"Croft's a drug company. Did Dr. Rathbone have access to large quantities of drugs?"

Snell, recognizing he had won the brief battle of wills, acknowledged Washington's retreat by answering in a conciliatory tone. "Dr. Rathbone was a licensed physician. He had access to any pharmaceutical, in virtually any quantity. There would be reports to be filled out, but access would not be a problem."

"Mr. Snell," Washington said with uncharacteristic

sensitivity, "in our business, we see people who've been shot on a regular basis. Sometimes the shooting's an accident. Most of the time it's 'cause of a family quarrel; people argue, tempers flare, out comes a gun and someone gets shot. That's one kind of murder. Then we see the kind that was committed on Dr. Rathbone: cold-blooded, gangland-style. Most of that kind of murder is about drugs. The victims are dealers or users. The M.E. will tell us if Dr. Rathbone was a user. I'm gonna guess he's clean. Then the other possibility is that he was somehow involved as a pusher: a dealer or supplier."

Snell was frowning. He didn't like the line Washington was taking, yet he made no outburst.

Washington, the gloss off his conciliation, continued, "I won't ask if you think Dr. Rathbone was in any way involved in dealing drugs. He was, I don't think you'd know. If you did, I'm not sure you'd tell me straight." He held up his hands to stifle Snell's eruption. "No offense. Just not in your best interest to admit something like that." One upraised hand reconfigured itself into a pointing finger aimed at Snell's nose. "No, you wouldn't admit it, but I'm gonna find out, Mr. Snell. I'm gonna send a team in here to look at your drug usage records. I'd like you to cooperate. If you don't, I'll get a warrant. Either way, I'm gonna look at those records." He paused and his jaw began to grind.

Snell's glare was hostile.

"What about it, Mr. Snell? You gonna cooperate?"

Snell felt tricked. This cop was going to invade his company with a battery of clerks. He could fight them, but Washington was right. It was a simple matter to get a warrant. He might delay them for a day or two, but in the end they'd be in here.

"All right." He nodded to Washington. The hostility had not dissipated, but his corporate training was thorough enough for him to mask his feeling. "You can send your people in, but they'll only have access to the drug records, not to the research."

"You're the boss," Washington said. The interview was over.

■

Once the doors to the executive suite swung shut behind them, Calvin Washington said to his partner, Brady, "That guy's hiding something."

"Yeah," said Brady. "He made me feel inferior, cheap. Know what I mean?"

"Probably didn't like our tailor." Washington grinned. "I watch a guy's eyes when I talk to them. I can tell when they're lying or holding back. This one is doing one or the other. I'll bet you a week's pay on that."

Washington walked, with long slow steps accented by a distinctive swagger, toward the guard stationed at the elevator. "Where's the lab?" he asked.

CHAPTER 4

THE INSIDE of Croft was a maze. From the outside, the building didn't seem imposing: a two-story structure with a small penthouse. Inside, it felt cavernous. Brenda, not knowing where the corridors led, moved quickly from the employee entrance into the bowels of the structure. It was a mistake. The halls lacked signs. Without reference points, direction became an abstract concept. One hallway looked like any other; only the spacing between the doors and their numbers changed. How would she find Chinsky? To ask would reveal her trespass.

She wandered into an area that seemed to be administrative offices: secretarial desks set off by partitions. Behind each desk was the door of a private office. Would Chinsky have an office? Or would he work in a laboratory? She walked purposefully past the desks, as if she belonged there. Most of the secretaries ignored her. When she did catch an eye, it was accompanied by a friendly smile. She passed a small group talking in hushed tones, probably about poor Dr. Rathbone.

Well, getting to Chinsky required creativity.

"Ugh," she said in a loud, exasperated voice as she approached a small work pod housing a pair of secretaries. Brenda stopped in front of the desk of the younger one and threw up her hands. "I'll never figure out this place! Can you help me?" she appealed to either or both. They looked at her uncomprehendingly. "I've only been here a week, and my boss sent me to give some papers to Dr. Chinsky. This place is so confusing. I'm lost." She looked plaintively from one to another of the upturned faces.

"Who are you looking for?" the older secretary asked.

"Dr. Chinsky," she answered.

"Where does he work?"

"Ohhh," Brenda said, screwing up her face, "that's part of my problem. My boss told me, but I forgot. And even if I had remembered, I'd never know how to find it in this place."

"No problem," the younger one said as she pulled out what looked like a small directory. She flipped through the pages. "Here he is, Chinsky, Luke, MD. Is that him? He's the only Chinsky listed."

"It must be," said Brenda with a sigh of relief.

"He's in lab four. That's on the lower level. Take the elevator"—she leaned over her desk to indicate the direction of the elevator. It was back in the direction from which Brenda had come—"to the lower level and then take a right. It's next to the cafeteria. You can't miss it," she said brightly.

"Oh, thank you," Brenda gushed as she started back toward the elevator.

The secretaries exchanged a glance as if to say, good help is hard to find.

■

The elevator door parted to reveal the pretty face of Brenda Byrne. Her lustrous red hair haloed creamy, sun-touched skin. The green-gray eyes peeked through oversized round glasses while a straight nose, sporting a band of light freckles, ended in a slight pug. Her mouth, a bit wide, framed a devastating smile. She had the rugged look of a tomboy, which was close to Chinsky's ideal of beauty. She was the last person he expected to see standing there, waiting for the elevator. She made no move to get on.

"Luke!" Brenda exclaimed, her hands flying to her mouth to silence the fleeing yelp.

He stood there, like a dunce, not saying anything.

She moved toward the elevator as the doors began to close. Divining her intention, he shot out his arm to hold the door from squeezing in on her.

"What are you doing here?" he finally asked.

"Oh." She sighed, relief audible. "I found you. I came to see you. I need your help."

Without reason, the premonition of trouble, which had evaporated during his meeting with Snell, re-formed itself near the edge of his consciousness.

■

Chinsky was becoming increasingly frustrated.

Brenda had badgered him into agreeing to help her. He liked her in part for her easy, laid-back manner and her interest in sports. She took his mind away from the routine of experimental research. But in the month or so they had been dating, she had never shown this aggressive side. He wasn't sure he liked it. But he did like her—at least the old her—and as she had been quick to point out, his help didn't cost him anything. Still, he had the vague feeling he was being used.

Now, going through Rathbone's papers, he found nothing significant. Chinsky had gone through most of the file cabinets and they were either empty or contained travel vouchers, personnel records, old clippings, and the like. Had the man done nothing serious? If he did, where were the files? He stuck his head out the door and called, "Mary, could you come in for a moment?" She responded instantly. He was surprised she had stayed the day; her grief at Rathbone's death was profound.

Mary Cray and Rathbone had worked together for over fifteen years. As he had climbed the corporate ladder, she accompanied him. Now, or at least until this morning, she was acolyte of the king, queen of the research secretaries. She wore her power well and was matronly but efficient. On more than one occasion she had helped Chinsky through some administrative quagmire that would have otherwise brought him—unfavorably—to Rathbone's attention.

Entering Rathbone's office, she poked at the corner of an eye with a tiny, crumpled, tightly grasped handkerchief. There was nothing left for the cloth to absorb; her tear ducts were pumped dry, but she still felt the need to dab every few seconds.

"Mary," Chinsky said gently, "I've looked through all Dr. Rathbone's files and they contain nothing but routine paperwork. Do you have any idea where he kept the files of the projects he was working on?"

She nodded her head and moved to a cabinet he had already inspected. "In here," she said in a weak voice. "It was the only cabinet I didn't have a key to." She sniffled. "He was very insistent that we observe all security regulations. Otherwise, I think he would have just given me the responsibility for filing. He hated filing. Most of the time he put things in the wrong file and then couldn't find it." Ignoring what yesterday would have been a breach of security, she pulled open the top drawer. "Here, it's open," she said, surprised.

"The key was in the desk," Chinsky said apologetically.

Mary fingered the files. "This doesn't belong here." The indignation of a professional overcame her grief. "These are papers he kept in the desk." She whirled on him. "Did you move them here?"

"No," he blurted out defensively, surprised at the accusation. "I haven't moved anything."

Mary opened then next drawer and briskly flipped folder after folder. "These are the clipping files. I keep them in that cabinet over there," she motioned to a credenza file against one wall. "What are they doing in here?" The remaining two drawers were also loosely filled with files that belonged elsewhere.

Mary went over to the closet and opened it. On the floor was a small stack of booklets. Other than that, the closet was empty. Chinsky had looked at the booklets earlier and found they contained nothing but old scientific clippings. "There were two boxes in here packed with clippings," she said. "I was about to have them transferred to the morgue." The morgue was the file depository where seldom-used records were kept. "I don't understand." Her grief was replaced with puzzlement.

Chinsky took her by the shoulders and forced her to look straight at him. "What are you telling me, Mary? Has someone been in these records?"

"It seems that way," she said in a calm, more reflective voice. "I don't know what records Dr. Rathbone kept in this file cabinet, but I know it was full. He always complained about it, and on a few occasions when he had it open, I could see what a mess it was. Besides, I know that my records have been moved. They were never in that cabinet." The word "that" dripped with disdain.

"Could Dr. Rathbone have moved them"—he paused, trying to find the right way to ask the question, one that would not provoke another bout of sniffling—"last week?"

She thought about it for a second, then gave a slow nod. "He could have. He could have come in on Saturday; he sometimes does that." To Mary, Rathbone was still alive. "But"—now she shook her head emphatically—"he's never done anything like this before. Why would he empty all of his confidential files? Where would he put them? Why would he fill the cabinet with old files?"

Good questions, Chinsky agreed. Why, indeed?

"Mary, is there another place he keeps his records?" He spoke slowly now, giving her time to reflect. "In a lab? In the morgue? At home?" At each question she gave a tentative shake of her head.

Chinsky pressed. "Where does he send files when a project terminates?"

"That depends. If it's a closed project, which no longer requires confidentiality, he dumps the files on his table and I send them off to the office of the major investigator. Every once in a while, though, he packs a file on his own, seals it, and then has me walk it to the vault in the morgue." Mary was becoming distraught again. "Dr. Chinsky, I don't understand this. It isn't like him."

"Mary," Chinsky said with authority, "I need your help in this. I've been asked to review Dr. Rathbone's projects. To do that I have to locate his files. You, more than anyone, would know where he would be most likely to send them." He gave her a small, gentle shake. "So, come on. Think hard."

She shook her head with determination. "It's not like him. He wouldn't do this." She broke free of his gentle grasp and walked to the credenza file and looked in it again. "I don't understand it."

"Neither do I," said Chinsky.

There was a rap on the door and a head poked its way in.

"You Dr. Chinsky?" it asked.

Chinsky, brow knotted at the abrupt intrusion, nodded.

"Good," the lanky black man said as he pushed the door the rest of the way open. "Sergeant Washington, Homicide. I went down to your lab, and they told me you were up here. Can we talk?" Chinsky saw there was a white man behind Washington, shorter, more his own height and build.

"I'd better get back to my work," Mary said, as if important duties awaited her.

"Yes, go ahead," Chinsky said. "I'll call you if I need anything. And why don't you check on those files?"

"Moving right in?" Washington said. "Talked to Mr. Snell. He told me he gave you Rathbone's job. You didn't waste much time. By the way, this is my partner, Detective Brady."

Chinsky wasn't sure whether it was the words or the tone, but his dislike of Washington was immediate.

"He gave me a job to do, and I'm doing it," he said abruptly.

"Don't get testy, Doctor. Just want to ask you a few questions."

Chinsky had the feeling there was purpose in Washington's rudeness, as if he were trying to provoke him.

"Ask," he said.

"How long you been here, Dr. Chinsky?"

"Ten years."

"Before that?"

"I served a residency at Michigan. Before that I was at Northwestern Medical School."

"First job. Hmmmph." Washington made it sound surprising. "Ten years later you're acting chief of research."

"That's right," Chinsky said, waiting to see if the

policeman had a snide comment to offer. He didn't. Instead, the sergeant changed the subject.

"How'd you and Rathbone get along?"

"Pretty well. We had some differences, but on the whole he supported me, and I respected his work."

"That so? You had a pretty big argument with him last week."

Chinsky scowled. Did everyone know about that? It was irritating. "We had some words."

"About what?"

"I told him I wanted to work more independently. He wanted me to work on team projects."

"That's nothing to get excited about." It was said flatly, without inflection, as if to contradict.

Chinsky's jaw clenched involuntarily. What was this guy after? "It was important to me," he said.

"Must have been important. People heard you yelling at one another. You normally shout?"

"No." Chinsky shook his head sadly, recalling the scene they had made. "No, I don't. I was irritated at the time. An experiment was going badly. I felt I could make faster progress if I worked on my own. Rathbone disagreed."

"Doesn't seem like something to shout about."

"I don't think either of us realized we had raised our voices." The bile rose in Chinsky's throat. What was he getting at? "This is nonsense. You're reading more into this than is there."

"What am I reading into it, Dr. Chinsky?"

"Damn it," Chinsky said, raising his voice, "that's what I mean. I make a statement, and you question it."

"That's my job, Dr. Chinsky. Sort of like your job, I imagine." Washington seemed to relax the intensity of his probe. "What's so important about working alone on these projects?"

Chinsky accepted the redirection and became more conversational. "It's probably not important to most researchers, but I accomplish more when I don't have to worry about other people's work."

"I take it Rathbone didn't agree with you."

"Well, yes and no. He knew I was right as far as my work went. He wanted me to spend more time with other team members, to help them out."

"And you didn't want to."

"I already told you that. I like to work alone."

"Why?"

"What has this to do with Dr. Rathbone's death?"

"That's just what I'm trying to find out, Dr. Chinsky. It would help if you'd just answer the question."

"I prefer to work alone. Leave it at that."

"If that's the case, why did Snell ask you to take over Rathbone's responsibilities?"

"You'll have to ask him."

"Did. He said Rathbone had a high opinion of your talent." Washington was silent a moment, as if reflecting. His jaw moved while his eyes stayed fixed on Chinsky. "Guess you're right," he finally said. "That is a question Snell would be in a better position to answer. What I can't understand, though, is why you accepted the job. It would seem to me that if you really wanted to work alone, the last job you would want is Rathbone's."

Chinsky nodded. The same thought crossed his

mind when he talked with Snell. "I thought I would have more control over my work if I were in charge. If not, I can always give up the responsibility."

Washington looked at him as if waiting for him to go on. The silence between them fell like molten silicon forming a glass wall. You could see through it, but if you reached out to touch, the hand hit hardness. Washington broke the silence.

"Dr. Chinsky, the thing that's strange is that everyone around here liked this Dr. Rathbone. Everyone is his friend. No one speaks ill of him. Only person who I've found who had any disagreement with Rathbone is you. I ask you about the shouting match, you tell me you want to work alone but Rathbone says no. Next thing, Rathbone is dead and you're acting chief. Doesn't square, Dr. Chinsky. Doesn't square."

■

Brenda, with uncharacteristic timidity, rapped gingerly on the glass of Jake Salley's door. He waved her in. The office had the same low diffused lighting as the newsroom. Ever since the paper had switched from typewriters to computers, with their gray cathode-ray screens, the light had been filtered, homogenized to save reporters' eyes. Even the slats on the blinds were closed to block the sunlight. It gave the place a dark, homey feel. Or, as some said, the atmosphere of working in a closed cardboard box.

"What can I do for you, Ms. Byrne?" the news editor asked in his brusque, businesslike voice. Jake Salley, like most editors, had more work than time.

The job promoted a conversational style which eradicated pleasantries and moved straight to the point.

"I have a story idea I'd like to talk to you about."

"Why me? Why not Gus?"

"It's not a story that falls in my normal beat."

"Have you talked to Gus about it? I don't want to get in the middle of a turf battle." Gus was Brenda's boss. Protocol dictated that she review all proposed assignments with him.

"I haven't talked to him. I was sure he'd disapprove, so I came directly to you." It was true. Gus Donovan had as many prejudices as cliches. One of them was that when sportswriting got in your blood, it tainted you for all other kinds of reporting. It was a chauvinism he preached to cub reporters, probably to preempt any thought of an eventual switch. As self-serving solace, he also held that to be good you had to have sportswriting in your blood. Ipso facto, good sportswriters could never become news reporters. He had said more than once that he thought Brenda one of the best. There was no chance he would sanction her doing a hard news story. None.

She read the scowl forming on Salley's face as a preamble to rejection, so she plunged forward before he could get it out. "I want to be assigned to the Rathbone murder, the doctor who was killed at Croft this morning. I went out there this morning with Billy. He did it as a favor to me; I've been bugging him to let me in on a story and this one just happened to break while I was around." She kept the words tumbling forward, figuring that without an opening he couldn't counterpunch. The more she

talked, the more arguments she could jab at him.
Brenda firmly believed that in a pinch the sheer number of words delivered could wear down an opponent.
"I have an inside lead on the story. A guy I date works
at Croft, and he worked for Rathbone. While I was at
Croft, I tracked him down. He's agreed to help me.
The way I figure it, I can do some inside reporting,
work on the human angle of how a murder like this
affects the people around the victim. We could add a
feature piece that will take an in-depth look at how
it's affecting the company, maybe even the profession
and—or—the city." She had not seen any softening
of the scowl. "This guy, Rathbone, was pretty well
respected. There will be a lot of interest, particularly
in the medical community.

"Chief," she pleaded, "there's a big story in here.
Rathbone was a big man, an important man, and he
gets his head blown off. Why would somebody kill
him? What else was he into? Was he mixed up with
drugs? Was this a gangland hit? Was there family
trouble? This is at least a two-person story. It's not
just me, Billy needs the help. How about it, Chief?
You know how much I want to break into hard news."
It came out in a rush. If she didn't get it out now, she
might not get the chance later.

Salley leaned back in his chair and gave her an
appraising look. "You've got balls; I'll say that." She
took it as a compliment.

"Look, Jake, I think this will make a great story. Let
me go after it."

"What about Billy? It's his story."

"I know. I know," she said with exasperation. "I

haven't talked to him yet, but I know he'll let me in on it. It would be a lot easier if I had your okay. How about it?"

He pursed his lips and shook his head. "I don't think so, Brenda. This is Billy's beat and we need you on the sports desk. It's not a story that deserves two reporters—not yet, at least. If you worked with Billy you'd be doing grunt work and we're paying you to write. You're good at what you do, why don't you just stick with it? Besides, like I said, I don't want to get into a pissing contest. Gus is a mean son of a bitch when he thinks his people are being seduced."

"I'll take care of Gus, and I'll do this story on my own time. You can't object to that. But I want to know that, if Billy approves, I get a byline."

Salley gave her a cool, blasé response. "What's up? Have you started dating a jock? Is this a way to get you out of a conflict of interest?" It only stoked the fire that fed the steam building in her.

"You bastard, that's a nasty, sexist comment, and I want an apology. I also want to do this story."

He gave her a grin to let her know he wasn't taking her outburst seriously. "I'll meet you halfway. You have the apology but not the story." Seeing she wasn't going to buy it, he threw up his hands in mock defense. "Wait! I'll go one better. You get Gus's formal okay and Billy's agreement that he'll let you do more than grunt work and I'll buy the deal."

It cooled her steam but didn't satisfy her. "Aw, Jake, come on. You know Gus will never officially buy it. Give me a break. I'll get him to let me do it on the side, without admitting that I'm defecting. The for-

mal part can come later"—now she flashed him a
huge grin—"after you've made me an offer to join
the news team as leadoff batter."

The charm had little effect. "Sorry, Brenda, that's
the deal. Take it or leave it. It was more than you had
when you walked in. Now, unless there's more, get
the hell out of here so that I can get some real work
done."

With effort she stifled the riposte that sprang to
her lips. It was true. She had more than she had
started out with, though not as much as she wanted
—which was a page one byline. Further arguing, at
this point, was not going to help her get it.

"It's a deal," she said.

CHAPTER
5

CROFT'S EXECUTIVE suite was as still as the meadow upon which it looked. The calm environment extended past the bounds of the building. A plate glass wall allowed a lazy eye to extend the green of the carpet to the rolling countryside. In the distance, a stand of maples separated the Croft land from that of its neighbor. Inside, pastels and muted earth tones enhanced the serenity. It was a nice place to work. The slow pace and the breezy, piped-in music created a bucolic ambiance.

Rarely did the occupants of the suite display emotion; never, even through the trauma of yesterday's events, excitement.

Alice Murcheson's calm demeanor masked the hurricanes that often raged within her. At the most elementary level of daily routine, she fought to balance the demands of the people who had to see Snell with the available time. The demands always lost. There was never enough time.

The turbulence of the last week, starting before Rathbone's death, had churned the storms within her to force 10, the nautical measure of a sixty-knot blow, but to let it show would, by her standards, be crude.

Her reserve was a seawall protecting the peaceful meadow from the floodtide of emotion.

Murcheson was as graceful, sleek, and functional as the furniture surrounding her. At forty, she had learned that for a chief executive's secretary, looking and sounding good were as important as being good. She looked, sounded, and was good. Like her setting, she was unflappable. Because of her cold, businesslike approach, the regular visitors of the suite had dubbed her "Alice of the Arctic." She knew of the tag and both liked and ignored it. She was more interested in knowing what made these high-powered people who paraded past her desk tick. She had honed her ability to read the moods and motives of executives who fancied themselves inscrutable.

Chinsky burst through the door of the executive suite. The force of his entry created enough wind to ripple papers on the three desks.

To Murcheson, the book named Chinsky read trouble. With strides that belied his five-foot-eight frame, he covered the fifteen yards to her desk in fifteen steps. His face was a thundercloud. His voice, lightning.

Without preamble he snapped, "I want to see the boss."

"I'm sorry, Dr. Chinsky," she said with a sweet but unyielding smile, "he's on a long-distance conference call just now. Would you mind waiting a few minutes?" She motioned toward a comfortable chair. "Perhaps I can get you a cup of coffee."

"No. Tell him I need to see him now." He continued to hover above her, hands clasped behind his back. She raised her eyebrows ever so slightly. This was extraordinary behavior for one so unaccustomed to the executive suite. At least he looked better today in a lab coat than he had yesterday.

From experience, she knew that when one of these high-strung doctors was about to do battle over some real or imagined slight, they often became bull-like. In Chinsky's case, he was more bulldog than bull. It was medical school, she had long ago decided; part of the curriculum was to make them believe they were gods: omnipotent, bull-like gods.

"Why don't I give him a note to let him know you're waiting?" she calmly asked. Then politely, ignoring his bad manners, she added, "Won't you sit down?"

He didn't. She batted her lashes and gave him her closed-lip Miss Congeniality smile, turned, and went into Snell's office. Christ, she thought, all I need right now is another flap. She had her hands full getting the routine back to order while managing her own private turbulence.

In less than a minute Murcheson was back. She ignored Chinsky's bulldog look and said, "Mr. Snell is just finishing up his call. He'll see you in just one second, Dr. Chinsky." Then apologetically, "You won't have long, though. Mr. Snell does have an appointment in just a few minutes." Flashing her smile again, this time with teeth showing, she said, "You will be a dear and let him keep his schedule, won't you?"

Chinsky cleared his throat and gave her a disdainful look. He was not in the mood to be put off by pleasantries. Just then, Snell opened the door and said in a hearty, good-old-boy voice, "Luke, come on in. I'm glad you came by. I was about to call you."

"We need to talk," Chinsky said.

"Of course," Snell said graciously, ignoring the curtness. "Come on in." He closed the door behind them and motioned Chinsky over to a small seating arrangement in an intimate corner of his office. "How are you coming with sorting out Dr. Rathbone's projects?"

"What projects?" Chinsky retorted, still standing. "There's nothing in Rathbone's office but administrative paperwork."

"Well, a large part of what Dr. Rathbone did was administrative."

"Mr. Snell, what I'm telling you is that there's not a shred of project work in Dr. Rathbone's files. They've been cleaned out, and I want to know why. You ask me to take over Rathbone's work, check his files, and then you clean out the place. So what's going on?"

"I'm not sure I know what you're talking about."

"Look, Mr. Snell, I'm in no mood for games. I didn't get much sleep last night trying to sort this out, but when I finally did, it came down to you—or someone else pretty damned high up in Croft."

Snell looked perplexed. "Dr. Chinsky, I would like to understand what it is you're trying to tell me, but I'm having difficulty. Why don't you sit down and start from the beginning."

"The beginning is your asking me to review Dr. Rathbone's projects."

"And?"

"And there are no projects. At least none that I can find any files on."

"Why, that's impossible. Dr. Rathbone was working on at least a dozen efforts—not himself, of course, but through teams such as yours."

"Well, that's what I thought too. But there's no record of anything in his office and his secretary swears that his files have been rearranged."

"Rearranged?"

"Moved. Things taken out of one place and put in another. Junk filed where the confidential records were usually kept."

"You're not serious."

"I'm serious. And you know as well as I that with the security in this place those records could not have been moved without an order from you. Especially after his death yesterday."

"You think I had Dr. Rathbone's records moved," Snell said incredulously. "That's ridiculous. Why would I do such a thing?"

"I thought you could tell me that."

"Well, I can't. If what you say is true, I'm as perplexed as you."

"What I say is true. Believe me." Snell was making a good act of it, but it didn't square. Chinsky had pondered the problem overnight. Snell didn't want him to work on Rathbone's projects. That was a blind, for reason or reasons unknown. But Snell did need someone to temporarily sit in Rathbone's seat, and Chinsky was the chump. Give him the power and prestige of the chief's job temporarily. Stop the infighting for the job that was certain to occur and settle the troops down during the crisis. Then, after the crisis, appoint somebody else, removing the mantle of power. In the meantime, make sure that chump Chinsky doesn't upset anything by cleaning out all of Rathbone's files. Crude but effective. There seemed no other answer. Snell was playing him for a fool. "What I don't understand is, if you didn't want me to go through those records, why did you assign me the responsibility?"

"Dr. Chinsky, I assure you; I wanted you to handle the projects. That is the purpose of your assignment."

"Okay then, you explain it."

"There must be some logical explanation. It is possible Dr. Rathbone moved his own data for his own reasons. Perhaps," Snell said ominously, "it has something to do with his death." The words hung heavily in the air. Snell, pushing his point, lifted the dark quiet by saying, "Perhaps, although I would be the last to believe it, Dr. Rathbone had something to hide."

Chinsky was at a loss for words. It was plausible, given the violent nature of Rathbone's death. But it was awkward to hear Snell, yesterday's friend, mouth such thoughts of David Rathbone.

Snell, now confident, blasé, continued with his speculation. "Perhaps he conducted some tests and had second thoughts or felt his records could embarrass him."

Snell's proposal was preposterous, yet possible—especially the suggestion that his death and the records were linked. As Chinsky processed the rationality of Snell's suggestion, his shifting conclusions played across his face. Doubt, outrage, plausibility each took their turn on the epidermal stage. The alternative Snell suggested was repugnant, yet rational. The scientist in him could not reject the theory out of hand. But he knew Rathbone. They had worked together for a decade. They shared success and failure, hope and frustration, anxiety and satisfaction. It was out of character. On the other hand, Snell knew Rathbone more intimately. Instead of a decade, they had spent their lives together. And it was Snell who put voice to the speculation. Maybe Snell knew better, had more data. Chinsky could feel his hand tugging furiously at his beard, but deep inside himself the echo of his intellect shouted, "This is not in Rathbone's character."

Snell warmed to his hypothesis. "This wouldn't be the first time something like this has happened. You remember the fellow a few years back, brilliant, respected? He published fabricated findings in the *Journal*, made speeches, was an instant celebrity. Only after others tried to replicate his work, and couldn't, was he challenged." Snell raised his voice for emphasis and became more animated, more dramatic. "Then he admitted the fabrication. Oh, yes." Snell sighed. "But by then the reputation of those around him was in ruin, guilt by association. Sure, he had excuses. They all do. The pressure to produce results, to publish, to gain recognition sometimes plays havoc with professional values. Sometimes, under all the pressure, even the strongest personalities snap. Sometimes, because of overzealousness, people do things that are not in the company's best interest. It's possible, Luke. It's possible." Snell became reflective. "I don't even like to suggest it about David. He was my friend, but he was under great pressure. And, though I hate to say it, it's possible."

"I just can't believe it of him," Luke said emphatically. "It would be totally out of character."

"Well, I would be inclined to agree with you, but as you say, the records are missing." The inflection of the sentence placed the onus of accusation on Chinsky.

"It's not that I say it," Chinsky bristled afresh. The aura once surrounding Snell was dissipating. "The records are missing. That is a fact."

"Well, I believe you," said Snell soothingly. "The question is what to do about it?" Then, taking executive control, he answered his own question. "What I will do is call security and get them on this. We'll conduct a full investigation. There may well be some other explanation that hasn't occurred to either of us, some quirk of coincidence that gives the ordinary a sinister look." Snell walked back to his desk and picked up the phone. He held the module in one hand, the handset in the other. "Alice," he said, "get me security."

Chinsky turned away. His fingers massaged his eyes, trying to force order to all this. Where was the pattern? Snell said into the phone, "This is Bradley Snell. We've had a report of some missing records. I'd like you to contact Dr. Chinsky and start an investigation."

As the executive talked, Chinsky slowly, silently, turned around. Snell's long, erect back was to him; the finely crafted wool of his pinstriped suit coat was unmarred by wrinkle or bulge. The executive's head gently undulated to the rhythm of his words. His long right arm holding the phone gestured emphasis to the unseen audience. Chinsky saw all of this, but his eyes fixed on the phone and the hand that held it. He blinked his eyes clear once, then again, to make sure what he saw was actually there. Snell's slender, patrician fingers cupped the instrument and his manicured thumb held the phone's plunger down. Chinsky's eyes darted to the phone's other clear plastic plunger. Snell's gestures and the transparency of the nub made it difficult to focus. What made it more difficult, he realized, was that it was not there. Snell's pressure on one side of the plunger depressed the other side as well. Snell, Chinsky realized, was speaking into an empty phone.

Hot blood of resentment cascaded from temples to toes. Snell, the powerful executive he feared—and for a moment trusted—was trying to deceive him. Before his eyes. And badly. Rage, the urge to confront, added fuel to the resentment. With his throbbing jaw clenched, he closed his eyes to blank the scene and hold composure before temper triumphed. Through force of will he turned the waterfall of hot blood to crystal ice: cold, hard, unfeeling. When he opened his eyes they reflected his interior: determined yet confused. Why, the question reverberated, was Snell doing this? He needed to know. He needed to sort it out. But later, when he could think, not now.

Snell finished the charade and turned to Chinsky with a confident smile. "There," he said. "As soon as security hears anything, they'll let you know. I don't know what the trouble is, Luke, but they'll get to the bottom of it. In the meantime, I have an appointment." The corporate chieftain stood up to signal that the meeting was over. Chinsky, without a word, got up, turned, and left.

■

Alice Murcheson was always surprised at the skill Snell demonstrated in calming the raging bulls who entered his office. Usually they exited, as had young Dr. Chinsky, far calmer than when they arrived. She noted, though, that while Chinsky was restrained, his face was still a thundercloud.

She gave her boss five minutes to refresh himself before announcing Ben Proxy's presence. In those five minutes he would dictate notes of the meeting with Dr. Chinsky and splash water on his face to refresh himself. The man was so cool on the outside. She wondered if the interior housed a cauldron. After all their time together, she didn't know. What she did know—was just learning—was that what appeared was not always what was. Proxy knew him better. He would help her make sense of it. Ben Proxy was Croft's vice president of marketing. More significantly, as far as she was concerned, he was her special confidant.

The thing most people first recalled about Ben Proxy was his blondness. His hair was the color of Dom Perignon, without the bubbles. What it lacked in color, it made up in volume. The full mane, bushy brows, and thick beard gave him the look of a lion. Those who had seen him naked knew that mats of tightly curled blond hair covered his chest and pubes. The hair on his forearms and shanks was just as dense and only slightly less curly.

Where sun had penetrated the hair, it had toasted his skin a pale cinnamon. Unlike many blondes, his eyes were brown. Under a beard, his lips were thick and full. Over it, a short pug nose gave him the character of a boxer.

Although not tall or particularly muscular, he made a striking presentation. Like a good model, clothes looked better on him than on a mannequin.

This morning Proxy, standing in front of her desk, looked imperious. He had chosen a dark navy blue suit from his custom collection and paired it with a blue tie with small white polka dots. For dramatic effect, he always carried an ebony walking stick with a gold handle in the shape of a scaled serpent. The drama was redundant.

It was common knowledge that they went places together. But in all respects they worked at maintaining an appearance of being nothing more than close friends. There were some who speculated about their relationship; indeed, some who had furtively probed to see if it went further than hand-holding. The probes were always gently and tactfully turned aside. To the world, and in fact, they were friends—very close, very good friends—intellectual intimates, confidants. Nothing more. Both preferred it that way.

Tonight, though, Ben had to be more than that,

she thought. She needed someone to help her figure out what was going on.

"It's important, Ben," she said. "Please be there on time."

The elegant man gave her a reassuring smile.

■

As special as Murcheson's relationship with Proxy was for her, for him, it was not unique. All Proxy's friends were special, including Bradley Snell.

Ben Proxy came as close to being a friend as Snell allowed. Snell hired Proxy soon after receiving his first real promotion at Croft. They learned the business together. Proxy had become Snell's alter ego, a willing, able subordinate. Snell repaid Proxy by being an effective mentor. Lockstep, they moved up through the corporation, Proxy usually a promotion or two behind, but always there, ready to fill the job Snell vacated. Snell taught Ben almost everything he knew. Ben did everything he was asked.

While loyalty is an archaic concept for most business associates, the two travelers had developed something akin to it over their years together. The climb to the top is usually along the cliff. If, in reaching for a handhold or firm footing, a fellow climber goes over, that's business. Each knew that if survival demanded, one might sacrifice the other. Yet the relationship between them was such that if there were a third climber, he would go over first. Even if it meant giving a small push.

Snell opened his office door and beckoned to Proxy. "Come on in, Ben."

"Right," Proxy said to Snell. He finished up his conversation with Alice by reminding her that he would pick her up at six.

Before she could mention it, Snell told her to reschedule his next appointment. The meeting with Chinsky, he said, had put him hopelessly behind.

Closing the door, Snell motioned Proxy to the chair vacated by Chinsky. "Ben, we have a problem," he said. "Did you see Dr. Chinsky leave while you were waiting?"

"The rube in the lab coat? Is that who he was? He looked a bit upset."

Snell raised an eyebrow and shrugged off the comment. "I assigned him to take over some of David's responsibilities," he said, "including giving me an update on current projects."

Proxy waited for his boss to get to the point.

"He just told me," Snell continued, "that Rathbone's files are missing."

A grin cut across Proxy's champagne beard. "Is that so," he said. "The rube is efficient."

"Or maybe," said Snell, "you're not efficient enough."

"What do you mean?" Proxy asked with a defensive surliness.

"Twenty-four hours after I put him in charge, he's in here telling me that records are missing. Didn't I tell you not to make it obvious?"

"I filled the file cabinet with some old reports I found in his closet. What more do you want?"

"It's what I don't want that's happened. I told you

to get those records out of there because I didn't want to answer questions about them."

"If you wanted the records kept quiet, why did you put this guy in charge of reporting on Rathbone's projects?" There was only a hint of rancor in his voice as he rebutted Snell's rebuke.

"It might have been a mistake," Snell said, regaining his characteristic grace. "Before he was killed, Rathbone gave me an evaluation of Chinsky. He said that even though Chinsky was a brilliant analyst, he didn't like to work with other people. I made the assumption that—with his lack of people skills and the predictable departmental infighting—it would take him a while to get organized. Bad assumption. He just ignored the people and dug right in."

"What's so important about those records?"

"Nothing significant. Rathbone was doing some private research. He cut some corners that could embarrass the company. With all the publicity about his death there was a good chance that his indiscretions would find their way into the press. I don't want that to happen."

"So you had me move them. I wondered what was so urgent."

"Now you know."

"Well, it makes sense. These reporters get on something and they won't let go. Okay, so we've got a problem. What do you want to do now?"

"Put Chinsky off the track. You took all of the files. Some weren't sensitive. Send some of the records back to him."

"How do I know which are which?"

"I'll sort them out. In the meantime, you buy some time."

"How?"

"That's up to you."

Deep inside Croft, in lab four, in his cubicle, Chinsky sat hunched over, elbows on knees, sorting out what he thought he knew. His fingers curled in his beard. His tongue hurt from the bite he had given it as he left Snell's office. The quick clench on his teeth had prevented him from blurting out an accusation before he had time to think it through.

Snell had lied to him, that much he knew. Snell was somehow involved in the rifling of Rathbone's files. That could mean that Snell was also involved in Rathbone's death. But if Snell wanted to take the files, why did he ask Chinsky to catalog the projects? He had to know that the task would expose the missing files.

The *brinnng* of the phone interrupted his thoughts.

"Dr. Chinsky," he said into the speaker.

"Dr. Chinsky? Oh, good, ummm, you're the one I want to talk to," the earpiece said back to him. "This is Knowles over in security."

Chinsky's eyebrows rose noticeably. This was the Knowles that Snell had never talked to. Or could he have been mistaken about the finger on the plunger?

"Yes, Mr. Knowles?"

"Mr. Snell told me you thought some records were missing."

"That's right," acknowledged Chinsky.

"Must have been some misunderstanding. We

picked up the records Saturday. Dr. Rathbone wanted a new filing cabinet, a fireproof one, so we took charge of the records in the meantime. Too bad about Dr. Rathbone. Can't figure out why anyone would want to do that. Doesn't make sense. Y'know what I mean?"

"No, it doesn't make sense," said Chinsky.

"Well, anyway, about the files, I'll have 'em back in Dr. Rathbone's office tomorrow—unless you need them sooner. Or unless you want them somewhere else."

"No, tomorrow in Dr. Rathbone's office will be fine. Just lock them in the old file cabinet. I'll have Mary, Dr. Rathbone's secretary, make sure it's empty."

"Okay! Can do, Dr. Chinsky," Knowles said jauntily as he hung up.

Chinsky was perplexed. This was surrealistic. Had he been mistaken in Snell's office? He didn't think so. But here was this Knowles calling him. There was still something strange about all this. Elbows back on his knees, hair clenched in his hands, he thought about it. Then it came to him. If Rathbone wanted the files switched to another cabinet, why, in Mary's words, would he fill the cabinet with old files?

■

Across town, at the Detroit Westin, Horst Spangler sat in his room reading *The Detroit News*. He had already finished the *Free Press*. The reports of the two papers coincided: the police weren't getting anywhere. The newspaper stories gave him a feeling of confidence. Their accounts matched Duke's precisely. He took another sip from a bottle of Dortmeister.

Stepping over the mental brook of resentment that flowed naturally across the downhill terrain of his psyche, he reflected that he had done well to select Duke. Specialists, even though they were more expensive, always worked out better than ordinary thugs. The Dutchman, he thought, did a particularly clean job, surgically executed. He laughed at his little joke. And best of all, there was no link to him, Spangler. Everything had been handled by public pay phone or through cutouts. Duke was wise enough to take payment in untraceable diamonds and was already on his way out of town.

All bases covered. No loose ends.

Maybe, for once, the boss would be pleased; he, too, appreciated good craftsmanship. His lips curled in the snarl of a meat-deprived Doberman. The boss had made him hire someone to do the wet work. It took the fun, the excitement, out of this dull job. The thought stirred ugly resentment in him. He was paid for handling things himself. Now he felt like a messenger boy, nothing more. His lips twitched in disgust.

Christ! Any way you cut it, it was a shit job. He hated being holed up in this small town masquerading as a metropolis. The central city wasn't worth pissing on. And all the goddamned action was spread over twenty suburbs. It was a hard place to make connections in, though he had made some in the year he had been here. Not that the boss cared. "Watch

Croft," the big man had ordered. "Get an inside contact. Keep informed." He had done it, but apparently
not well enough. For the better part of a year nothing
happened. Then, during the last few months, the
boss started demanding weekly reports. Still there was
nothing to report. Then the order to contract Rathbone out had come. It was a surprise. Both the sud-
denness of it and the instruction that it was a contract. "Why?" he had protested. "Do as you're told,"
the boss had said. The words still rankled. He wasn't
sure whether the resentment was caused by the rebuke or the fact that the order had taken him un-
awares. He was supposed to be the man on the scene.
He was supposed to know what was going on. And he
had not. Maybe his inside snitch wasn't well enough
connected. If not, who was?

CHAPTER 6

DETECTIVE SERGEANT Washington sat with his over-size feet propped on a gray metal linoleum-topped city-issue desk. His swivel chair was precariously balanced on two wheels. A wrong move would land him on the dingy, gray vinyl tile floor. It had happened once. An irate ex-partner had kicked the wheels out from under him. Since then, no one had been brave —or foolish—enough to duplicate the feat.

"You know, Brady," he said to his partner, who, too, had his feet propped on a desk, "trouble with this case is there doesn't seem to be a motive. Why would someone drill a hole in Rathbone's head just for the hell of it?"

"I tell ya, Cal," Brady said, "there's a drug connection we don't know about. When we find it, we'll find the motive. This thing is just too professional to be anything but a paid hit. No reason for anyone to buy a hit unless there's a lotta money involved."

"Maybe. Maybe not," Washington said, his jaw moving rhythmically. "Remember that guy from Bloomfield Hills who paid to have his wife taken out?"

"Yeah, but that guy was a weirdo. This guy was straight. Everything turns up straight on him. Good reputation. No visible family problems. Plenty of money. Everywhere we turn, we turn up Jack Armstrong."

"'Cept for the argument he had with that Chinsky character," Washington reminded him.

"Yeah, except for that. But that don't mean that everyone who has an argument is a murder suspect."

"Most guys who have an argument don't get killed three days later."

"Naw, it still doesn't figure," Brady said. "Ballistics said both slugs came from a custom .44 Magnum; that usually means a pistol. But, given the pattern and direction of the bullet holes, I'd say we're looking at a rifle. Rifle, that caliber points to a pro. You use a pro, you need time to set up." He shook his head emphatically. "Couldn't do it in three days, not unless you already had connections. Nothing we got on Chinsky says he has connections."

Washington just sat there, thinking, listening to his partner talk, moving his jaw. Finally, he said, "We'll see. We'll see," and went on thinking.

■

Two stories above lab four, in the executive suite, Proxy replaced the handset in its cradle. That, he thought, took care of the mystery about Rathbone's missing records. A self-satisfied smile graced his beard.

Next, he would have to see what was troubling Alice. A nice piece, but sometimes she could be bitchy and aloof. He hoped this wasn't one of those nights.

■

Alice Murcheson sat in a corner booth of the Red Fox restaurant. The red leather upholstery felt cool to the undersides of her thighs. As usual, the light was dim enough to shade her from the casual observer. According to local folklore, and in fact supported by police records, this restaurant had served the last meal to former labor lord Jimmy Hoffa.

She had left early for her rendezvous with Proxy. For all her executive power, she had a very small circle of friends. Still fewer were the people to whom she could talk. Her family was virtually nonexistent: a brother who worked in the Flat Rock Mazda plant and a father who retired to a trailer on a one-acre lot near Ocala, Florida. Neither would understand the high-powered maneuvering of the life she lived. Her life was her job. And her job had taken her to a station where she had no peers within the company. Though rewarding, her life was more lonely than that of the chief executive. . . . She needed someone to talk to.

Most people within the company saw her as a conduit to Snell. Easy association with them usually ended in disappointment when she couldn't—or more accurately wouldn't—satisfy their political objectives. She had long since learned to shun fraternization with Croft people. But Proxy gave her an outlet. Proxy was an anomaly. Proxy understood, was a part of, her corporate world. Yet his relationship with Snell was such that she could never threaten him. That simple fact allowed the two of them to be friends. They both worshipped at the same altar.

She looked at her watch. What was keeping him?

This last week had been a nightmare. First, there was the deceit she had discovered, then poor Dr. Rathbone. Her nerves were like stressed, coiled wire; first a weak outer strand would snap, then without warning the increased tension would explode the remaining strands in quick succession. All week she had been trying to work up enough courage to confront Snell. The outcome of voicing the accusation she harbored might mean a clearing of the air. More probably, it would mean her job. Not an insignificant risk. Losing her job meant losing her corporate life with its perks, power, and prestige. But he had deceived her. That was intolerable. She had found one rationalization after another to put it off—until Rathbone's death.

Thinking back, ironically, her irritation had started with Proxy. She didn't mind working late hours or even on weekends; it came with the territory. Not many private secretaries earned sixty-two thousand a year. She was worth the money. Though she sometimes thought that when all of the hours were added up, she would be earning less than the janitor. Still, she wasn't complaining. There were other compensations. The surrogate power the job gave her was, at times, more exciting than the money. Although she seldom abused it, she could create major problems for any Croft executive who crossed her. Few did. She liked the work.

She knew more about the company on a day-to-day

basis than most of the executives. She read every
piece of mail that came into, or went out of, Snell's
office. As a routine part of her job, she parceled out
work assignments to various Croft vice presidents.
Not directly, of course, but she culled correspondence
and forwarded what she thought they should handle
in Snell's name. Reciprocally, every VP wanted a
piece of Snell's attention. She listened to their re-
quests and made priority judgments. In many ways,
she was more chief of staff than secretary. She
screened his calls and visitors and audited his telephone tape system. She attended all board and special executive meetings. She delegated the produc-
tion of agendas and minutes to her clerical staff, but
reviewed them for style, content, and accuracy.

A job like hers required commitment twenty-four
hours a day, every day of the year. It was what she
had aspired to. Yet the rewards had their price. Occasionally, like the weekend before last, she felt comfortable taking two days off in a row. That weekend
should have been hers. With Snell in Europe, the
odds were fairly good that the time would be uninterrupted. She made plans: lunch with a friend, a visit to
the Art Institute, a little shopping at Somerset Mall
—from stores instead of catalogs for a change—a
show at the Fisher and then late dinner. But thanks
to Proxy, the weekend plan never happened.

He had called at noon, just as she was leaving. He
needed to reach Snell. "Help me find him," he
pleaded. She agreed, but only after she had had
lunch.

For some reason, Snell had told Proxy he was going

to California. She knew better. She had made the reservations for Zurich. From experience, she knew Snell trusted Proxy, told him everything. But if Snell didn't want Proxy to know where he was, that was his business. She would not be the one to call the lie. Had she been smart, she chided herself, she would have taken Snell's itinerary home. She had not. Saturday afternoon found her sitting at her desk, going through her files to find where he was staying. As it turned out, the itinerary didn't help her.

She hadn't booked him into a hotel. What she had told Proxy was true, he was staying with friends. Trouble was, she didn't recognize their names. It would take a bit of research to identify them, but she solved thornier problems every day. The easiest way to track them down was to look them up by phone number. Snell's phone and address list were on both the computer and Rolodex.

She flipped on the computer and called up the phone directory. With a few keystrokes, she sequenced them numerically. International numbers, with their three-digit 011 prefix and two-digit country code, headed the list. She pulled out a phone book and looked up the code for Switzerland. It was 41. Turning back to the computer, she advanced the list until the 41 country codes were displayed. There were two numbers, both corporate offices. One was in Bern, the other in Geneva. There was no entry for Zurich. A frown creased her brow as she tried to recall Swiss geography. She didn't think Zurich was close to either city. She pulled out an atlas and found the map of Switzerland. She was right. She was confused.

Both of the other cities had major airports. Why would Snell fly to Zurich when his only contacts were across the country? Even though Switzerland was a small country, it was mountainous, so a drive to Bern or Geneva would take a the better part of a day. Sitting in a slow-moving car was not Snell's style. He must be seeing someone in Zurich. Someone he had kept hidden. A purple tinge of resentment colored her inner vision. It couldn't be. He trusted her. There was another explanation and she would find it.

Well, if the data wasn't in the computer, it could still be in the Rolodex. She hated the Rolodex. Leafing through it was a time-consuming task if you were looking for an isolated bit of data. With a sigh of resignation, she started flipping through the hundreds of cards on the rotary file, looking for a Zurich address or telephone prefix.

Her search netted nothing. With more than a modicum of exasperation, she made a mental note to chide him about keeping her informed. She thought he was better trained than this.

She went into Snell's office and opened his desk. In practice it was simply an extension of hers, or vice versa. She found his telephone book. She had been the one to type in most of the entries, but here and there were names and numbers penned by Snell. She sat down at the desk and started the tedious task of paging through the entries. A half-hour later she finished the Z's. There were no Swiss numbers not already on her computer.

There were, however, a half dozen handwritten entries that had caught her eye: all foreign, all unknown to her. She had noted each and now proceeded to check them out. It was strange that the number in each case was listed by itself with no name or company designation. So unlike Snell. Most of his entries were as complete as hers.

She looked up the country codes in the AT&T directory. They were from a strange mix of places: one from France, two from Germany, one each from Taiwan, the Netherlands, and Japan. She checked the numbers against those on her computer screen to see if there were duplicates. None. In fact, there was no entry in the computer for the Netherlands.

The numbers aroused her curiosity. She was supposed to know what was going on. Obviously, she didn't.

Her first thought was that these were numbers of women he was seeing. She quickly rejected the idea, not because it was out of the question, but because she was privy to Snell's little affairs. She had the names of women he saw in four cities. She sent them birthday and Christmas gifts in his name.

She called the long-distance operator and asked for the identity of the city codes. She then asked for the name of the party to whom the number was assigned. Sorry, she was told, that was against company policy. She pleaded that she was a secretary who had scrambled her computer files and needed to straighten out her boss's phone book. He would kill her if he found out. The telephone operator was not swayed. Murcheson begged. The operator offered to call her supervisor, then gratuitously told her it wouldn't do any good, all the parties were registered as unlisted. Murcheson thanked her and said it wouldn't be necessary. At least she had identified the cities.

Five of the cities the operator had given were easy for her to place on her mental map of the world: Paris, Hamburg, Taipei, Amsterdam, Yokohama. The sixth she had never heard of. She turned back to her atlas to look up Friedrichshafen, Germany. It was located on the Bodensee, a short air-hop from Zurich.

On impulse, Murcheson dialed the number. It took a few minutes to make the connections. She was surprised at the speed, then remembered it was Saturday. The automated electronic system had plenty of excess capacity. The phone rang six times. She was about to hang up when the other side picked up. "Ja," the voice answered.

"Hello," she announced. "My name is Alice Murcheson. I am Mr. Bradley Snell's secretary. I would like to reach him. Is he there?" It was a gamble, but she had tried long shots before and had made them. If she were lucky, the afternoon could still be saved.

"Mr. Snell is not here," said the voice. And after a moment, "He has left. It is late." My God, she thought, it must be evening in Germany. They must be hours ahead of us. It was; they were.

"I'm sorry," she said. "I didn't realize how late it was." She decided to try to solve the rest of the puzzle. "I really do need to get in touch with Mr. Snell. Can you tell me how long ago he left and where I might reach him?" There was no response from the other end. She let the silence hang in the air. Still no answer. It was she who finally yielded and broke the impasse. "I need to find him. Can you tell me who you are, where it is I'm calling?" The hand attached to the voice at the other end hung up the phone. The click was not violent, but it had a deliberate finality to it. Murcheson held the phone in front of her face and said, "And up yours, too, buddy." It was as close as she ever came to profanity.

She sat back in her chair. Now what? As an afterthought, she vowed that Snell would do some explaining when he got back. The wrath of a wife scorned is mild compared to that of an offended secretary. Snell was in for a bad time.

Then, she remembered the tapes.

Snell's phone was connected to a voice-activated tape recorder. Each morning as she came in, she routinely changed the tape and used a high-speed duplicator to rerecord it onto a master. The tapes were filed chronologically. If an important conversation needed to be transcribed for the record, she would copy it from the tape. Most of the time, though, the tape was its own record. She pulled out the tapes for the last week. If Snell had set this meeting up, there would be a record of his calls on tape. From it, she could trace his unscheduled—at least by her—itinerary.

She started with Wednesday, the day before Snell had asked her to arrange for tickets to Zurich. She played the tape, fast forwarding when she knew the conversation was irrelevant to her purpose. Wednesday turned up nothing. Not far into Thursday she caught an odd snippet. She backed it up and listened to the whole conversation.

"Ja," said an accented voice, which she thought she recognized from her recent call.

"Joseph, this is Mr. Snell. Set up a meeting immediately."

"Yes, sir. Shall I call you back with the arrangements?"

"No, unless there are problems. Understood?" Snell sounded like he was ordering a dozen shirts from his tailor.

"Yes, sir."

"Very well. I'll expect everything to be in good order," Snell said, and hung up.

Murcheson played it back twice more. This was the damnedest thing, she thought. Unlisted numbers. An unannounced destination. Orders to an apparent lackey in a remote German town. What is going on? Who are the others with whom Snell was to meet? Could they be the other telephone numbers? Her professional pride was wounded. Now she had to find out what was going on. Proxy's need to contact Snell became secondary to her purpose. In coming to that conclusion, she made the second biggest mistake of her life.

The first had been making the call to Friedrichshafen.

■

Proxy stood in the arched medieval oak doorway of the Red Fox. Murcheson sat at their regular table in the lounge.

"You're late," she said in her frostiest voice.

So, she was irritated with him. Too bad. He enjoyed her company when she wasn't being a bitch. For such a pretty woman, she had the tongue of a snake: swift and stinging. Oh, well.

"Yes." He flashed his broad smile. "Couldn't be helped. What's wrong?" he asked as he took a seat next to her. Without waiting for her answer, he gave a high sign to the waitress for his regular drink.

"Ben," she said pleasantly, "you've known the boss for a long time. You're probably closer to him than anyone in the company." He nodded agreement. "Something is going on, and I need to talk to you about it." Proxy's curiosity was aroused. Was Snell banging Murcheson? She was classy enough, but it was bad policy to play with subordinates. Many did, though. Never him. He had his rules. So, he thought, had Snell. Was this another surprise?

"Before I can talk with you, though," she went on, "I need your word that this will stay between us. Promise?" Her eyes pleaded with his. Her body strained, barely under control. This was a different Alice Murcheson. The one he knew was hard, cold, analytical.

"Sure," he promised. "Whatever it is will stay between us. Why don't you tell me about it?"

She nodded, took a deep breath and started. "Ben, I've worked here for twelve years. Eight of them for Mr. Snell. During that time I've done everything I've been asked, usually more. You know that; you know how I work." Proxy saw it coming. She was in love with Snell, he thought.

Even though Alice and Ben had been friends for a long time, the relationship was not emotional. Other than friendship, Proxy had no feeling of love—or anything akin to it—toward her. And he could not imagine her having such feelings toward him. Reason told him that one day she would become emotionally involved with someone. His surprise, he admitted to himself, was that it was Snell. Now, he speculated, she had found that Snell was playing around. He remembered the line, "Nor hell a fury . . ." brought a faint smile to his lips. Well, at least he knew what it was about, or so he thought. He liked to anticipate conversations so he could control them.

"Part of what keeps me going, what drives me," she said, "is that I've always felt there was absolute trust between Brad and me." Small pools of tears began to well in the underlids of her eyes. She blinked to hold them back and wiped with a tiny handkerchief. Despite a quivering lip, she went on with a resolute voice. "When I called you it was because I wanted to talk about some information I found last week. I've been a wreck since then. I've been trying to see if I could make sense of it, but it just gets worse." She shook her head. "I need your help." She pushed away another emerging tear. "Has Brad ever talked to you about me?"

An awkward question, thought Proxy. Was she trying to find out if he knew they were fucking? Probably. Proxy measured everyone's ethics by his own low standard. But Snell had never said anything to him. Might as well play it straight, not let her know that he had guessed her secret. "Sure he has. He recognizes that without you, he'd be lost. He may make the decisions, but you run the office, and he knows it. He lets everyone know it, not just me." The compliment had some effect. A feeble smile tried to break out of her frown.

"Thank you, but that's not what I mean." The smile hadn't made its way out. "Did he ever tell you that he had to be careful around me, that he couldn't trust me?"

This was not the direction Proxy expected the conversation to travel.

"No," he said instinctively. There was something she was trying to get out. One wrong answer on his part and it would stay locked inside with the smile. Women talked to women about sex with abandon. The same talk between women and men was more difficult. "If Brad gives any impression at all, it's that he trusts you implicitly."

"That's what I felt. That's the same impression he gives about you. Why would he lie to both of us?" Proxy's bearded jaw dropped. He could feel the widening of his eyes. Lied to both of them? Lied to *him*? This was not what he expected. Where was the sex confession, the undying love scorned? What did this have to do with him? A frown forced his mouth shut and his eyes back into his head.

"What do you mean? How did he lie?"

"He lied to you. He didn't exactly lie to me. He just kept secrets. Which is the same thing, when it comes to trust. I know everything about that man. I know about his girlfriends."

Proxy squinted his eyes in surprise. This wasn't about sex, he thought. A part of his curiosity dissolved, another part crystallized.

"I know his opinions about every director on the board. I know," she said with a wry smile, "who is going to get dumped a year before it happens. But last week, I discovered there's a lot I don't know." The last was said with scorn.

Proxy focused on her earlier words. "How did he lie to me?"

"You remember last Saturday, when you asked me to find him, you said he told you he was going to California. I knew it was a lie when you said it. I felt smug. He trusted me more than he trusted you. Maybe that's why I felt so bad when I found he was keeping secrets from me too." Proxy didn't know which to ask about first, the lie or the secret.

"Where did he go?"

"Germany. A little town called Friedrichshafen." He could feel her watching him closely to see if there was any reaction to the name. There wasn't. Proxy was perplexed, unknowledgeable.

"What the hell was he doing in Germany? We don't have any operations there."

Murcheson swallowed hard, as if to build resolve. "That's what I thought. At least until I started tracking him down." She told him about tracing Friedrichshafen through the telephone numbers, about her call confirming Snell had been there, about the tape and his conversation with a man named Joseph, and about her decision to open the safe. "In all the years I've been here I've never been in that safe more than two or three times. Most of the secure documents are in another safe in my office." It seemed important for her to let him know that im-

portant matters left in her hands were secure. "Mr.
Snell kept some cash and a few personal items in
there. But I never believed he would keep business
secrets hidden from me by putting them in his safe.
It's as though he doesn't trust me."

"You may be overreacting." What was the big deal?
Snell didn't owe her anything; she was just a secretary. Still, he was curious about what it was she could
have found to provoke this kind of response.

"I don't think so. Look at these." She pushed a
small stack of papers and four cassette tapes held
together by a rubber band toward him across the top
of the cocktail table.

He thumbed quickly through the papers.

"Alice, these look like copies. Is this the way you
found them?"

"No. I made the copies. It took me all week to get
everything together without being noticed. I put the
originals back in the safe. I wanted to have these in
my hand when I tell Mr. Snell what I think of his
secrets."

Proxy considered that. Snell didn't like surprises.
Or confrontation. Especially from a subordinate. "I
don't think that would be such a good idea," he said.

"I'm a confidential secretary. He's not supposed to
keep secrets from me. When something comes up
and I don't know about it, I look like a fool. When
you called and I didn't know how to handle the situation, I felt stupid." He had never seen a forty-year-old
woman pout. It wasn't pretty.

"Take my advice, Alice. Forget it. You'll be a lot
better off in the long run."

"Read the papers," she said. "Listen to the tapes, then tell me to keep quiet." She took a deep breath, then voiced the suspicion that had gnawed at her the past two days. "I think this may have something to do with David Rathbone's murder."

He looked at her with disbelief. Was she serious?

"Do me a favor," he said. "Don't talk to the boss until I can go over these and we can talk again."

"Ben, I have to talk to him. This has been eating at me for a week. Either he trusts me or I quit. There's no middle ground."

"I understand," he said reassuringly, "but you called me and said you wanted my advice. I can't give it to you until I go through this stuff." He motioned to the tapes. "In the meantime, just keep your lid on."

She considered his words. "I know you're right," she said. "But I don't know if I can. Every time I see him, I just want to blurt it all out. I resolved to do it over the weekend. If it weren't for poor Dr. Rathbone, it would be out by now."

"But it isn't. And now you've gotten me involved. If you want my input, you have to give me a chance to listen to these. If you can't trust yourself to hold your tongue, stay away for a few days. Call in sick. Can you do that?"

She looked at him uncertainly, then nodded.

Proxy's dilemma was whether he should talk it over with Snell before or after Murcheson had her shot at him.

CHAPTER
7

NOT MANY CABS cruised the Brewster project anymore. Charlie, like a little boy crossing the street, looked both ways before he left the protection of the front stoop. St. Antoine Street was clear as far as he could see. His caution was not for cars, but for the gangs that prowled the neighborhood. He turned north and walked toward Mack Avenue, where cabs occasionally cruised.

His joints didn't seem to hurt as much today. Maybe it was the warmth of the sun. It was a grand day, just like in the islands. It had been a long time since he had felt the toasting heat of the island sun. He wiped the sweat from his forehead with the soiled turquoise scarf he wore loosely knotted around his neck. The feel of the scarf on his brow took him back to the city of his birth.

Though he didn't know it at the time, Samuel had given him a going-away present, one that he would share with many acquaintances over the next few years. It wasn't much, just a tiny, invisible virus.

That was a long time ago.

Charlie flagged a cab going east on Mack.

Six months earlier, when he went to the clinic, he didn't need a cab. Even though it was cold, he could walk to the bright new clinic run by the university. Then, he knew he had something bad. His head hurt all the time. The cough wouldn't go away. The food wouldn't stay in him. His fatless body lost twenty pounds in three months. But worst of all, he ached. It was always with him, the ache. The weariness wouldn't go away. It was the ache that overcame his dislike of doctors.

The white doctors were nice, but as far as he could tell, they didn't help much. He was a little afraid of them. Three times in Haiti he had seen a doctor. Three times they gave him bad news. Worse, they had told him to change his life. It wasn't what Charlie wanted to hear. So he stopped going. This time, though, the hurt was great enough to overcome his fear.

The clinic was pretty with its Karol Appel primary-color paintings on the corridor walls and the sweeping fabric sculptures in the enormous window wells. He was surprised such a fine building was there for poor people. It was a far more elegant establishment than any he had known in Port-au-Prince, even better than the rich hotels he had once frequented in New York and Pittsburgh and Cleveland and Detroit. And it was big. In the center of the building was a hole ten stories high. By craning his neck he could see the sky through the glass roof. Once he had taken the elevator to the very top floor and looked down. People scurried through the connecting corridors, up and down halls, like little white and green ants. Sometimes it seemed there were more people here than in all of Port-au-Prince.

In the fifth floor reception area he sat on a modern overstuffed armless sofa and waited for someone to see him. He'd come here sixteen times and never seen the same doctor twice. Some of them barely spoke English. None of them spoke Haitian or even French. No matter, they had the air of authority and wore starched white coats. And as far as Charlie could tell, they gave good treatment. The pills made the ache go away for a little while.

For all its modern decor, the clinic was untidy. Its clientele brought the habits of the streets inside. Cigarette butts, candy wrappers, styrofoam cups, and a broad sample of the throwaway artifacts of a disposable world littered the floor. By his seventeenth visit Charlie knew the routine. He walked through the familiar corridors, took the crowded elevator to the fifth floor and signed in at the reception booth, using childlike block letters. Then he took a seat and waited.

"Brun," the clerk called. "Brun, you're next." The sound of his name snapped Charlie from his doze. As always, his first urge was to walk out, to leave. But the effort of rising brought the ache back and pushed away all thoughts of retreat. He meekly followed the clerk. Pills lay at the end of the routine and with them a brief respite from the hurt.

Once inside, things moved quickly. A nurse in a once starched uniform hustled him into a cubicle. Off came his clothes. They gave him a blue paper gown to hide his nakedness; he stood waiting, protected only by the flimsy paper and his socks. The doctor came in and asked a few questions while he thumped Charlie's chest and felt his neck. Without seeming to consider the answers, the doctor announced that some tests would be taken, then walked out. Charlie had stopped expecting more. The nurse, whom Charlie thought a shrill bitch, took some blood, some urine, some X-ray pictures. She told him to come back in three days. They didn't even give him pills.

"Where my pills, mon?" he asked the nurse.

"The doctor didn't prescribe any," she said. "He wants to see you again."

"They always give pills. You know, for to take away the hurt."

"Not today, Mr. Brun. Besides, you'd only sell them on the street." She gave him the shrewd look of a well paid, secure suburbanite.

He had done that once or twice, but not lately. Now he needed pills more than money. "No. I need pills. I hurt."

She looked at him suspiciously, but something in his face or perhaps his manner caused her to relent. "I'll ask the doctor," she said. "Wait here."

In a moment she returned with a small vial of medication. "Here. This will last you until your next visit. Be here on time."

Three days later, still weak and tired, he was back. This time, the same doctor attended him and showed more interest. He wanted more tests taken. "Would Charlie mind taking a cab to another clinic?" the doctor had asked. Charlie wouldn't mind. The nurse gave Charlie a ticket for the ride, and another to get home, then sent him off.

A cab, one of six waiting in a queue in the clinic's circular drive, took Charlie's Medicaid chit and headed toward I-75. Once on the expressway, the cab joined the northbound flow of traffic. Charlie sat back on the ripped vinyl seat and watched the blur of buildings flow by. The big turquoise-and-black Coon DeVissor sign told him they had passed out of the city. Even without that, he could see the character of the buildings change. Now they were less shopworn, had more glass. The cab's sharp turn west, as it approached Big Beaver Road at full speed, threw Charlie's frail body against the door. Less than two minutes later another sharp turn, this time north, pushed him to the opposite door. This new clinic was a long way off, he thought.

As the cab traversed Troy, the landscape opened up. The buildings were set in pastures of green with carefully trimmed trees. Rust-colored bark outlined the plantings. The taxi slowed to take the exit ramp to M-59 west. Charlie marveled at the expanse of the Silverdome. He had seen it on TV, but it looked much larger in real life. The cab slowed to fifty, made its way through Pontiac, then into the open country.

The speedometer popped back up as they sped past small but comfortable homes, larger and more expensive homes, undeveloped vacant acres, an occasional farm, and then into the rolling green hills of the Oakland County countryside.

The driver turned down an oak-lined road, which wound around a hillock. On the other side, in front of a marble-and-glass building, a cool, clear fountain fed a manufactured lake. One would have to look closely to see the small chrome letters on a discreet sign identifying the building as the Croft Pharmaceuticals, Inc. Medical Research Clinic. An even smaller line of letters read, AFFILIATED WITH WAYNE STATE UNIVERSITY, THE DETROIT MEDICAL CENTER, AND HURON VALLEY HOSPITAL.

Charlie didn't bother to look that closely. He knew he was in the wrong place. This was a place for people who had money, and while in the old days Charlie strutted with the best, he now shied away from any hint of extravagance. He needed what he had just to survive. Did the driver have the right place? he asked. Yes, this was the address. If Charlie wanted, the cabbie would wait while Charlie checked it out. Charlie wanted.

He walked up the wide marble steps. As he approached them, the ten-foot high plate-glass doors were opened by an invisible doorman. Charlie's eyes nervously darted around. A huge, circular white marble desk and low-slung leather-and-chrome chairs were the only furnishings in this room, which was clearly as big as the Empire poolhall. Charlie stood just inside the doors, uncertain whether he should advance or retreat. A pretty young woman sat behind the desk.

"Can I help you?" she asked. Although she spoke in a conversational tone, her voice carried quite clearly in the stark surroundings.

"They sent me here," said Charlie, extending the envelope with the papers the nurse had given him.

"Please let me see them," she said. Charlie took the remaining steps necessary to place them in her hand. She looked at the papers, then up at Charlie. "Mr. Brun, please have a seat. I'll tell Dr. Rathbone you're here. He's expecting you."

"I have to tell the cabbie he can go."

"That'll be fine," she said.

Charlie walked back toward the oversize door. The invisible doorman swung it open again. He walked out and waved to the driver. By the time he had walked back to the reception desk, a tall white man with slightly graying hair was coming through a door that Charlie had first thought to be a mirror.

"Hello, Mr. Brun," he had said. "I'm Dr. Rathbone. Won't you come this way?"

■

Now, months later, Charlie was feeling better. All because of that Dr. Rathbone. Charlie would have to tell him that.

The cab took the now familiar route to Croft. Charlie handed the cabbie his Medicaid chit, and without paying much attention to the building, walked the corridors to the examining area.

He smiled at Renee, the nurse on duty. They had become old friends after the first few visits.

"Hi, Charlie," she said. "Good to see ya. What can I do for you?"

"This is my day," said Charlie.

Renee's hand flew to her mouth. "Oh, my!" She bit the right side of her lower lip as her hand came down. "Didn't they tell you?"

Charlie stared at her.

"Didn't you get a call?" she asked after a moment.

He knotted his brow, perplexed at the question. He didn't have a phone. Well, there was a phone, but no one ever answered it. It was in the entry of his building. They had wanted a number in the beginning, so he had copied that one down and gave it to them. "I don't have a phone," he said.

She took his arm and moved him to a chair. "Sit down, Charlie."

He sat and looked up at her, waiting for an explanation.

"Dr. Rathbone is dead," Renee said in a gentle, quiet voice.

Charlie gave her a half grin. She was putting him on.

"He was killed two days ago—Monday." It was a whisper. She had a hand on his shoulder to allow the shock of the news to pass like electric current from him to her.

"Killed?" he asked, this time with dawning comprehension.

She nodded. "Someone shot him."

Charlie's face reflected his disbelief. *Naw*, he thought. *They shoot people where I live. They don't shoot people out here.* "But I'm getting better."

She closed her eyes, quietly took a deep breath, and said, "Charlie, let me see if I can get another doctor to talk with you. Okay?" She pushed down on his shoulder as if to press him into the chair. "You wait here. Don't move. I may be a few minutes, but don't leave."

■

It was a long shot. The only doctor who had seen these patients was Rathbone. Her only option was to call his office and see if anyone had been assigned to take his caseload. To be out of Charlie's earshot, Renee went into the little glass-walled cubicle that served as her office and dialed Rathbone's office number in the main building. "Come onnnnn," she said impatiently as the phone rang for the third time.

"Dr. Chinsky's office," Mary answered at the other end.

"Is this Dr. Rathbone's office?" Renee started to ask, then caught herself. "Wait. I know he died," she added quickly. "I'm trying to reach someone who would know about taking care of one of his patients."

There was a slight pause at the other end, then Mary said, "Dr. Rathbone doesn't . . . didn't . . . normally see patients. But Dr. Chinsky is handling his work now. Perhaps you would like to speak to him?"

Thank God, she thought. "Yes, let me talk to Dr. Chinsky." Renee leaned over to see out the door. Good. Charlie was still where she had left him.

Using the interoffice tracking-and-paging system, it took Mary less than a minute to track Chinsky. She connected him directly to the nurse.

"This is Dr. Chinsky," he said.

"Dr. Chinsky, this is Renee Stanton, the nurse at the Clinic examining station. Can you come here? I need you. One of Dr. Rathbone's patients is here."

■

In ten minutes Chinsky traveled the half mile of underground corridor separating Croft's small clinic from the main laboratory. He had only been in the clinic a few times and then only as part of a tour.

In her office, Renee Stanton explained that Charlie was a regular patient who Dr. Rathbone had been treating.

"For what?" Chinsky asked. He didn't know Rathbone, or any of the researchers, personally treated patients. That was usually left to the clinical specialist responsible for trials.

"I don't know," Nurse Stanton said. "Dr. Rathbone kept his own records. All of his cases were confidential."

"Get me the chart," he ordered.

"It's in the computer," she said. "We don't keep hard copies." She was looking at him apologetically. "I guess it has something to do with security."

"Fine," Chinsky said with a hint of annoyance. "Call up the chart and get me a printout."

"I can't," she said. "I don't know the code, the password. If you know it I can get it. Dr. Rathbone always called up his own records. He handled all the input too."

Christ, thought Chinsky, what other surprises was Rathbone going to leave him?

"Is that normal procedure?" he asked.

"No. It was just Dr. Rathbone. He was very sensitive about his project. I offered to help more than once, but he always refused."

"Is there anyone around here who can get into these files?"

"Maybe someone in information systems. One of the nurses quit a few months back and they were able to open her files. Do you want me to call them?"

Chinsky was annoyed. "Get me the damn chart. I don't care who you have to call." The thundercloud passed. "I'm sorry," he said, "this is just all so unusual. Look, while you're doing that, I'll talk to the patient. What's his name?"

"It's Brun, but he likes to be called Charlie Brown."

"You're kidding," he said.

She shook her head. She wasn't.

"Put him in the examining room, then get his chart."

CHAPTER
8

THE DAUM NANCY lamp cast a faint glow. Acid-etched glass threw wispy reflections of an orange lily. The unetched areas projected a deep orange glow. Yet there was light enough to clearly make out objects.

The room was large, sparsely furnished. The cadmium-orange light made the silk of a Tabriz, hung above a simple walnut bombé desk, shimmer. Across the room, the green LED of the stereo pulsed as Bernstein paced the New York Philharmonic through Debussy's "Prelude to the Afternoon of a Faun." The volume was just loud enough to wash the room with shallow waves of sound. The water in the mattress of the oversize, canopied bed moved with the rhythm of "Prelude." Above, hidden in the canopy, a plate-glass mirror cast amber reflections on the lovers below.

The man slowly ran his tongue down the inside thigh of his lover. Fingers intertwined and clenched as the gentle sensation sent waves of alternating ice and heat through the writhing body. He worked his way back up slowly, lovingly, gently over thigh, stomach, breast, and neck. Through the journey he rarely pressed hard into the flesh; the touch went no deeper than the length of the downy hair.

In the dim light, their bodies glistened with the

dull sheen of perspiration. Lips met; mouths opened and tongues played. As they kissed, their hands explored: fingers slid into the cracks and crevices formed by their bent bodies. The man arched his back as his lover slipped down his body until lips surrounded his manhood. Slowly, with practiced strokes, the lover went down on the excited partner. The man's head lolled back over the side of the bed as he thrust his pelvis up to match his lover's engulfing downstroke. He opened his eyes and saw the beauty of their naked bodies in the canopied mirror. His eyes rolled back in his head. He came. Even then, his lover didn't stop. Finally, he reached down and touched the side of his lover's face and in a guttural, German-accented voice said, "Ben, that is enough. I'm raw. Give it a break."

"Relax," Ben Proxy said softly. "Lay back, enjoy." Then, with a pleased laugh, "This is when you like it most, when it hurts." And he took the man into his mouth again.

■

Proxy lay cradled in the muscular crook of Horst Spangler's arm. The orange glow washing over both of them gave their skin a rich, tanned, erotic look. Neither had spoken for the past ten minutes. Proxy broke the mood. "That was so good. I wish you could come more often."

"I thought I came quite often." Spangler smirked.

"No, you beast," Proxy said, giving him a knuckle to the ribs. "I mean to my place. Here. So we can be together. Oh," Proxy said petulantly, "you know what I mean."

"I come here as often as I can. You know that."

"Sometimes I think you have another lover. It makes me jealous."

Spangler shook his head, "No. Before, maybe. But not anymore." It wasn't a lie, but it wasn't the truth. At the moment, Spangler had no other male sex interest, certainly none that he would characterize as a lover. But had he wanted one—either for pleasure or profit—there would be no hesitation. The words were said to reinforce Proxy, to maintain the useful relationship.

Proxy turned serious. He liked to talk after sex. It made him feel closer to his mate. Spangler would have preferred to turn over and fall asleep, but again he catered to Proxy's wish. The boss had said, "Find out what is going on in that company." It had taken Spangler less than a month to find the golden veep who had both Snell's ear and a penchant for cocks. A fortnight of surveillance gave Spangler a list of the Croft vice president's haunts. In the next week they crossed paths once, then twice. On the third crossing Proxy took Spangler home.

"Do you think we'll get it?" Proxy clenched his teeth, grimaced and answered his own question. "Oh, I hope not. I've been faithful ever since we started. I just hope I didn't get it before we met." It was the prayer of every gay man gone monogamous.

By the time they met, Spangler and Proxy had, between them, tasted the fruits of a thousand lovers, mostly men—sometimes two or three a day. Spangler took his sex as an outgrowth of his need to dominate men. Proxy had no need to dominate. For him men were just, well, more comfortable. He took his comforts seriously, and like a bee in clover found pleasure skipping from flower to flower. During this last year that had changed—at least for Proxy.

Spangler still saw both men and women, made love with them, used them. Women satisfied the commonplace lust within him, but men—even apart from his special use for Proxy—were a special thrill. He could slap a woman and she would whimper. Some men were like that too. The ones he liked, like this one, would slap back. The pyramiding frenzy of rough, even brutal, play would end in submission—never his—then orgasm. It was so much better than the tepid response of women. Who knew, he might have eventually found Proxy even if the situation hadn't dictated it. The main reason for his current abstinence, though, was the increased caution of the gay community. A good man was getting harder to find.

"Don't worry, you're the only man I sleep with," Spangler said, skirting the issue but addressing Proxy's concern, AIDS. Spangler didn't fear the disease. He expected to die young. If not from a bullet, then from a bomb. A disease that lingered for six or seven years before killing was in all likelihood too slow to do him damage. If he caught it, he would invoke his own solution: violent death would claim him. It was the only way to go. Besides, he naively thought, women were not a threat. It only worked the other way around. "And, hey, don't worry. If we have it, it's too late to do anything about it." He gave Proxy's head a squeeze and reached over for a cigarette.

"Did you hear about those guys from Fire Island?" Proxy asked.

Spangler hadn't.

"Six years ago seven of them spent the summer together in a house. They were all famous. One was an author. Another one did commercials. They all lived together and had a marvelous time. Now they're all dead. One of them had slept with that guy, Gaetan Dugas, the Canadian airline steward." Dugas was reported to be patient zero, the source of the North American epidemic. "He gave it to one, who gave it to the others. Now they're all dead. Somebody should have killed that guy, Dugas. Then this would never have happened."

"Somebody should have," Spangler agreed.

The mood was getting depressing. Spangler rolled over to his side of the bed and started to get out.

"Don't worry about it," Proxy said, to lighten the atmosphere. "By the time we get it, someone will find a cure. Remember"—he laughed—"I'm in the pharmaceutical business."

■

"It's the damnedest thing," Chinsky said to Brenda as they sat at Foxy's horseshoe-shaped bar. "This Haitian that Rathbone has been playing doctor to comes in for his regular visit. Hell, Rathbone never saw patients. None of us do. I told the nurse to get the chart —the documentation of the patient's history and treatment plan—and she tells me it's locked in a computer. We sent out for a technician to unlock it so we can see what's going on."

Brenda alternated between jotting notes and munching on free popcorn.

"Finally, an hour after I've sent the patient home, the technician comes up with the password."

"And?" said Brenda.

"And there were no charts, no records, no file, no anything on him. As far as the clinic is concerned, he never existed. The only thing in the file under Rathbone's password is an amortization schedule and spreadsheet on a boat he was planning to buy. You picked the right murder to do a story on. This is weird."

"Can I use it?" she asked.

"I don't even know if the patient is for real. He likes to be called Charlie Brown, though that's not his real name. He says it sounds more American. He's an interesting person. I spent an hour talking to him. It sounds as though he's been on a protocol under Rathbone's supervision, but Rathbone would never give treatment without developing a chart. He was too good a technician and administrator."

"Tell me everything. Every last detail," she demanded.

"I'm not sure I can. I've never treated patients, but they were pretty heavy in med school about patient privacy. I'm not even sure I should have told you as much as I have."

"C'mon, Luke," she wheedled. "We're dealing with murder here. And you said you'd help."

"Maybe I shouldn't have said that. Besides, I didn't know patients would be involved."

"Look, Luke," she said sternly, "I'm not just a reporter off the street that you happened to bump into. I thought we had something going!"

He could see their positions hardening. Too bad. He liked Brenda. A lot. But their relationship was embryonic. Whether it would go beyond camaraderie was still to be determined. Even so, there was the issue of patient confidentiality.

"Hey, lighten up," he said. "Just because we've dated doesn't give me license to break trust with a patient."

"You're right," she said, sensing the tension. "I don't really want you to tell me anything that would violate your relationship with Charlie. Tell me what you can. If that's nothing, okay, I'll accept it. On the other hand, I'm pretty good at asking questions, stimulating thought. Maybe just by talking together it will help clarify the situation."

He tugged on his beard.

"Look," she said, "let's go to my place. I'll fix dinner and we can talk—or not—at your pleasure. What do you say?"

He wasn't sure if this was a trap, but the idea appealed. "Okay," he said. "On two conditions."

"Name them."

"First, no pressure." He waited for her to agree. She did. "And, whatever I give you about the situation is between you and me. It doesn't get into your story."

"That's not fair, Luke."

"That's how it has to be," he said.

"Let's do this. Whatever I write, you can see before it goes in. You can be the umpire, censor what you like, call balls and strikes. If you think I've said something that oversteps the bounds, say so and out it comes. Fair?"

"You're asking for a lot. Once you have something, the only thing that keeps it between us is your word."

She looked at him hard before responding. "Yes, I am," she said.

"Sorry," he said. "I have a tough time trusting people. Not you specifically, people in general."

"Want to talk about it?"

"Not really."

"Come on, Luke," she prodded him gently. "Talk to me."

He took a long drink from his glass. This was uncomfortable. He didn't like sharing what was going on inside. He could say no and walk away. He had done it before when women had gotten too close. But they did seem to have something going. He wasn't sure he wanted to walk away just yet. He could change the subject. Agree to her scheme. That was all she wanted anyway. But that meant trusting her. Maybe she was right. Maybe he could share his concerns.

"Sometimes," he said hesitatingly, "I feel as though I'm alone in the world, even though I'm surrounded by people. They're there, but I can't trust them. If I do, they'll betray me."

"Oh, Luke. That's a terrible way to feel."

He smirked. "Intellectually, I agree. But it's the way I am."

"Why? What caused this?"

"Look, forget I brought it up. This is my problem, not yours. Anyway, I've just always felt distrustful of people. Depend on people, they let you down. It's easier just to rely on yourself."

"You trust me, don't you?"

"I haven't needed to trust you with anything yet."

"But if you did, you would; wouldn't you?"

"I don't know." There was a long pause. The seconds of silence were like bricks in a wall being built between them. "Look," he said, "this discussion makes me uncomfortable. Let's compromise. I'll tell you what I can. You write what you need to, but show it to me before you go to print. I'll take the veto power you offered. We'll see how it works."

"I'll buy that," she said, glad for the lessening of tension.

"Let's go," he said, pushing himself away from the bar but thinking, this will change our relationship one way or another.

The conversation during the fifteen-minute trip from Foxy's was trivial. Both stayed away from Charlie and the Rathbone murder.

Brenda lived in a Southfield condo development. On two previous occasions they had ended the evening at his apartment. This was the first time Luke had been here. The inside of her place, with its dark green chintz and Louis XIV furniture, was far more stylish than the outside.

"What can I fix you?" she asked. "Wine or a Jack Daniel's?"

"Some wine," he said.

She poured them each a glass of Mondavi Chardonnay, then sat beside him on the sofa. "Now," she said, "tell me about Charlie Brown." She leaned over and pressed the record button of her tape recorder.

"Do we really have to record this?" Chinsky asked.

"It's a lot easier—and less businesslike—than taking notes."

He accepted that. "I really don't know that much about him. The only information I have is what he told me. That, and my examination of him. He's a very sick man.

"I kept trying to take his history—to collect the basic facts of his physical antecedents—and he insisted on telling me stories about his life. He lives in the inner city and travels out to the clinic at Croft expense. Takes a cab. He's been doing that for six months.

"I gave him a physical exam. I could see shingles on his face. They covered his shoulders, chest, and back."

"What's a shingle?" Brenda interrupted.

"Actually, it's herpes zoster, a segmental inflammation of the dorsal root. A lot like chicken pox, but very painful."

"The chicken pox helped. You lost me with the rest."

"I'll try to keep it nontechnical. Actually, I was trying to do that with shingles."

She made a face.

"His lymph nodes—small glands in the neck, arm-pits, and crotch—were quite swollen. He's very thin." He paused. "Is this helping you?"

"Maybe. What's wrong with him? Why was Rath-bone treating him?"

"At this point, I don't know the answers to either of those questions. I've ordered some tests taken, and they should begin to tell me something. The interest-ing thing is that the symptoms he has are for infec-tions and neoplasms that are generally short-lived. My initial diagnosis was acute herpes, but after some research, I think Charlie has a virus that's affecting his immune system."

"AIDS?" she asked, in a subdued voice.

He nodded his head. "I think so."

CHAPTER
9

CHINSKY SAT LOOKING at the lab reports spread over his desk top. There was no question about it, Charlie had AIDS. The ELISA test was positive.

The more he studied the reports and literature on the disease, the more perplexed he became. Most of the publications had come not from Croft's library but from the files in Rathbone's office. "The articles," as Mary put it, "that the chief was always clipping and saving." During his initial review of Rathbone's files, he hadn't noticed the heavy emphasis on immune systems. Now, though, it was apparent that Rathbone's papers focused on various aspects of the disease, its history, and efforts made to control it.

Riotous speculation swirled through his researcher's brain. Was Rathbone engaged in secret research? If so, why? There was nothing secret about the virus. It was the number-one priority of the National Institutes of Health. Congress had appropriated a billion dollars for research. Money was there for the taking. Croft was no stranger to government grants. But generally, applications for grants were well publicized within the company. The main research effort of any venture was carried out by teams under Rathbone's direction, but the chief of research rarely got involved with the actual process of investigation. Why was he delving into this so deeply? And was he acting on his own?

Chinsky looked up from the papers; his thoughts meandered to Brenda. She was right about one thing: her questions helped clarify issues. She was a good interviewer. A shame it was wasted on those jocks.

Their talk last night had been comfortable. She was easy to be with. He forced himself back to the test results.

Perhaps he was being too quick in his conclusion. The ELISA test confirmed that HIV antibodies were present, not itself a definitive confirmation of viral infection. To be sure, he would have to order a Western Blot. That took a bit more time. But now that he knew what he was looking for, the search would go faster. He reached over and picked up the phone.

■

Two floors up, Ben Proxy was also reading reports: Murcheson's. *These are notes*, her paper started, *on about a half dozen meetings. The meetings are between members of what appears to be a secret organization, consisting of the top people in pharmaceuticals. For reference, there is an attached list of people and organizations.*

He flipped to the back page and checked the list. He recognized most of the names. It was an international group, and all the big boys were there.

They meet about twice a year, in places like Friedrichshafen. There's another place in Brazil and one in Hong Kong. The notes on the meetings go back

*four years. Usually, they deal with keeping drugs off
the market or limiting competition. For example, the
reason we're doing so well with Priden is that everyone
else agreed to let us have the market.*

Proxy had wondered about that. Priden was Croft's
brand name for a pindolol-based beta-adrenergic
blocking agent, used to treat high blood pressure.
They had introduced the drug four years ago and had
a virtual monopoly ever since. Margins were extremely high and sales brisk, a true cash cow. Proxy
had often wondered why the competition had not
come after them. *Each of the attached reports con-
tains a summary of a meeting as it was dictated by Mr.
Snell. I transcribed the summaries from the dictation.
Interspersed with the dictation are telephone recordings
of conversations with various people I believe to be connected with this venture. These were not transcribed,
but are available on the tapes themselves. The tapes are
numbered in what I believe to be the chronological order in which they were recorded.*

Proxy flipped through the transcriptions and read
them quickly, trying to take in their flavor. As he did
so, long-standing marketing mysteries vanished. Here
was the reason they had never pursued a competing
product for Avco's nonsteroid analgesic, which had
made such an impact on the sports world, or
Wahlbanger's nicotine mint, which had captured the
"stop-smoking" market.

They were all here.

Slick, thought Proxy. Slick, but illegal.

This stuff is dynamite.

∎

It was on the last tape.

Proxy hit the stop button. With frenzied motions he rewound the tape a few feet and played it again. Then again.

Snell's voice came through clearly. "It was decided that a cure or vaccine to bolster the immune system against opportunistic attacks is unacceptable." *Unacceptable. Unacceptable!* The word, delivered in Snell's impersonal monotone, seemed to shout at him. Snell's voice went on. "A way will have to be found to limit all meaningful research until such time as various government grants are maximized and the market reaches a size to sustain a significant profit level."

Unacceptable. Limit research. Government grants maximized. Market size. Significant profit level. His thoughts whirled, confused, unbelieving. *The bastards!* He played the tape again, this time straight through to the end. Snell summarized some additional points of the last meeting before Friedrichshafen; but no further reference to the heinous decision.

"I need to talk to him about this," an agitated Proxy said out loud. "He has influence. He can get them to change their minds. We need help. We need a cure, a vaccine, anything." Proxy paced the room, his hands flailing. There has to be a mistake, Proxy thought. He can't be a part of this.

Vaguely, through the haze of his anxiety, a memory began to pound on his subconscious like a drop of water on a rock. It had something to do with Rathbone. With the files. There was something in the files he pilfered from Rathbone's office that had to do with AIDS. He hadn't looked at what he was taking, he had simply emptied the cabinet—as Snell had directed. Then, after Snell's barbed criticism that he had taken too much, he remedied the error by sending back all but a single box full of files. There was something there, something that caught his eye as he sorted the patient records from the rest. Out of curiosity he had looked at a patient record to see if he could figure out why these records were so important. It was all mumbo jumbo to him. But the drop kept pounding. There was something there. He needed to find out what it was.

Grabbing his coat and cane, he flew out of his office. Halfway out the door, he remembered Alice's notes and the tapes, both sitting on his desk. He wheeled around, grabbed his briefcase and dumped the papers, tapes, and tape recorder into it. Then he was gone.

■

It was seven when Brenda got to Luke's apartment. She had covered a rare afternoon ball game. The Tigers, uncharacteristically, managed to lose in the ninth. The late-inning surprises were what kept her and the fans there "till the fat lady sang."

She had stopped off at her apartment to change clothes and take a quick shower.

As her cab approached the canopied entrance of Luke's Troy apartment, she began to redirect her focus from sports to news. The story was taking shape.

The fact that Rathbone had been working on something to do with AIDS created intrigue. The question was, how could she use the information? Not even the police knew about this angle. Chinsky only had circumstantial evidence. Based on what she had, Croft could deny everything and she would strike out. Not at all what she wanted. She needed more. Luke could get it for her, but first she had to do some groundwork. She needed to develop the story in a way acceptable to him, and he was not an easy person to work with. It was as if he resented another person's involvement. His reaction to her suggestions was resistance and suspicion. Christ! He was trying to be a one-man basketball team. His shooting was great, but without teammates his passing was terrible. She would have to handle him carefully.

Gus was being a regular curmudgeon too. He had reluctantly agreed to let her follow this story and then had practically doubled her assignments. Only when she told him to shove it had he relented and gone along. She wondered if she meant it. Would she give up her job if he had refused to cooperate? Well, that was something she didn't have to answer—yet.

From a business perspective, this relationship with Chinsky was beginning to pay off. By luck, he had reached her just before she left the newsroom for the ball game. All he said was that he needed to talk to her. That was enough. She would take the opening in his line and drive a fullback through it. *No wonder he's paranoid about working with others,* she laughed to herself, *with friends like me around.* Yes, she thought, we are becoming friends. Apart from the help he was giving her, she was beginning to like him. We live in a strange time, she mused. People became lovers first, friends later. On her rating scale he fell somewhere between a teddy bear and a fuzzy Dustin Hoffman. A very high rating.

She directed the cabbie to the resident entrance of Chinsky's glass-skinned high rise. The building also doubled as an office. Although she had been here before, this was the first time she had arrived by herself, or in daylight. The mirrored glass shell gave the building a space-age look. Not bad for a struggling doctor, she thought. He only looked like he was struggling. Ten years with Croft had paid handsomely— without the expense of going into private practice.

"Good evening, miss," the doorman greeted her. "Can I help you find someone?"

She recognized the doorman, Albert, from the other times. Chinsky said he was just there for show, to impress the visitors. The residents, he had told her, usually entered through the underground, completely bypassing the lobby. She still had the magnetic card he had given her after the second visit. Clearly, the good doctor had been out to impress her, since they had used the front entry both times. Well, for her money, Albert did add class. "Yes," she answered, "I'm here to see Dr. Chinsky."

"Yes, ma'am. Is he expecting you?"

Class went only so far. What the hell business was it of his whether she was expected? He was probably supposed to keep the riffraff out. Did she look like riffraff? "Yes," was all she said.

"Would you like me to ring?"

"I can handle it," she said.

The marble foyer sported a cathode-ray tube built into one wall, an electronic version of the old-fashioned buzzer system. She found Luke's name and punched his code into the keyboard. She could feel a scanning camera show him who was at the door. It was like being undressed in public. She turned to it and flashed a smile. The impulse to moon the camera was strong. Perhaps if the doorman were not there—well, another time. The latch on the glass door buzzed and she pushed it open.

The elevator ride was swift and noiseless.

"Hi," Chinsky said, as he opened the door.

If the building failed to match the Chinsky image, more so the apartment. The same thought had struck her on her first visit, before she knew he was a doctor. She was surprised. And pleasantly.

"Hi," she said back.

He ushered her into a large foyer. A series of three Russell Keeter paintings of anatomically perfect, though limbless, nudes in rich, sensuous colors gave impact to the walls of beige travertine marble. A small DeGuisti bronze on an illuminated pedestal was the only object on the entry floor.

The living room was two steps down. The far wall was glass. At night, she remembered, the view of downtown Detroit was like fireflies on an August farm. Now, in the abating light of day, a haze cast a soft luster over the homes and businesses stretched out on the relief map twenty stories below.

Chrome, leather, glass, and marble were the predominant textures of the room. The gunmetal-blue tightly knit wool carpet was accented with rich, red-toned Oriental area rugs. It was sparse, functional, elegant.

It was on their second meeting, the first time she had been here, that he began to reveal that his manner was a facade used to cloak the genius in him. She had asked him casually about the furnishings and found him schooled in their background. Yet he passed it off as something of little interest to him. "I had it decorated," he had said. "I like it, but I don't pay much attention to fashion. Had I done it myself, it probably would have been early K mart." She began to sense that the self-deprecation and his casual dress and manner were studied understatements—no, mis-statements—meant to lull others into accepting him. She sensed he was a special person, one who had to work hard at relationships.

This evening a rhythmic Stan Kenton tape played softly in the background.

"Thanks for coming on such short notice."

"I wouldn't miss it for the world, sport. You're my ticket out of the locker room."

"Can I get you something?" he asked. She took a glass of wine.

"Is this you?" she asked, holding up a picture of a clean-shaven Chinsky against a backdrop of mammoth pines.

"Yeah. Taken up North."

"You look so different without the beard. Nice, but different. I mean—"

"Actually, it was on that trip that I started growing

it. I do a little camping up North; backpack, stuff like that, in the Upper Peninsula."

"You do?" she broke in. "Which part?"

"Around Sault Sainte Marie."

"We used to have a cabin near Cheboygan. I love it up there! I'm just a city girl with country roots."

"The land is beautiful but rugged, about as wild as you'll find in the Midwest. It's nice just to get away, chop wood, live off the land, rough it. You can get lost up there."

"You go alone?"

"Once. But usually with a couple of college buddies."

"That's something I'd like to do someday."

"Who knows, maybe next summer."

"I'll put it in my book."

"Do that." Chinsky refilled their wineglasses and settled back on the sofa. After a while he said, "I got the lab reports back on Charlie. He tested HIV positive. It looks like he has the virus."

She just said, "Oh."

"I've also been going through Rathbone's office files. He has a lot of literature on immune systems. And I don't know if I told you, a lot of the missing stuff showed up." As an afterthought he added, "Not all, but a lot. Anyway, it seems as though he was devouring everything printed on the subject. I thought that unusual, since his duties are largely administrative. The research is pretty much left to the investigators who make up the teams."

"Didn't he supervise the research?"

He nodded. "Yeah. But to administer a program he

only needed to know the pathology of the problem, the general protocol, and the economic cost-benefit ratio to administer the research. The stuff he assembled goes way beyond that. Besides, as far as I know, there aren't any teams at Croft working on any immune-system related studies." He tugged at his beard. "As I said, it doesn't fit. That's why I wanted to talk to you. I thought your questions might add a different perspective, one that could trigger a connection." It was a revealing statement. He was asking her to join him on the court, then passing her the ball.

"Count me in," she said. "Before you go too far, though, I have a confession to make. I'm woefully ignorant when it comes to AIDS. I know there's been a lot of stuff in the newspaper and on TV, but I've pretty much ignored it. I thought it just didn't affect me."

"Well, except for my general reading to keep up— and the crash course I've had in the past few days— I'm probably in about the same position relative to the specialists."

"What I don't see is why it's so difficult to find a cure."

Chinsky smiled at the statement. "From what I've read the researchers have made good progress so far. Most people have no idea how little we, the scientists, know about the human body. In many respects we're no more knowledgeable than nineteenth-century scientists. On the other hand, do you realize that this disease was not even identified until 1981?" Her look told him she didn't. "When you consider that, things are moving pretty rapidly. To give you some idea of how fast things are progressing, consider that by 1984, in only three years, two doctors, one French, the other American, positively identified the virus. That's amazing progress."

She nodded as if she understood.

"By 1985 AZT, an unpatented drug developed by a guy named Horwitz—who, incidentally, is from Detroit, a chemist—as a cancer-fighting agent, showed that it could kill the virus in a test tube. But a test tube is a lot different from the human body. Besides, it took until 1987 for the FDA to authorize the use of AZT for the most advanced cases of patients with AIDS-related complex. And it wasn't until late 1989 that they allowed AZT to be used for mild cases. Still, the progress has been phenomenally fast. But so far, no cure. No vaccine."

"What's the difference?"

"A cure will halt and reverse the direction of the disease. A vaccine helps the body resist infection in the first place. Remember Salk's polio vaccine? It virtually wiped out that disease by stopping the spread."

"Back a minute ago you said this AZT was unpatented. Is that the case with most drugs?"

"Lord, no! It's a jungle out there. If someone has something that might work, they patent it to protect their manufacturing and marketing rights." He could see the quizzical look on her face. "AZT was developed in 1964. It didn't work as a cancer drug, so they never took out a patent. At that time, no one had ever heard of AIDS. Besides, that was over twenty-five years ago. A patent is only good for seventeen years."

"Okay, I understand. But now you've found a lot of literature concerning AIDS in Rathbone's files and you've confirmed that Charlie has it. So what?"

"Well, Rathbone's files, even with the emphasis on literature concerning AIDS, wouldn't normally raise my interest. Perhaps he was just following it as an intellectual exercise. But a few days ago, when the missing files were returned to Rathbone's office, there were no files on Charlie or any other patient."

"Do you know there were other patients?"

"No. It's just a guess on my part, but, I think, an educated guess. Remember when I told you about my conversation with Snell? I didn't think he was talking to anyone on the phone. Then, a few hours later, I got a call from a guy in security named Knowles who told me he had the files."

She nodded, waiting for him to continue.

"When the files were returned, I put the literature from Rathbone's file cabinet back into the boxes Mary said they had originally been packed in. Then I put the files security delivered into the file cabinet. Even before I started looking through the files, something seemed odd. I remembered something else Mary said when I first looked at Rathbone's files. The cabinet was supposed to be crammed full. Rathbone complained of having trouble getting any more into it. After I filled the files"—he stood up and spread his arms so that his hands were about two feet apart—"there was still about this much room left."

"So," she said, "they didn't give you back all of the files."

"It doesn't seem so. And, while the record on

Charlie might be large, I can't imagine it taking up"
—he looked down at his still outstretched hands—
"this much space. There are more records somewhere. I'll bet on it."

"Why not call up Knowles and see if he has another box that he failed to return?"

"I did."

"And?"

"There's no one by the name of Knowles working
in security."

Brenda's eyes widened; the freckles on her cheekbones were stretched taut. Her mouth formed a silent
Oh. "You think Snell set this up," she said out loud.

"That's what I thought at first. Maybe still do.
Maybe Snell knew that Rathbone was doing something illegal. When he was killed, Snell could have
had the records confiscated to protect the company."

Brenda nodded. It made sense. "Is that what you
think happened?"

"I don't know. There's another piece of information," Chinsky said. "When the lab sent the tests
back they also sent me copies of the prior tests on
Charlie. Apparently, whoever took the files and
blanked the computer forgot about the lab computer."

"And?"

"And Charlie's pattern of tests show definitively
that his disease is in remission."

CHAPTER
10

CHINSKY RESOLVED to keep his temper in check. He sat in a cinnamon-colored leather armchair and looked at Snell across the broad expanse of a fine-grained walnut desk.

"Well, Dr. Chinsky, what can I do for you?" Snell said in a businesslike tone. Snell appeared uncharacteristically rushed. There was little small talk. Chinsky, who had demanded an audience, was ushered in unceremoniously.

"Mr. Snell, something is going on here that I don't understand." The researcher, unaccustomed to confronting authority at this level, was stiff, formal. "As you requested, I've been following up on Dr. Rathbone's work. What I've learned makes me believe that you're holding something back. Something, I think, that is very important. And I'd like to know what it is and why."

Snell leaned forward across his desk, supporting his weight on his elbows. His hands were clasped, prayerlike, before him. He said nothing, waiting for Chinsky to continue. The silence had its effect.

"First, Dr. Rathbone's records were missing from his office. When I complained of that to you, they reappeared—or part of them. Supposedly—and at your instruction—a security man named Knowles called and told me the records had been moved for safekeeping. I checked with security and no one named Knowles works in the department. Besides, when you were making the call, I noticed that your finger was on the plunger. You were speaking to a dead phone. I don't know why, but I didn't say anything at the time."

Snell's face registered no sign of surprise.

"A few days ago," Chinsky continued, "I received a call from the clinic telling me one of Dr. Rathbone's patients was there to see him. It seems no one—including Rathbone's secretary—outside the clinic knew he was seeing patients. Apparently, someone screwed up. No one told the patient Dr. Rathbone was dead. The nurse in charge of the clinic called Dr. Rathbone's office for instructions. She got me. When I went to the clinic, I asked for the patient chart. The nurse told me all records were computerized. When we finally managed to break the password and get into the computer, there were no records. The files had been wiped clean. Nonetheless, I talked to the patient and ran some tests. It was clear from the results that the man is suffering from a number of opportunistic diseases complicated by an immune deficiency. He has AIDS."

Snell was passive.

"Whoever was confiscating and destroying records —at, I suspect, your instructions"—at this Snell's face muscles tightened—"apparently overlooked the historical lab profiles. The lab sent me not only the results of the latest test, but those they had previously run. The disease was clearly in remission when Rathbone died."

Chinsky paused and stared at Snell, waiting for a response.

Snell leaned back in his chair, not breaking eye contact, and said nothing.

"Mr. Snell, I believe you knew of Dr. Rathbone's work, and for some reason you're trying to keep it secret. I didn't ask for this job, you gave it to me. But now that I have it, and since the secret appears to be coming out, I think you owe me an explanation."

"Have you shared your hypothesis with anyone?" Snell asked.

"I don't see what that has to do with it!" Chinsky answered. "Something is going on and I need an explanation."

Snell appraised him. "Dr. Chinsky, it's important that I know if you have discussed this with anyone but me. Answer me that and you'll get your explanation."

Chinsky was tempted to deny his conversations with Brenda, but that would have paired him with Snell. "Yes," he said. "I've discussed it with a friend."

"Who? Someone associated with Croft?"

"No," Chinsky said, "a woman I see from time to time. She has nothing to do with the company."

"May I ask her name?" Snell asked with the nonchalance of a trained interrogator.

Chinsky became suspicious. "I don't see that it's relevant," he said.

"Trust me," Snell said.

"Are you kidding?"

Snell nodded. "Touche," he said. "I would, however, like to know the name of your woman friend. Whether you trust me or not, it's important." His voice was imploring, reasonable. Chinsky conceded.

"Brenda Byrne," he said.

Snell made a note of it. "B-U-R-N?" he asked as he wrote.

"No," Chinsky said, "with a Y. B-Y-R-N-E. Now, about that explanation?"

Snell ignored the question. "Anyone else?" he asked.

"No," Chinsky said coldly. Snell acknowledged the curt answer by a slow nod and a hard stare.

After a moment, Snell pushed himself away from his desk and rose. Silently he walked over to a walnut-paneled cabinet on the far side of the office. Opening the door, he reached for a cut-glass decanter and glass. The silence exaggerated the time. Pouring, he finally asked of Chinsky, "Can I get you a drink?"

Chinsky shook his head at Snell's well-tailored back, then said, "No."

Snell turned and faced Chinsky. There was a slightly amused look on his face, his lips curled at one end to form a wry smile. "Dr. Chinsky, you are a very clever man, a clever researcher. That's probably why David thought so highly of you. And you're right, it was foolish of me to try to keep a part of Dr. Rathbone's work from you. But, when you hear the rest of the story, perhaps my actions—and yes, deceit—will be understandable."

It was Chinsky's turn to be expectantly silent.

Snell took a deep draft from his glass. "David

Rathbone was my dearest friend, but I'm afraid he got himself, and possibly us—by us I mean you, me, the company—into something that is clearly beyond our capacity to handle. I believe it had something to do with his death.

"I could share my suspicions with the police, but if I do so, it will mean certain ruin for Croft. I'm not willing to risk that. We do too much good here. And there are too many people whose livelihood is inexorably linked with the survival of this company. And, of course, while we do have a responsibility to society, our first responsibility is to do what's best for the company."

"What happened to 'doing the right thing'?"

"After you've heard me, I think you'll agree that this is the right thing."

Snell walked over to the desk and perched on the edge closest to Chinsky.

Chinsky tilted his head to watch Snell's face. The exposure of his neck made him acutely uncomfortable.

"A few months ago," Snell went on, "I became aware that Dr. Rathbone had been quietly working on developing compounds that affected the immune system. I didn't pay much attention to it. From time to time one thing or another caught his interest and he pursued it. That was his job. Sometimes his hunches were spectacularly right. At other times, nothing came of them. I never really knew when he was working on something by himself or when he devoted a half dozen teams to the effort; as I said, that was his job.

"Three weeks ago Rathbone told me he believed he had developed an agent that would reverse the effect of AIDS." Snell showed a wry smile. "I was elated. If he were right, this would be the discovery of the century. Not only would the effect be to reduce a plague that was consuming the heart and mind of our young people, but it would, in the process, create a fortune for Croft."

Snell was back on his feet, pacing. Chinsky was glad for the relief it gave his neck. So far Snell had told him nothing he had not already discovered, except, perhaps, the timing of events.

Snell's face and tone darkened as he turned back to Chinsky. "He also told me," Snell said with measured words, "that he was testing his compound on human subjects." He stopped and stared at Chinsky as if to assess the impact of his revelation.

There was none. Chinsky had guessed as much. "Do you know anything about the compound?" Chinsky asked.

"Not a lot," Snell answered. "Rathbone said he had developed an agent that produces an antibody that kills the HIV and encourages the regeneration of helper T cells. He never shared the composition with me, but he hinted that the dosage was extremely heavy."

Chinsky nodded, more as a sign for Snell to go on than as an indication of understanding or agreement. The full information would be in Rathbone's files. Then an irrational anger engulfed him. Damn it, what had Snell done with the records? "Why did you take the records?" Chinsky asked harshly. "And where are they now?"

Bradley Snell inhaled deeply through his nose and rocked his head slowly up and down, as if to say, fair question. "When I heard of David's death, the first thing that I remembered was our conversation concerning his viral research. He had used human subjects. As you know, that's illegal unless you have FDA approval." Snell gave a sad shake of his head. "He didn't."

Chinsky understood. Croft operated at the pleasure of the FDA. The government bureau set rigorous standards for the testing of substances on human beings, with good cause.

In the late 1950s and early 1960s, thousands of children in West Germany and Britain were born with arms and legs that looked more like seal flippers than human limbs. Still others lacked ears or normal body openings, or had eyes that were fused shut. Few survived. After intensive investigation, the source of the disaster was traced to thalidomide, a drug widely used as a sedative. The mothers-to-be took thalidomide to get rest, to calm their nerves during the trauma of early pregnancy. The short-term calm turned to long-term horror.

At the time, medical science believed the fetus to be adequately protected by natural means from the effects of drugs ingested by the mother. Medical science was wrong. The European pharmaceutical manufacturer who released the drug knew nothing of its terrible side effects. Testing had been inadequate.

Mothers and babies in the United States were

spared tragedy because the FDA insisted on prolonged trials before the drugs could be released to the public. At the time the agency was severely criticized as being unnecessarily cautious. Then the European disaster struck.

The episode had reinforced not only the power of the FDA but its conservative policy. Now the agency was so powerful that violation of their regulations could ruin a company and the people involved.

"Dr. Rathbone," Snell continued, "needed subjects who had contracted the disease. To find them he spent whatever money was necessary. The only reason I found out about the testing was because I questioned some expenses being incurred at the clinic. While he had not shared the fact of his experiments with me until then, he was too honest to lie when faced with a direct question. I asked. He answered." Snell shook his head. "I was shocked. More than shocked, outraged. I told him to stop testing immediately. He said he couldn't—or more forcefully, wouldn't." Snell paused, as if to collect his thoughts. "He said he had been conducting human trials for over four months and some of the cases were in remission. He was convinced he had a cure. From what you say, apparently he was right. We argued about it more than once. Finally, just last week, he agreed that we would share our basic research with the NIH and ask for FDA approval to conduct trials. By that time he knew what the outcome would be."

"I still don't understand," Chinsky said, "why you took the files."

Snell gave a self-deprecating smirk. "I panicked."

He paced over to the far side of the desk, placed both hands on it, leaned forward, and looked hard into Chinsky's eyes. "When I heard that Dr. Rathbone had been murdered, I knew there would be an investigation, and I panicked. I had the files removed from his office and the computer records destroyed. I never thought of the lab records, or they would probably have gone too. At that point, I was more concerned with protecting Croft than I was in producing a cure that would save a few fags and drug addicts."

Snell's last words startled Chinsky. They undercut the sincerity of the words. He could understand protecting the company, but why the disdain for the victims? A picture of a sincere Snell with his finger on the phone plunger flashed through Chinsky's head. His face must have revealed his thoughts.

"Forget that," said Snell quickly. "But make no mistake—the company is my first concern."

Another concern, triggered by Snell's comment, flashed through Chinsky's brain. "What did you do with the files—not the computer files, the other ones. The ones you had taken from Dr. Rathbone's office?"

"I had them destroyed," Snell said.

It was the answer Chinsky had feared. For a moment he mulled the enormity of what Snell had done. Of the hope Snell had mindlessly snuffed. The red dust of anger clouded his eyes. A cyclone of disgust swirled from deep within him. "You bastard," he said with the sharp blast of a gusting gale. "You stupid, greedy, self-centered bastard. You've condemned thousands, hundreds of thousands of people to death." Chinsky was on his feet. He had had enough.

"They condemned themselves," Snell said calmly, ignoring Chinsky's vituperation. "In any case, it serves them right. I'm sure they killed Rathbone."

The comment brought Chinsky up short. "What do you mean?" he demanded.

"Rathbone was using contaminated drug addicts as subjects. Obviously, he offended one of them in some way, and they killed him. Who else could have done it?"

"I don't know," Chinsky said, the storm momentarily quelled by the analytical problem so casually thrown in his face. So consumed was he with tracking the professional aspects of the mystery that his analysis had not led to speculation about Rathbone's death. He had vaguely linked the two, but the priority of the technical puzzles had dulled his sensitivity to the cause of his chief's death. Now Snell's pairing of cause and effect made him address the issue.

"Luke," Bradley Snell said in the honeyed tone of his best corporate voice, "you're right to be angry. You're a researcher. Your role is to find cures, solve problems, save lives if you can. My role is different. It's to keep this company alive. As callous as my action seemed to you, keep in mind that had I not taken the action I did, we might not be here next year or the one after that to find the next vaccine. And I'm not speaking hypothetically. That detective, Washington, has launched an investigation of our records. Had I not acted, he would have made the link between the cure and Rathbone. The report to the FDA would have been a routine affair and we'd be out of business. Whether you like it or not, that," Snell said with authority, "will not happen now."

Chinsky stretched his five-foot-eight frame as high as it would go. Stepping deliberately, he came as close to Snell as he could while still looking him in the eye. "Don't bet on it," he said.

■

After Chinsky had gone, Snell sat at his desk, thinking. Things were not progressing as he had hoped. Proxy was right. Putting Chinsky in charge of Rathbone's projects had been a mistake.

What to do now? Take Chinsky out of the job? He could do that. But what would it accomplish? Chinsky was onto the cure. With or without authority, the tenacious researcher would pursue answers. To questions that Snell preferred be left unanswered. He could fire him. On the outside, out of control, would he go to the police? The newspapers? Probably. Better to keep him in the company, under observation. And, to the degree possible, under control.

Chinsky, like Rathbone before him, was acting irrationally. Why were these people trying to destroy what he had built? Why were they trying to destroy him? Didn't they understand? He sighed. For scientists, they had such limited vision. They were nothing more than narrow-minded technicians. Weisel would know how to deal with them. But why Weisel? Why not himself? That was what this was all about: power, money, prestige. If he was ever to replace Weisel, he would have to act boldly and decisively.

And where the hell was Alice? She was never sick.

For her to be out upset his routine. Damn her. Was she conspiring against him too? She wouldn't. She needed him. They all needed him. Still, it was the wrong time for her to be ill. She should have known that.

After a few minutes, he opened a desk drawer and pulled out a private phone. It took a few minutes for the international operator to put him through. The phone only rang once in the quiet villa in Friedrichshafen. When the other end answered he simply said, "Joseph, this is Mr. Snell. Have Mr. Weisel contact me." Joseph acknowledged the command and they both hung up. The call had lasted less than fifteen seconds.

■

The problem, Proxy brooded, was not that Snell lied. But that he had lied to *him*.

Brad Snell, his mentor, his trusted boss, had hired him straight out of college.

Proxy unquestioningly believed the loyalty went both ways. It was a matter of faith.

One weekend ago, the weekend before Rathbone's death, he had hurriedly packed the file cabinet contents and carted them to an unused storage room at Croft. He didn't ask why Snell wanted the files removed, it was enough that he wanted it done. Nor did he ask why when Snell told him to return everything but the patient files to Chinsky. He obeyed without question.

Now, after listening to the tapes, the questions formed in his mind.

He had to know. Without thinking, he scooped up Murcheson's cache and went to the Croft storage room. The files were as he had left them. Unceremoniously, he dropped to his knees and flipped the lid off one box. His anxious fingers nibbled through the file tops. Nothing. The next box was more promising. It held Rathbone's notes. He knelt on the dusty floor, coatless, reading the dead man's journal. The pain from the pressure on his knee bones was dulled by the adrenaline flow of anticipation.

Even though he had spent most of his business life talking to doctors—both researchers and clients—his technical vocabulary was not up to this. Most of Rathbone's data was unintelligible to him. But he understood enough to follow the thread of the discovery. The initial speculation—hunch, some would call it—led to hypothesis. Rathbone's tight, precise handwriting recorded how he had culled records, identified cellular response patterns, categorized them, and speculated further. Once, twice, he despaired when a promising hypothesis proved inconclusive through incomplete data. Then, the decision to conduct his own trials. The search for subjects. The winding path of developing complex formulas, tests, reactions, pathologies, glazed Proxy's eyes, but he pushed on. The last entry, made three days before Rathbone's death, confirmed what Proxy guessed.

"The cure works," Rathbone had written, "that much is clear from the tests. Snell, however, is being unreasonable. He knows I can present the data without reference to the human trials I have conducted, yet he vacillates. We need to act. The world needs to know that there is a solution to the problem of AIDS and that it exists not in some distant future, but now. I will talk to him again. If he continues to resist an announcement, I will make one regardless."

Rathbone was right. The market was right for a cure. There were millions to be made. This could be the hottest product of the year, of the decade. The U.S. market alone was worth a few hundred million. Hell, they were getting four dollars a dose for AZT. Given the frequency of dosage, that was nine grand a patient per year—and AZT didn't cure a damned thing. From what he read, it was clear Rathbone had a cure. He had tested it. It worked. And it was cheap. They could manufacture the stuff for peanuts. Eight doses a week apart and the disease was in remission. They could wipe out this epidemic in a year. There was no reason to hold back. The only outcome of delay would be more dead people, mainly gays who had contracted the virus early. More pain. More suffering.

He paged back to what looked like the formula to the cure and folded the corner of the page. When he had time he would need to photocopy it. But what about now? What about Snell?

Snell had no right. But then, maybe there were things Snell hadn't told him, things that would make Snell's course the right one. After all, the boss had a twenty-year track record of being right. Proxy's rise in the company was testimony to that. Was it fair to question Snell now?

Jesus, Proxy pleaded to himself, *what should I do?*

Proxy could hear the ghost of Rathbone's voice echo in his ear.

"The cure works. . . . Snell vacillates. . . . Snell resists. . . . I will talk to him again."

Did he?

Is that why he is dead?

And Proxy knew. It was.

Proxy stared at the journal, but no longer read the words. He heard Snell's taped voice, *"A cure . . . is unacceptable. A way will have to be found . . ."*

A way had been found. And he was part of it.

Snell, he knew, killed Rathbone. If not himself, then through someone. And he, Proxy, had helped— if not in the murder, then in the effect.

■

Brenda unobtrusively wandered over to Billy's desk in the newsroom. He sat there, phone between his right shoulder and ear, entering words into the processor that sat on his desk. Whoever was on the other end of the phone was a despised enemy or close friend. Brenda sat herself on a corner of the desk and waited for him to finish.

He slammed down the phone receiver and typed furiously for a minute or so, then looked up at the smiling Brenda. "Damn," he said, "it's getting tough to get a straight answer out of some of these bozos. What can I do for you, babe?"

She bristled inwardly at the epithet, but ignored it externally. She needed this sexist bastard. "Just thought I'd check on the Rathbone story. Anything new?"

"Naw, the cops are tracking the drug angle, but the last time I talked to Washington it wasn't going anywhere. How 'bout you, catch anything?"

She shook her head. "Nothing. I talked to Dr. Chinsky, but he didn't give me anything I could use. I may do a column or two on how Rathbone's death has affected the research capability of Croft. What do you think?"

"Put it together and we'll look at it."

"I can use Chinsky as a source. He's taking over for Rathbone."

"So your boy doctor makes out on the deal," he said with a smirk.

"Billy, what is it with you? For such a good reporter, you're really a jerk at times."

"Goes with the territory, I guess."

She turned serious. "I need a really good computer hacker. Someone who knows how to reconstruct files, and all that. The only one I could think of was Barney in DP. I talked to him, but I don't think he can help me. Any ideas?"

"I dunno. Why, whatcha do?"

"Not me. Dr. Chinsky. He was playing around with a terminal and thinks he blanked some files."

"Why doesn't he get someone at Croft to help him? They've got plenty of money."

"That's what I suggested," she lied, "but he's so embarrassed that he doesn't want anyone to know about it—new to the job and all."

"Christ!" he said. "What a loser."

"Billy—" she said.

"Okay, okay. Look, you know who you might try?"

He looked at her expectantly. "Jerzy. Florence Jerzy. You remember her. She used to work here before she went to work for the Department." In Billy's jargon, the only department that counted was the Detroit Police Department.

Brenda brightened. "You're right," she said. "That's great. She was really good. Thanks, Billy." She scooted down from the desk, leaned over, and kissed his forehead. "Love ya!" she said.

■

It took Brenda less than ten minutes to get from the *Free Press* building to Thirteen Hundred, where Jerzy worked. Security was tight. It took another fifteen minutes to find her once she was inside.

A blue-uniformed receptionist took her name and called Jerzy, who came to fetch her.

"It's been a long time," Jerzy said, giving her a small hug.

"Too long," said Brenda. "By the way, Billy sends his love."

"I'd be afraid to take it," Jerzy laughed. "That guy is so horny, he must have every disease on the street. Is he still trying to hustle every skirt in the office?"

"He makes the noises, but his batting average approaches zero. I don't really think he's serious, it's just a macho act."

They took an elevator to sub-level two.

"Don't you feel like a mole?" Brenda asked.

"You get used to it. In my business it would look the same if I were in a penthouse. The windows make temperature control hard, so we do without them."

Jerzy's cubicle was one of twenty or so in the sixty-eight degree subterranean complex. She showed Brenda the mainframe, in its own expansive glass cubicle. Except for the uniforms, it reminded Brenda of the newsroom with its phosphorescent CRT terminals and diffused overhead light.

"Well, what can I do for you?" the policewoman asked.

Brenda had worked out her story with Chinsky to give it a ring of authenticity. He had insisted that the nature of his discoveries thus far remain secret and that no lies be told in securing help. Beyond that, their agreement was that if she could find a hacker who could be trusted, he would get them access to the Croft computer.

"A friend of mine over at Croft, the drug company, has had some files erased. The stuff he's working on is very controversial and he's not sure if it was accidental or on purpose. He'd like to get the data back, but he's not sure he can trust anyone in the company."

"Croft. Isn't that where the research guy was just murdered?"

"Yes," said Brenda. This was the tricky part she and Chinsky had anticipated. "But the data involved here has to do with the clinical side of the operation and not research."

"Oh? I didn't know they had a clinical side."

"Yeah. It's small and not highly publicized. They treat patients with unusual disorders as part of a coop program with the university and the medical center."

"Is this his data or someone else's?" a suspicious Jerzy asked.

"His. He's the doctor responsible for these patients." It was stretching the truth, but given Chinsky's appointed role, technically accurate.

"Are you sure this has nothing to do with the case under investigation? If it does, I can't get involved; actually, I'd have a duty to report it."

"We don't think it does." Again, technically true. At this point, she rationalized to herself, they had no *factual* reason to believe that Rathbone's records were connected to his death. On the other hand, it didn't take a great leap of imagination to link the two.

"What has this got to do with you? Are you working on this for the paper? I thought you were a sportswriter."

Brenda laughed disingenuously and avoided the essence of the question. "I am. The doctor involved is a good friend of mine. We were talking about the problem one night and I volunteered to help if I could."

"And now you're volunteering me," the analyst said with amusement.

"Not unless you agree to help. You're a first-round draft pick, but you have to sign the contract."

"I'm not sure I can help. Do you have any details?"

"Are you signing up?"

"Whoa, girl. You're pushing."

"You're right, but I really don't want to get into details—not that I have a lot—if you're going to tell me no. You can understand. This is sort of sensitive."

"I understand, but you need to know where I'm coming from. Even if I agreed to help you and signed

a contract in blood, I'd back away if I thought anything about the situation was illegal—or even under-
handed."

Brenda shook her head vigorously. "There's nothing illegal. He just needs to get to some records."

"That he has a right to see?"

"That he has a right to see," she acknowledged.

"What kind of records?"

Brenda accepted the fact that if she was going to
get any help from Jerzy, she'd have to share what she
knew—short of telling her about Chinsky's hypothesis.

"Patient records. For some reason a group of
records has been deleted from the computer and he
can't call them up."

"Why not just reconstruct them from the hard
data?"

Brenda gave her a quizzical look.

"The paper files," Jerzy explained, "printouts,
data-entry forms, stuff like that."

Brenda understood. "From what I know, there was
no hard data. Everything was kept on the computer."

"Boy, is that dumb," the computer expert said.
"And there are no backup files?"

"No. To maintain confidentiality, there was only a
single record."

"That's crazy," she said. "Even a novice knows
enough to back up files. An electrical storm or a
power failure can wipe out an entire data base."

"Well, maybe there were backups. I don't know.
But if there were, they're gone too. You'd have to ask
Luke."

"So Luke's the guy. Luke who?"

"Luke Chinsky."

"Is this serious?" asked Jerzy, slipping into girl talk.

She's going to do it, Brenda thought. "It might be," she answered with a knowing smile.

CHAPTER
11

It was 11:50 p.m.

The clock radio erupted in sound disproportionate to its size.

Spangler swung his bare legs over the side of the bed. "Get out," he said to the still prone, naked brunette. Two cigarette burns, remnants of his game an hour back, showed on her thigh.

He picked up her clothes from the chair and threw them at her. "I'm finished with you. Move."

The woman grabbed her clothes and ran toward the bathroom. As she passed in front of him, he caught her arm and whirled her toward the door. "Out. I want you out."

"I'm going," she whined. "Just let me get my clothes on." Pulling free, she started back toward the bath. He caught her again with one hand and pushed her to the door.

"Out. I have no more time for you," he said, in his accented English. He jerked the door open with his other hand and shoved her into the hall. She clutched her clothes, trying to hold on to all of them and still cover herself.

"You were a lousy fuck anyway," she spit out at him as he closed the door on her.

That, he thought, was her problem.

It was five minutes to midnight. The musky smell of sex hung in the air. Spangler turned off the radio, went to the window, and opened it. The cool night air wafted across his bare, muscled torso and washed the heaviness from the room. He pulled on his pants and sat down at the desk in preparation for the call.

He was breathing heavily, and it was not from the sex. His palms had the wet slickness of anxiety. Though he never let the thought meander to his consciousness, he knew that Herr Weisel owned him as completely as one could own a useless trinket.

He picked up the phone and dialed his master.

Once placed, it took only a few seconds for the transatlantic connection to be made.

The signal rang once before a deep, cultured voice, which Spangler recognized, answered.

"It is me," Spangler said.

"So it is, Horst. So it is. What can you tell me?"

"Everything seems calm."

"That is not what I hear."

Spangler went clammy. Who would Weisel hear anything from?

"What is it you hear?"

"There are problems. Two more problems that need solving."

"I am close to the situation, and I know of no problems."

"Horst, are you listening? I am telling you, there are problems and they need taking care of. Do not tell me everything is calm when it is not. Are you listening? Do not tell me that."

Horst said nothing, but his breathing was heavy.

"Now I will tell you what to do," the bass voice said. "Are you listening?"

"Ja." The word was clipped, terse.

"You are to solve the problem as you did the last one. Do you understand?"

"Ja."

"Hire somebody to work on it. You are not to do it yourself. Do you understand?"

"Ja."

"And Horst, the last time was untidy. It was *Unordnung*. Do you hear me, Horst? It was left all over the street. Not natural. This time your people must solve the problem naturally."

"I understand, mein Herr."

"Good. Good, Horst. I will send you information about the problems in the usual way and you will take care of it. Do you understand?"

"I will see to it," Spangler said.

"And Horst, do not let this get out of hand. I would not like that. Do you understand?"

"Ja," he said.

"Good. I am leaving it to you. Do what you must, but do not let this get out of hand." A pause. Spangler said nothing. "That is all then," the husky voice said. "It has been nice talking with you. Good day— or I should say, good night. It is night there, is it not?"

"Ja," Spangler answered again, but by the time it took to finish his short response the voice on the other end had hung up.

Horst Spangler reached over for a pillow and used

it to wipe the beads of perspiration that had formed on his brow.

He picked up the phone again and called the bell captain. "This is Mr. Burger in 724. The last girl you sent up was a pig. Send me another one. This time, make her good."

■

Spangler, thought Herr Weisel, was a good man. He followed orders, was efficient, and never made excuses. A good man. Snell was a good man too. But was he beginning to act recklessly? The man had ambition, but limited creativity. Perhaps a bit greedy; perhaps a bit grasping. Neither in themselves bad traits for an executive—if they could be controlled. Should he talk to Snell? To some of the other members? No! It was wrong to judge. So long as Snell didn't threaten the rest of them, he was free to do as he pleased. Besides, as concerned as Herr Weisel might be, he was not there, on the scene. Snell was. It was his opportunity, his problem. Let him solve it. Snell was an executive. It was up to Snell to handle the situation. Snell *was* handling the situation. If it got out of hand, Horst would report it. He had full confidence in Horst. When he called, it would be time to worry.

■

Alice Murcheson peered through the tiny viewer in her door and saw Ben Proxy. She quickly undid the chain lock and let him in.

"Ben, you look terrible," she said.

It was true. His tan Palm Beach suit was soiled from carting the file box; his once-starched shirt was open at the neck; his champagne hair lacked its coifed precision. But it was his expression that prompted her comment.

"Can I come in?"

"Certainly." She opened the door wide and he walked in.

"Ben, what's wrong?" she asked with growing concern.

He looked at her closely, with suspicion. "You know what's wrong. You gave me the tapes. You listened to them."

At his reminder of the tapes, anger seemed to well in her. "I haven't been back to work since I talked to you. I called in sick. I won't work for that man until he apologizes. I know it's irrational, but it's how I feel."

He looked at her quizzically. "Don't you know what's going on?"

"I know he hid things from me."

She had heard the tapes but not made the connections, thought Proxy. She truly did not comprehend; her issue was not his issue. His customary snideness was gone, replaced by the first confusion he had felt in a decade. Her initial revelation of Snell's lie to him was as great a shock as she felt at the lack of trust. But now his outrage at the initial deceit was supplanted by the horror of the cure suppressed, the murder committed. And yet, Snell was his friend. His mentor. His protector. Alice was back where he had been this morning, concerned with relationship, not effects, with rapport, not consequence.

"Alice," he said, smoothing his hair with his fingers, "I've listened to the tapes. There is some very dangerous information on them. I would have destroyed them, but they belong to you."

"Is that what's upsetting you?" she asked. "His club? The fact that he's getting together with his secret little group?"

"It's more than that, Alice. It's more than that." If she didn't know what was going on, it would be best not to involve her. A genie out of the bottle never fit back in again. "Look, I would strongly suggest you not discuss any of this with the boss. I think it would be a good idea for you to destroy the tapes and your notes. Forget you ever heard them. Believe me, they're dangerous. And Alice, stay away from work for a while. For a few weeks at least. Promise me that."

She looked at him as if he were babbling gibberish. He straightened his tie and pulled it tight, getting ready to go. "Promise me, Alice."

"That I won't go back in?"

"Not for a while. And destroy the tapes."

"Without them he can deny everything."

"Forget it, Alice. Let it go. Stay away for a while so whatever you feel can fade. It's important. Will you do this for me? For our friendship?" He held both of her hands in his. He had never acted so intensely with her.

"What will I say? I've already taken off too much time."

"Go to a doctor. Have him say you're suffering from nervous exhaustion, anything. Just do it. Okay?"

Her eyes searched his, looking for more of an explanation. He gave none. He could give none that would make sense to her without telling more than he dared. He could be wrong. He didn't think so, but it was possible. Bringing her into it would only complicate things.

She closed her eyes and breathed hard. A squeeze on his hand signaled her assent. "Okay," she said.

"Everything—your notes, the tapes—are in there," he said, pointing to his briefcase. "For your sake, get rid of them."

■

The phone rang a dozen times before anyone thought to answer it and then only when it began grating on the ears of the semipermanent occupants of the steps outside the building. The first instinct of the fifteen-year-old tough who picked it up was to rip the cord from the wall. Then reason, or more likely the memory of a past need satisfied, saved the phone.

The vestibule smelled of urine and cheap booze. Not many calls came in over that phone, but the out-traffic was heavy. It was the only place on the block where residents of the once-respectable building could call their pushers. As pay phones went, it was one of the most profitable in the Bell System.

Everyone in the neighborhood knew Charlie, including the step-sitters, but it took a few minutes for them to decide who should climb the three flights to let him know he had a phone call. Had the call not been a novelty, it is likely that no one would have bothered. But someone did. Then it was Charlie's turn to be surprised.

Charlie Brown picked up the handset dangling from the pay phone. "Charlie," the caller said, "this is Dr. Chinsky from the Croft clinic."

"Hi, Dr. Chinsky."

"Charlie, I need your help."

"My help?" It seemed strange that Dr. Chinsky would need *his* help. But if he wanted something Charlie could give, it was his.

"Charlie," Chinsky said again, as if the repetition of his name would bridge the communication gap between them, "did Dr. Rathbone ever give you any papers? Anything at all?"

"Papers?" the Haitian said. "The nurse gave me papers. Always a ticket for the cab."

"Anything else?"

"No. Nothin' else."

"Think hard, Charlie." Charlie thought.

"Maybe. A paper about insurance. I didn't have any."

"Was it all printed up like a form, or did it have handwriting or typing on it?"

"I can't remember."

"It's important, Charlie."

Charlie shook his head. "I can't remember. But I can look at it and see, if you want."

"You still have it?" Chinsky's voice was excited, elated.

"I think so. I think it's in my room."

"Can you get it, Charlie? Can you get it and tell me if it has any numbers on it?"

"It's in my room, upstairs. I'll have to get it."

"I'll wait. Go get it." Charlie didn't argue. Who was he to tell the doctor that he'd have to climb three flights up and back whether he had the paper or not? He owed these people. If they asked, Charlie would do. He lowered the receiver carefully so that it wouldn't bang against the wall, and let it dangle as he started his trek up the stairs.

∎

He wondered why the doctor needed the paper. They had everything at the clinic. It was a wonder they ever needed anything. He liked Dr. Chinsky. Not as much as he liked Dr. Rathbone, but Dr. Chinsky was nice. He was kind. Gentle. And the nurse, Miss Stanton, she was nice too. They were all nice at the clinic. Too bad about Dr. Rathbone. He hoped the dead doctor had not taken a taste of salt, *goute sel* in Haitian, to wake up the zombies. Maybe he had. Maybe that's what Charlie was, a zombie raised by Rathbone's salt. The idea chilled him. He shook it off. The doctor was dead. Leave it there. Forget about the old ways. Still, it was too bad. Everyone had to die. Everyone had to eat. Everyone had to have sex. He smiled. Everyone especially needed sex. He wondered if Dr. Rathbone and Miss Stanton ever had sex together. He didn't think so. Maybe she did it with Dr. Chinsky. They were more alike. And if Dr. Chinsky had to have it with a woman, that Ms. Stanton looked fine to him. Most men liked having sex with women. He didn't understand it. He had tried it with a woman once and it wasn't nearly as good. He wondered if Dr. Chinsky had ever had a man.

As he worked his way up the stairwell, thoughts of sex brought him around to his visit last night with Raymond. He had wanted sex. He knew Raymond did too. They had been so good together so many times. Yet he, because of lack of strength, and Raymond, because of fear, had spent the evening in pleasant conversation. That was enough for Charlie. It had been a long time since he had talked like that.

Charlie hated pain and Raymond feared it. Most of the talk had focused on the times they had had together as friends, special times of love, outrage, tenderness. But Raymond kept bringing the conversation back to pain, the pain of his sickness. "Does it hurt? How? When? Do pills or medication help? When did it start? Does it ever go away?" Charlie didn't like to talk about it, but he told what he could. The pain was bad. The raw nerve ends inside his body screamed every time they were assaulted by the normal process of living. Just to think about it made it hurt again, and he didn't deal with the thought of pain any better than he did with the pain itself.

After a while he had dozed off. Raymond covered him with a blanket. He hadn't needed it. Raymond's apartment was warm and his night sweats made him throw it off, but it was nice to have someone care. Raymond kept putting the blanket back over him. In the morning it was clear Raymond had kept vigil. That warmed Charlie almost as much as the blanket. Raymond still loved him. He expected Raymond to invite him to move back in, but the offer never came. Still, it had been a good night, and as he walked home that morning Charlie was as happy as he had been in a long time.

The last few days had worn him down. The climb up three flights made him gasp for air, his lungs radiating arcs of fire. The stairs seemed higher than they were this morning. He sat for a moment before looking for the paper. He wasn't sure if he had it, but there were very few places to look. He had few things to hide or places to hide them in.

He found it in the tin box, his frail vault for important things. His bony hand pushed aside a month-old lottery ticket, some letters from the Department of Social Services, and a dog-eared passport. The computerized printout, on a blue standardized insurance form, was halfway down the pile. Taking the paper, he started back down toward the phone.

■

The wait seemed interminable to Chinsky. His ear felt swollen from the pressure of the receiver. He started to hang up a half dozen times, then checked himself. Better a red ear than a dead end.

He didn't believe Snell's explanation. Had he destroyed the records, he would have destroyed them all. In that case, there would have been no records for the mysterious Knowles to return to Rathbone's office. The records were still out there somewhere.

But what if Snell were telling the truth?

What if Rathbone's files were destroyed?

Then what?

If Snell had destroyed the formula, then he, Chinsky, would have to piece it together from what was left. Once a trail had been blazed, it could be followed. The signs might be faint, the footprints shallow, but they would be there. He would follow Rathbone's path and reach the same destination. One way or another he would find the formula for the cure. He knew it existed, and that was enough.

After leaving Snell, he had reviewed their discussion. The explanation was rational yet unsatisfactory. The gain from making the cure public—especially with Rathbone dead—seemed greater than the risk Snell feared. He searched for a motive to explain the bizarre events that were surrounding and confounding him.

The motive always brought him up short. What did Snell have to gain? The profits from a cure would be enormous—why surrender them for the imagined threat of FDA action? Either there was a greater danger Snell was hiding from him, or there was more profit to be made from suppressing Rathbone's cure. From what Chinsky could see, Snell was obsessed with the well-being of the company. Chinsky interpreted that to mean profit. How, he asked himself, could Croft make more money by ignoring Rathbone's cure than by acknowledging it?

Of one thing Chinsky was convinced, nothing happened in isolation or without cause. His problem was to unravel the mystery and make the cause visible. His last ploy, unless Brenda could come up with someone to crack the files, was to find a paper trail that led to other files—like the one in the lab. Everything had a code. Maybe if he could find the code for Charlie, he could find the agent Rathbone used and from there reconstruct the formula for the medication causing the virus to go into remission. It was a long shot, but there were few alternatives. Research had taught him that success most often follows thorough, methodical work. List all the possibilities, then follow each to its end. It was time-consuming, but it worked.

Charlie interrupted his musing with a clatter as he retrieved the dangling phone.

"You still there?" Charlie wheezed.

"I'm here. Did you get it?"

"Yeah. Man. Let me get my breath." Chinsky realized that he had put Charlie through an ordeal.

"Take your time, Charlie. Take your time."

"I'm all right," he said, wheezing again. Chinsky wasn't as sure as Charlie seemed to be. In labored words Charlie told Chinsky, "It has numbers typed on it. And my right name, not Charlie Brown, the other one, Brun."

"That's great, Charlie. That's great," an elated Chinsky said. Maybe the long shot would pay off. "Now, I need one more favor from you. I need that paper. Can you bring it to me? I'll pay you."

Charlie sighed. He hated the long trip. But he owed these people. "You don't have to pay me, Dr. Chinsky. You've already helped me. I'll bring it out. When do you want it?"

"Now, Charlie. Now."

■

"There are two of them," Spangler said into the pay phone. Three small stacks of quarters sat on the shelf, waiting to be fed into the phone. "This time it must be done subtly, not like the last one."

"What was wrong with the last one, fer Christ's sake? I thought you liked the way I did it," Duke's voice whined.

"I have no complaints," Spangler responded quickly. "If I don't like your work, I will tell you. These are different. They must be handled differently." Spangler bristled with the irritation of having to pass on instructions. These were jobs he should have handled himself. His feelings were none of the Dutchman's business.

"So tell me," Duke said.

Just then the operator cut in. "That will be one dollar and fifteen cents for the next three minutes." Spangler reached for the pile and fed twenty quarters into the machine. "You have thirteen minutes," the operator said pleasantly.

Her interruption reinforced Spangler's distrust of phones. He gave Duke Van Allen the instructions in guarded words, not sure he was making himself clear. After eight minutes his only thought was to get off this phone. He had been on the open line too long. Not that he had much to fear; pay phones were notoriously difficult to bug. Yet he instinctively distrusted anything he could not fully control. He tried to end the conversation. "I've made reservations for you at the Ramada on Telegraph Road in Southfield. I will call you there. We will talk more then."

"Wait!" Duke yelled into the phone.

"What?" Spangler shot back. He wanted off the phone.

"How much? What's this worth to you?"

"The same as last time."

"Last time there was a bonus."

"Make these look innocent and you get the same bonus."

"For each one?"

The Dutchman was getting greedy. "No. For both."

"Bullshit. You want special treatment, you gotta pay for it. The same bonus on each one."

Spangler closed his eyes in disgust. He hated quibbling about money like a Belgian washerwoman. He could haggle and the price would come down. He could impose his will on this hireling, but he wanted off this phone, now! "The same on each one," he said, and angrily slammed the handpiece into the switchhook. The son of a bitch better make it look good, or it would be a long time between jobs for him.

■

She couldn't bring herself to do it.

Proxy had made her promise to destroy the tapes. And the notes. But they were all she had to show Snell's perfidy. It was one thing to stay away from the office. Hard as that was, it was harder to imagine letting the situation go on without resolution.

The office was more a home than home to her; she certainly spent more time there than she did in her condo. When Proxy first suggested she stay away, she didn't think she could do it. But she had. And she intended to keep on doing it until—until she didn't know when. She would trust Ben's advice—unless she disagreed with it. She would be sick for another day or two. Then, if Ben had not resolved the situation, she would confront Snell. For that she needed her evidence.

She emptied a pair of brown suede pumps out of their box and used the thin white tissue paper to wrap the cassettes. She laid her typed notes on the bottom and put the shoes back in on top. The wrapped tapes fitted snugly in the pumps. Then she placed the box back into the stack she had pulled it from. It was, she thought, a perfect hiding place.

■

The assignment appealed to Duke. He knew the territory and it would take some real craftsmanship to bring off hits that would look like two unrelated, unplanned homicides. One—perhaps both—could be a suicide, an accident, or manslaughter. There were a lot of choices. It would take some thought. He liked that. The price was right too. Foreigner or no, Spangler was the kind of guy he enjoyed working for. He let you do your own thing, never interfered as long as the job was done right. And tough. If necessary, he could do his own stuff. You could respect that. The guy was no pansy.

Spangler didn't give him a lot to go on, just two names and addresses. He would have to get a picture of the guy so that he could recognize him. Spangler said he was short with a brown beard. Getting a picture wouldn't be so hard. These doctors all belonged to the medical society and they published directories with pictures in them. That's how he had made that other doctor, Rathbone.

If Spangler kept him in this business, they would have to start a new medical school in Michigan.

Somebody really must have pissed somebody off to call for three hits. And one of them a broad. That was unusual. Usually they left women out of it. Well, that was their business. His was to do the wet work. As long as they paid and let him do it his way, he had no fucking beef.

Detroit was four and a half hours away. He could make that this afternoon. Might as well get a fix on this guy, a visual ID, which meant the medical library at the U. He could save some time by stopping in Ann Arbor on the drive over. The university town was on I-94, forty-five minutes outside of metro Detroit. Good. He liked that. It was efficient. Then, depending on the time, to the lab or the guy's house. Shit. What's the rush? This was going to take a few days no matter how he worked it. Stop, he told himself, and smell the roses. Life is too short to be always running. He would hit Ann Arbor, then go to the Ramada to take Spangler's call.

CHAPTER
12

Naked, Proxy got out of bed and turned the music down. He could feel Spangler's eyes watching him. It made him strut just a bit and pull in his washboard stomach. He liked being watched. The music, though, was too loud for what he had to talk about.

Spangler was an animal. Vicious, cruel, primitive. He was sure Spangler was capable of killing, maybe had killed. Nothing he'd said, but something Proxy could sense, smell. Ironically, he was also warm, understanding, and sensitive. Sometimes, after they had made fierce love, Spangler would recite poetry to him. He was partial to Stephen Crane and Lawrence Ferlinghetti, but sometimes it would be his own. While his words had grace, they were seldom sweet. Proxy never knew whether he would get the lion or the poet. It was part of the excitement, the attraction of this man.

The sex tonight wasn't very good. Proxy was distracted. Spangler didn't seem to mind, maybe this was one of his reflective nights. Proxy hoped so.

"Horst," he said, sitting down on the side of the bed, "I need someone to talk to."

"What's the problem, Golden?" It was Spangler's

name for him. Horst was the stud and Proxy was, well, simply Golden.

"It's something at work. Something I don't know how to handle."

"Tell me."

Proxy scooted up on the bed and leaned back against the headboard. He drew his crossed legs in close to him. "It's Snell, my boss. I've mentioned him to you, but I've never told you how important our relationship is. It's not *our* kind of relationship," he said in hurried clarification. "He's straight. He knows I'm gay from something that happened years ago, but he never mentions it." Proxy struggled to find words to describe an affinity he had never voiced before. "He's only three years older than me, but he's like a father."

Spangler grunted. Proxy wasn't sure if it was in understanding or derision.

"He hired me into the company. He's the only boss I've ever had. I'm not sure I could work for anyone else.

"When I was getting started, he showed me the ropes, not only the job but the politics, the strategies of moving in a company. When he got promoted, I got promoted. He always took care of me.

"Once, when I was in Alabama on a field visit, I got a little drunk. At the end of the day we used to go out, have dinner, a few drinks, and unwind. That night it was just me and Roger Parsons; Parsons was the field rep for Alabama. We wound up at a local bar and talked about the company. I was an insider. I knew what was going on; he didn't. Roger started

spouting off about some corporate execs, telling me
how good they were, how they were real comers. The
guys he was talking about were real assholes. They
stood a better chance of getting the Siberia territory
than a promotion. He was full of shit, and I told him
so. When I got back to the office, there was hell to
pay. Roger had called the assholes and they had gone
to their boss, who was also Snell's boss. Snell was
brought in and called on the carpet. Snell heard it all,
then demanded an apology from Roger, who, he speculated, was obviously too drunk to remember what I
had actually said. At the time Snell didn't know what
the facts were; he didn't care. I was being attacked.
That was enough for him. In the end, I got the apology. A year later both Roger and the assholes were
gone."

"Nice touch," said Spangler approvingly.

"Yeah, that's what he's like. If you're on his team,
he's on yours all the way. Whenever I had a problem,
we could talk about it. Not just company problems,
personal problems. Except for sex. I never talked
about sex to him. That's probably why I feel like he's
my father," Proxy laughed.

"The advice he gave me was always good. Well
reasoned. Snell has an exceptional mind. Sometimes
I didn't take his advice. One way or another he would
find out, but he never criticized my judgment. Nor
did he turn me away the next time I showed up looking for more advice. He just worked with me and gave
me what he had. I could take it or leave it.

"It worked the other way too. Especially after the
Alabama incident. He would tell me his plans, his

strategies. He would think out loud and I would react to whatever he said. There were no secrets between us, particularly when it came to the company."

"So what's the problem?" Spangler asked impatiently.

"Did you ever see *Death of a Salesman?*" A head-shake said Spangler hadn't. "It's a story about a traveling salesman who's lost his job. On the surface, the story is that the loss of the job is killing him. Underneath, it's a story about a father and a son. They had a perfect relationship. The father was the son's ideal. The boy was a perfect son. Then, without explanation, the son left home, drifted, and became estranged from the father. In the end it came out that the boy had walked in on his father while the old man was on the road, fucking a broad. It destroyed the relationship. The father had cheated on the son. I feel like the son, Biff. Biff was his name. And Willie Loman was the father. I'm Biff. Snell's Loman."

"Well, Biff, what's the problem?"

"Let me get to it in my own way. I need to talk." He realized it was true. The talking was as much a part of his need as the sorting of issues.

"You remember the other night, we talked about AIDS? I said not to worry; I worked for a pharmaceutical house. We do a lot of research, some of it basic, some of it applied. I usually get involved with the applied research because of the marketing issues, but I have a fairly good fix on what's happening on the basic side. A lot of companies have put a lot of money into immune-system research, hoping to cash in on the AIDS hysteria. There's a lot of government grant money floating around too. We haven't paid much attention to it. It's bothered me. Probably because I'm personally at risk. But I haven't made an issue of it. Probably because I don't want anyone opening closets. Except for Snell, no one in the company knows I'm gay. I've worked hard to keep it that way. I even date Alice Murcheson, Snell's secretary, to maintain the facade." Proxy's legs were getting cramped, so he extended them. Spangler gave him a look that said get on with it.

The timbre of Proxy's voice changed, becoming less authoritative, less secure, more like he had to get it out in one breath or not at all. "I'm pretty sure we've discovered a cure for AIDS."

Spangler rolled around to look at him full face. Now the killer eyes said, *tell me more. And do it quickly.*

"The doctor who was killed, Rathbone, had some files. I saw them. After Rathbone was killed, Snell made me take them from Rathbone's office. Apparently, he worked on his own and developed a cure. I don't know whether it works or not. Rathbone's not here to say, but everything seems to fit. The thing is, Snell didn't tell me about this—even though he knows I'm gay. And I know he knows. He's the one who told me to move the records. He knew exactly which records to take." Proxy sat, not saying anything. Building courage. "I also think he had Rathbone killed."

After a moment Spangler broke his eyehold on Proxy and dropped his head as if in deep thought.

Proxy started up again in a steadier voice. "But

that's not the problem. I can rationalize why it might be right to remove someone who's in the way. The fact that Snell may have had Rathbone killed is not important."

Spangler's head snapped back up.

"Just as Snell never told me about the cure, he never told me about a group he belongs to, some of the top people in pharmaceuticals. Together they control markets and regulate products." He made a deprecatory laugh. "I'm sure they've managed to double or even triple profits by working together. It's secret, illegal, and brilliant. But terribly risky. If word got out, all of the people involved would be ruined. I can even understand why he kept it from me, the stakes are so high." He sighed.

"How did you find out about it?" asked a fully alert Spangler.

"Alice Murcheson, Snell's secretary. She found out and told me. And I'm the only one who knows she knows."

Spangler's eyes narrowed to a razor-edge slit. "Why are you telling me this?"

"I need to talk to someone. I don't know what to do, and I thought by talking it through I would see the answer. Just getting it out helps me think." Proxy paused before starting again. "I can understand why he had Rathbone killed." He made a face. "Sure, I hate that it was Rathbone. If he found a cure, he's a saint. But saints get martyred. It was brutal, but I can posit reasons why I might have acted so, were I Snell. Nor is the fact that he kept this organization secret from me problematic. It was, at first. I was infuriated.

I was outraged that he didn't trust me. Then, the more I thought about it, the more I understood. The risk was just too great. It wasn't that he couldn't trust me. He couldn't trust *anybody*. No, my problem is more like Biff's. I still love him. Even though he has sinned, he is still my father. My dilemma is that I'm torn. I feel the cure must be made public. Too many lives are at risk: mine, yours. If I go public, I'll destroy Snell. If not physically, then symbolically as my father. I can't do that either." He was silent.

After a while Spangler broke the quiet. "Have you told this to anyone other than me?"

Proxy shook his head.

"Not even the girl, Murcheson?"

"No," Proxy said hoarsely.

"Golden, you do have a problem."

■

The night passed slowly for Proxy. In fits of intermittent wakefulness he kept replaying the tape of his life and the choices he had made, imagining how things would have been different had he made another turn here, a jog there. There were some things he would change, not a lot. But some things.

He wished he would have been stronger, more forceful. Great resolve was not his strength. He tended to take the easy path. He had followed Snell because that was the easiest way to the top. He loved life's pleasures and was reluctant to pass them up. That made resolve a challenge. Too many obstacles stood in the way of the good life. It was easier to walk around them.

By early morning, he knew he had only one choice. He was going to see that the AIDS cure was not suppressed. Snell would fight him. Discredit him. Expose him. Reject him. Destroy him if he could. So be it.

During his last walk into the foggy mist of sleep, Horst had left. Too bad; he'd wanted to thank him for listening.

■

Back in his hotel room Spangler, too, reached a decision. For him it was less difficult. AIDS was an abstraction, something that might never happen. His more pressing problem, in Proxy's words, was that the genie was getting out of the bottle. Now there were four problems instead of two. Would there be eight tomorrow? He had to stopper the bottle, quickly. Otherwise Weisel would be cross. Poor Golden.

CHAPTER 13

CHINSKY MET BRENDA and Florence Jerzy at Carlos Murphy's, a trendy restaurant bar—a cross between a yuppie watering hole and a singles bar—on Northwestern Highway.

Brenda made unceremonious introductions.

"Hi, Luke," Jerzy said. She held out her hand for a shake, elbow locked, fingers splayed.

Luke took her hand. The analyst was plain but attractive: an unremarkable face, brown hair manageably short, no more than five-foot-four, sturdily assembled.

"Shall we have a drink or go right to Croft?" he asked.

"Why don't we sit down and talk about the situation first?" Jerzy suggested.

"Good," Luke said. "I need a drink. I've been at Croft all day."

The decor of Carlos Murphy's was early brass with British-racing-green accents. Potted dracaena, marginatas, corn plants, and schefflera sprouted everywhere. Metal bentwood chairs surrounded tables covered with imitation fawn-colored suede. The focal point of Murphy's was the oval bar decorated with live humans in search of a good time. The charm of the place was that it kept the music to a reasonable level, so most people could hear what their partners said. For that reason it was considered more intellectual than most meat shops. "Killer Joe," sung by Manhattan Transfer rumbled over the loudspeakers. The trio found a table in the corner, out of the traffic pattern.

"I'm not sure how to start this," Chinsky opened. "What have you covered, Brenda?"

"Just that some of your computerized patient files have disappeared and you suspect sabotage. You've asked for internal help in recovering them, but nothing's come of it. Now you're down to two outs in the ninth."

"That's essentially true," said Chinsky. "While technically the patient files are now in my charge, they were personally compiled by Dr. David Rathbone, the doctor who was killed in Croft's parking lot Monday morning."

Jerzy turned to Brenda and gave her a reproachful look. "Didn't I ask you about this?" she asked, already knowing the answer.

"Uh-huh," Brenda conceded sheepishly. "But I knew that if I gave you all the facts, you'd turn me down. I thought if you could meet Luke and hear why this is important, you would help."

She wasn't buying it.

Brenda was penitent. "I'm sorry, Flo. Just listen to Luke, then decide if you can help. So far, you've only invested a trip out here."

Jerzy let her talk. She liked Brenda. She was smart

and had spunk. All the same, Jerzy had an odd feeling that, eventually, Brenda would get her into trouble.

"This is important," Chinsky broke in. "Why don't you let me tell you about it and then you can decide."

"Actually, I'm ahead of you on this," the analyst said. "I thought about it on the way over. It would be too much of a coincidence for this to be totally apart from the Rathbone killing. But I decided to hear you out first. More mistakes are made by people jumping to conclusions before they have the facts than by people who take the time to get all the information."

A smile spread over Chinsky's face. A prototype analyst.

"Thanks, Flo," Brenda said with obvious relief. She only hoped that Chinsky would tell enough.

In less than fifteen minutes, he briefed her on his examination of Charlie, the missing files from Rathbone's office, the lack of patient charts on the computer, and the confirming lab tests. It was a concise, factual, unemotional recitation, well suited to her particular analytical framework. He left out his conversations with Snell and the executive's role in moving the files. That was a separate matter he needed more time to think about.

Jerzy's reaction was similar to Brenda's: shock, awe, joy.

Her eyes said that there was no question but that she would help.

Chinsky went on. "I called Charlie to see if he had any paperwork with identifying code numbers on it. He did." Chinsky reached into the inside pocket of his tweed sport coat and pulled out a folded sheet of paper. "I don't know if this will be of any use at all, but it's a form used to determine if a patient has insurance." He pointed to a block of numbers on the form. "This is the control code of the patient," he said, then slid his finger to another block. "And this is Charlie's social security number. I suspect that if there are any files on him in the computer, they'll be listed under one of these numbers."

Jerzy looked up admiringly. "Not bad, Dr. Chinsky," she said.

"I'm not sure how many patients are involved. The nurse at the clinic says Dr. Rathbone saw about thirty patients. If all of them were part of this trial, then that would be the number. He may, however, have been working on other projects. After this, nothing would surprise me."

"Just one thing I don't understand, Dr. Chinsky—"

"Please, Luke."

"Okay. One thing I don't understand, Luke, is why you don't just contact the patients the same as you did Charlie. Wouldn't you be able to get to the root of the situation by testing?"

"Two reasons. First, we don't know how many different regimens were being tested. It could take us months to unravel that solely on the basis of lab reports. Second, there's the issue of FDA approval." And he told her about that.

"Okay," she said. "I buy it. There's one thing, though."

Both Chinsky and Brenda knew it was a warning.

"Based on what we find, I may have to report this. I can't give you any guarantee of confidentiality."

"Fair enough," said Chinsky. "I only ask one thing, and that's if you have to make a report, you allow us to cosign it. If that's okay, let's get started."

"Fair enough. Let me see if I've got it right. You think your files are still somewhere in memory or on disk storage. You want me to get them out. I may or may not be able to do that. It depends on how knowledgeable the person who altered them was and whether the intent was to destroy or just hide them. Do you know what kind of data base you're using—or the name?"

Chinsky's confused look was her answer. "Let's go over to your place and take a look," she said.

■

Croft headquarters was not intended to be a public place, especially after hours or on weekends.

In less sophisticated times, a human guard would have identified Chinsky and logged him and his guests in. Electronic monitors and computerized screening systems had long replaced most of the trusty but anachronistic watchmen.

Chinsky slipped his electronic pass into the card reader, and the machines automatically admitted him to the building. Deft maneuvering allowed Brenda to slide in as part of the same body mass. He used his card to open the door again and passed the plastic key out to Jerzy.

As the threesome moved down the corridors, they were followed by one of one hundred and twenty-six cameras that monitored the crucial areas of the complex.

In a small room one story below the surface, Fred Winarski, security technician, monitored the monitors. Along one wall of the security center, twenty TV screens made a surrealistic collage displaying flashing black-and-white images of vacant rooms and corridors.

On average, each screen was connected to six and one third cameras. Each camera flashed its image on the screen for ten seconds before surrendering its moment to the next camera. If he were fully alert, scanning each image as it appeared, Fred could devote a half second to each screen before moving to the next. During his first two weeks on the job, Fred had faithfully scanned the monitors, flicking his eyes across and down in a snakelike pattern.

Nothing had happened.

Occasionally, a cleaning person would dance a solitary waltz across the screen. Otherwise, the images were as interesting as watching a flickering wall. A wall, though, was less hypnotic.

A month after taking the job, Fred fell asleep. He awoke with a start to find that the same screens were blinking their same images on the same schedule. He felt guilty, but nothing happened: no cataclysm, no reprimand, nothing. The silent gray world of nighttime Croft went on without noticing whether Fred woke or slept, lived or died. Of course, if he died, it would be noticed—but not until morning. And then only because his body would be there to confront the corporate "them." That was nine months ago. Now, a seasoned veteran, Fred felt no guilt.

When Chinsky and Brenda passed briefly from one screen to another on their journey to the clinic, it was a major event in the dull monotony of the gray kaleidoscope. Or it would have been, had Fred Winarski been awake to see them.

■

Chinsky sat facing the computer terminal. His fingers beat nervously on the keyboard. He stopped and stared at the CRT. His hand reached up to tug at his beard. "Let's try this sucker," he said, as he felt behind the computer and snapped the toggle.

The hard drive whirred and booted the main menu. Jerzy pulled up a swivel secretary's chair and sat beside him while Brenda leaned over his shoulder to watch the screen.

"Good," Jerzy said, "you're using dBase IV. It's the same one we use downtown. Crackerjack program."

With a few deft commands, he found his way to the main files. He booted the data base and was pleased to see that the time-clock signature showed no changes had been made since his last sign-on.

He called up the catalog, then turned to Jerzy. "Want to take over?"

She scooted in front of the keyboard.

Surprising herself, she shivered with anticipation. Her delight in discovering hidden things was one of the characteristics that made her a good analyst.

She played with the keyboard for a few seconds,

getting familiar with some of the internal routines
and the command structure.

"How do you get into your files?"

"I use my password, then call up the appropriate
file."

"Do you have a master password and then secondary security levels or just the master?"

"There are levels. Rathbone's code was *Healer*. The
computer people said that a subdirectory had been
set up to be accessed only by the code *Dr. Virus*.
Once you're into the subdirectory the patient master
files normally have a primary code of last name plus
case number. A secondary code is social security
number."

Jerzy made a few keystrokes and was out to the
main menu, then back in to the program and out
again. "I'm assuming that your system configuration
includes a mainframe and interactive peripherals. In
other words, any number of people can access the
same files from remote locations as long as they have
the passwords."

"That's right. The computer room is on the next
level down, and we're all linked to it, enabling us to
transfer data anywhere in the building. So, if I have
experiments going on in two labs at the same time, I
can integrate the data."

"Does anyone else know your passwords?"

"They're on file with computer security. Company
policy. But it's possible that somebody could create a
code and not report it to security. My associates and
some of the key lab people know the master code, but
not my personal code."

"Not quite true, Luke," Jerzy said. "Look here." She had burrowed into the master program. The screen displayed listings. She nodded to the display. "This file is locked, but any password that's set up will only remain active for eight hours or sign off—whichever comes first—unless it's officially authorized. It's one of the controls the programming people use to make sure some guy doesn't come in and freeze up the system with an unbreakable password.

"That means it's most likely that someone inside the department altered the files, someone who had access to Rathbone's master and personal password—or who had the technical expertise to crack it. Let's see if we can figure out what this guy did." A string of computer instructions cascaded down the monitor's screen. For an hour she called up listings, reviewed them, and called up more. Brenda and Chinsky watched intently for the first twenty minutes. Then, like Fred Winarski, they felt their eyelids grow heavy. To give Jerzy room and to have space to talk, they backed away from the machine.

"Do you know someone who drives a blue Buick?" Brenda asked a shade above a whisper.

"No, why?" he asked.

"It seemed like one was following you from Murphy's."

"What do you mean?"

"I was the last one out of the lot. I notice other cars when I'm driving, who passes who and stuff like that. This Buick kept speeding up and slowing down. Sometimes he'd leapfrog Jerzy, sometimes he'd hang back."

"A lot of people drive crazy."

"You're right. Just my nerves, I guess."

Across the room, Jerzy stopped the flow and froze the listing on the screen. "Look," she said, "here's what they did. I'm into *Healer* files. This program is a random-number generator. It's a little program used in statistical sampling. They've patched your sub-directory for these files so that when you load it, it generates the numbers you've been getting on the screen. I think it's a worm."

They looked at her without comprehension.

"A worm is like a computer virus," she explained. "A virus spreads from program to program until it contaminates the whole system. A worm is more selective and only goes after certain programs. That's probably why nobody really got excited. Probably the only programs affected were those with the *Healer* password, and *Healer* wasn't here to complain. The question now is, What did they do with your original files? They could have deleted them or simply assigned different names under a different password. Depending on which technique they used, it may be easy or hard to find them." The analyst went back to staring at the screen while her fingertips punched in instructions.

"If they located your files under another password, we may be in trouble. We would have to break all the passwords, then examine the files. That could take days."

Brenda groaned.

"Is there a quicker way?" asked Chinsky.

"There may be. If they simply deleted your files,

they'll still be on the disk, even though you can't see them. What the computer does when you delete a file is set a little marker by the file that says 'pretend that this file isn't here.' Then, when you ask to see the directory, the computer only shows you the un-marked files. Hand me my bag," she instructed Chinsky. He did. She pulled out a half dozen floppy disks, leafed through them, and selected one, which she booted.

"I brought a master locksmith program with me that has an extraordinary undelete program on it. Let's give it a try." A master map of the disk appeared on the screen. It was a pictorial display of the used and empty sectors. She continued to manipulate the data, eyes darting from the keyboard to the screen. She toggled back and forth between the disk map and the listings. "The files are marked. The mark is also a signal for the computer to write over the file if it needs the space to save some other data. So the only information you can restore is data that has been de-leted but not overwritten. See those X's? They repre-sent active data. The dots are deleted data that has not been overwritten. Do you have any idea when the data disappeared, Luke?"

"I would guess it was about a week ago."

She stopped what she was doing and turned to him. "The day Rathbone was shot, right?"

"Yes," he acknowledged.

"Okay, Luke. Let's do this straight from now on. Either I'm in, or I'm not. No more bullshitting. Okay?"

"Okay," he said.

"Brenda?"

"Okay."

"Now," she said, "what about the date? This computer has a time clock that automatically logs a time to certain transactions. When you save or delete a file, it notes the time as part of its routine. I'm into the main memory of your CPU. It has a master index of all volumes and files that can be sorted by disk. There are hundreds of deleted files on the disk. That's good, but it creates a lot of work for us. It would help us narrow the field if we knew the approximate time it was deleted."

"Check Monday the thirteenth," Chinsky said.

"This month?"

"Right."

"Thanks," Jerzy said. "Any guess on the time?"

"Sometime after 8:00 A.M."

"Not too much activity on the thirteenth," she said.

"I can believe that," Chinsky said. "Not much got done around here that day."

Jerzy played with the data for a half hour or so. "Luke, take a look at this," she said.

Chinsky leaned over her shoulder to see the screen.

"Any of this look like the stuff you're after?"

He studied the screen and asked her to call up more displays. "No. I don't think it has anything to do with the files I'm after."

"Okay. Let's try the next one. There are only a few deletes for this day."

They went through the routine four more times

before they exhausted the bank of files deleted on the day of Rathbone's death.

"We can go forward, toward today, or backward. What do you think?" she asked.

It had been a few days after Rathbone's death before he had realized the files were blank. Tuesday and Wednesday were the logical days to check next. "How many files on Tuesday?" he asked.

"It was a heavy day. Probably catching up. About fifty or sixty files, I'd say."

"How about the other way, Sunday?"

She manipulated the keyboard. "About a half dozen."

Snell said he had the records moved immediately after Rathbone's death. Monday. There was no reason to think that any of the Sunday files were the ones he was after. Then he remembered Snell's thumb on the plunger. And there were only six files.

"Let's do Sunday before we do Tuesday," he said.

"Okay," the analyst agreed. "First I'll try this big one."

She moved the cursor to a file with 712k of data.

The computer went into what seemed like an interminable pause before a directory appeared on the screen.

Chinsky scanned it, moving from display to display, scrolling forward, then back. He moved Jerzy away from the console to get a better look at the data and easier access to the keyboard. He didn't know what he was looking for, but these were patient records. Strange patient records. Code numbers were entered where a name should have been. He pulled the folded paper from his pocket. The insurance form had Charlie's full name and social security number on it. Handwritten in one corner was the number 221260. The numbers in the name field had more digits. There was another number in a field in the top left corner. What seemed to be a record number. "That's it!" he shouted. In his excitement he gave Jerzy a robust slap on the shoulder, almost knocking her head into the monitor. "Sorry," he said. "But you've done it. See the field on the top left? It matches a number on Charlie's form." He showed her the insurance form.

"See if you can find the social security number," Chinsky said as he turned the keyboard over to Jerzy.

Jerzy moved the cursor and called up the record.

Six eyes scanned unlabeled fields looking for a nine-number series. "There," said Brenda. She pointed to a block on the right of the screen.

Chinsky read the numbers off the insurance form while Brenda confirmed them on the screen.

They matched.

"Great," he said. "Can you give me a printout?"

"Sure. Is there a printer around? Or do you want to scan some of the other files first?"

"You're right. Let's see if there are any nonpatient files that contain summary data or protocols."

She blanked the screen and went back into the guts of the system. Four of the five remaining files contained Rathbone's patient records. The fifth was a series of histograms of the white-cell count of different groups of patients. Chinsky studied them carefully. Most showed a steady decrease in count over

time. Some, including Charlie's, showed an increase.
"Flo," he said cautiously, "I think we may be onto
something. I'm going to need printouts of all this."

"Can do," she said.

"And Flo," he said cautiously, "is there any chance
these transactions were misdated?"

"None," she said. "The dating is by autoclock."

■

Outside, in the Croft parking lot, Duke waited in
the Buick he had rented at the airport. He liked
Buicks. They had class without the show-off-ness of a
Cadillac. Cadillacs were great for driving around, but
not for a job. Everybody noticed a Cadillac. Nobody
noticed a Buick.

Now he knew what Chinsky looked like. Not much
of a guy, especially for a doctor. He was small and
scruffy. Looked like a little mongrel. The women
looked a lot better, especially the redhead. What a
body! But which, he wondered, was Byrne?

Three cars, a Porsche, a Ford, and a Pontiac, sat in
a small still life, bathed in light from the parking lot
halogen lamp. Chinsky drove the red Porsche. Duke
had followed him from Croft to the restaurant and
back. It was an easy car to follow; not many like them
on the street. These doctors sure liked foreign cars.
Un-American. He saw them come out of Carlos Murphy's together. Then they went in different directions
to their cars. He stayed with Chinsky, who left first,
so Duke didn't know which woman paired with which
car. Once at Croft, Duke, cautious about being
sighted, hung back and again missed the pairing.

Less than thirty seconds work was needed for Duke to open the Ford door with a skinny flat metal bar. There was nothing in the glove or passenger compartments to indicate ownership. He got luckier with the Pontiac. The door was unlocked and the name badge on the seat belonged to Brenda Byrne, girl reporter. Too bad there was no picture. He hoped it was the good-looking redhead. She was nice, very nice. It would give the job spice, paprika.

CHAPTER
14

CHINSKY DOWNSHIFTED and took the corner at thirty miles an hour. The Porsche hugged the ground like a wet spot on pavement. He pushed the gas pedal to the floor as he started into the turn. He kept it down on the straightaway until the tach needle climbed into the orange, then threw in the clutch and shifted up, hit the gas, clutched, and shifted up again. The speedometer hit fifty-five and he eased off, bringing it down to just under fifty—a safe speed for the forty-mile-an-hour zone.

Brenda was following, but he doubted if she could keep up. Her ten-year-old Pontiac was more like a plowhorse than a trotter. She knew the way. Jerzy would find it easy enough to follow her.

He pulled the Porsche around the circular drive and parked under the canopy. The doorman welcomed him with a cheery, "Good morning, Dr. Chinsky." Chinsky looked at his watch. The doorman was right; it was past midnight. A hell of a time for a celebration. But after the night's work, they deserved it.

"Good morning, Albert," Chinsky replied.

"Would you like me to have it parked for you?"

"Don't bother. Some friends of mine will be here in a minute."

"That'll be fine, sir." Albert didn't like his driveway cluttered up with cars, particularly little red sports cars. He was more tolerant of black or dark-gray sedans. His preference was for Mercedeses or Lincolns. But even then he had the feeling that more than one automobile in the drive was a bit tacky. His spacious driveway was not a parking lot. At times, the residents had the uncomfortable feeling that Albert was tolerating them. The doorman winced as he saw Brenda's car. Jerzy, close behind her, had a newer model, but still well below Albert's standards.

Even before stiff-backed Albert reached her door, Jerzy leaned through the window and shouted to Chinsky, "Just one, then I'm leaving. Can I park here?"

"I'll handle it, miss," said Albert coolly.

As the trio approached the vestibule door, Albert belatedly called to Chinsky, "I let the telephone man in while you were gone, sir. He says everything is fine now." Chinsky spun in mid-stride. The velocity of the turn threatened to send his bundle of newly printed records flying.

"What telephone man?"

The usually imperturbable Albert showed some discomfort at Chinsky's sharp tone. The rule was no entry, unless authorized by the resident. People who lived here paid for their privacy as much as for the space. "He said that their monitoring system had traced a short to your phone line. It was creating problems on other circuits. He had proper identification, and I let him in." Chinsky's eyes bore into his. "I do hope I didn't create a problem, sir," Albert said.

"No," Chinsky said, but he was strangely perturbed. Distracted, he led the women to the elevators. "Do telephone repairmen work on Sunday?" he asked them.

"Are you kidding?" asked the analyst. "Since they broke up the phone company we're lucky to get any service."

"That's what I thought," he said. He was hyper. Too many things, unexplained things, were happening. Cool it, he told himself. Still, after Brenda's remark at the lab . . .

He punched the elevator button. Then again a half dozen times in quick succession, trying to prompt it into action.

"Slow down, Luke," said Brenda with a laugh. "You're playing Mike Tyson with that button. How bad do you need a drink?"

The elevator door opened. A little man in pastel-blue slacks and a silk sport shirt held a small dachshund on a leash. The dog liked the elevator. It took a bit of prompting for blue slacks to coax him off. Chinsky had an urge to grab the leash and pull the short-legged canine out; he resisted. The women gushed over the dog. Chinsky waited impatiently. As soon as they were in, he pushed the floor number and "close door" buttons simultaneously.

■

The ivory moon was a bashful sliver in the sky, coyly peeking from passing cloud cover. The night was black outside the aura cast by an infrequent streetlight.

Neither Albert nor his wards noticed the man with the binoculars watching their pantomime from an inconspicuously parked Buick. The man, though, noticed that Chinsky looked just like the pictures. He had been wrong earlier when he thought the guy looked like a mongrel. No, this guy was a hippie. That pleased Duke. Mongrels, he could identify with. Not hippies.

Chinsky left his key in the door as he bounded into the foyer. He took two steps and stopped. Brenda, quick on his heels, bumped into him. His eyes flicked from place to place, object to object. He took a cautious step, then another, toward the living room. He stood at the top of the steps, surveying the room. Everything appeared as it should.

He crossed over to another room and tossed open the door. Again, he studied the contents. Books covered the walls, except for a hollowed-out area that housed a PC and printer. A cabriole-leg walnut table, which served as a desk, filled the center of the study. All seemed in order. The brilliant red light of the answering machine beamed steadily. No one had called. Reflexively, he flicked off the master switch to the system.

He walked over to the computer and reached for his thesaurus. From under it he lifted a small stack of blue computer printouts. "They're okay," he said as he turned to show them to Brenda.

"What?"

"The lab records. Charlie's."

An oily coat of relief blanketed the charged edge of anxiety that had grabbed him downstairs. He paged through the papers to confirm that they were all there. He sat down at his desk and leaned back. False alarm. Brenda's comment about the Buick, the records deleted on Sunday, and the events of the week had him hyper. The telephone man was what he appeared to be and not some dramatic Sherlock. "My God, I was scared. I thought for sure they would be gone."

Jerzy, still standing in the foyer, was perplexed. Was the man paranoid? She didn't know him well enough to jump to conclusions, but it took no analysis to see he was edgy. Her short-lashed eyelids fluttered briefly as they involuntarily closed. Please God, she prayed silently, don't let me get into anything.

Brenda's rippling laugh brought both Chinsky and Jerzy back. "You sure know how to psych yourself. You okay?" she asked.

"I'm fine. I'm just a little worked up."

"I'll say," said Jerzy.

He shook his head. "For a moment I thought the telephone man was after something. I don't know why. Just a feeling." He shook it off. "Let's forget it. This is a celebration. What can I get you?"

"A beer," said Jerzy.

"It did seem strange," said Brenda, her breath heavy from the tension he had created, "especially after that guy I thought I'd seen."

"What guy?" Jerzy asked.

"Brenda said she thought she saw someone following me when we went to the lab. It's not a common route, nor well traveled. I thought it was a coincidence, but I guess I gave it more subconscious attention than I thought."

"Sounds like it. How about that beer, or do I have to get my own? Tell you what," she said jokingly, "you get the drinks and I'll check your phone for bugs. We just learned how to do that at the academy refresher course."

"You're kidding." Brenda laughed. "They sent you through the academy?"

"You bet. Marksmanship and everything. I could have had the job without it, but it adds a hundred bucks a week to the pay."

Jerzy unscrewed the mouthpiece from the living room phone. Her small mouth formed a shape to mirror the roundness of her wide eyes as she whispered, "Ohhhh." As her eyes made contact with Brenda's she raised a finger to her lips.

"All I have is Molson Light," Chinsky yelled from the kitchen.

"That'll be fine. Forget the glass."

As he came back into the room, he saw her pointing to the uncapped transmitter with a ballpoint pen. Brenda had a finger on her lips to silence him. He walked over and looked at Jerzy's prize. There, in his very own phone, was a tiny electronic bug.

The Electret microphone was a quarter inch in diameter. Its housing included a battery that drove a preamplifier to give it a range of about one city block —providing someone at the other end had a very powerful directional receiver. Electret, the Tiffany of bugs, is sensitive enough to pick up all but a whisper in the far corner of a large room. It has a frequency response wide enough to capture the entire range of the human voice, with decibels left over. But its resistance to magnetic jamming was what made it prized by professionals.

Jerzy whistled a long, low note in appreciation of the craftsmanship as she gently screwed the speaker cap back on and replaced the phone on the table. She motioned Chinsky into the other room.

Making small talk, one by one they checked the phones. All but those in the bathrooms had been fitted with what they believed to be bugs. Chinsky ushered the women into the bathroom and turned the shower on. "I saw that in a movie once," he whispered above the cascading water. "It's supposed to muffle voices."

They acknowledged the tactic.

"We've got to get out of here," Brenda said. "This place is wired. Someone is after you."

"No shit!" he said.

"Whoever did this was a pro," Jerzy said. "Those are very sophisticated devices. And I'll bet there are more to be found.

"I think you should call the police," Jerzy said. "Get this place dusted and nail the rest of the bugs. Until then, it's not safe."

"I can't go to the police. Not yet," Chinsky said.

"Why not?"

"It's a long story. This isn't the place."

"Try me. After all, I'm one of them. You had no problem using me."

"It has nothing to do with you or the police. It's

just that I don't like working with other people. There are some things I need to figure out and the police would get in the way."

"Excuse me?" Jerzy said in mock alarm. "Was I in the way?"

"He didn't want you in either," Brenda said. "That was my idea."

"Flo, I appreciate your help, but I need to work this out by myself. I need to find the formula and I'm afraid bringing in the police would signal my intentions to whoever is watching. I need time."

"Luke, you need to get out of here," Brenda insisted.

"I've no place to go."

"How about my place?"

"Or a motel." Chinsky wasn't being coy. Some unknown body was tracking him. After Rathbone's murder, it was easy to imagine that he was a target. His lurking paranoia only needed an excuse to surface. If he were a target, those around him were threatened. Especially Brenda. He did not want to expose her. There was something more than altruism at work, but he had yet to define it.

"My place is better. At least we can go there to talk and decide what to do." Brenda, too, was beginning to feel a need to protect him. Her protection, though, meant being together, rather than apart.

"Let's go," he said. "We'll work it out there. But not right away. Make small talk. I'll say I'm going to the office. You just grunt. I don't want them to know who you are."

"Grunt?" Jerzy said, unable to control herself. "You want her to grunt?"

He smiled and opened the door.

In five minutes, they were back in the lobby. Chinsky maneuvered Albert into a corner. "Tell me what the telephone guy looked like." Chinsky was half a head shorter than the doorman, but standing six inches from his body and staring up into his face, Chinsky was clearly the intimidator.

Albert, not used to ungentlemanly behavior, was uncertain whether he should be officious or submissive. A sharply honed survival instinct guided him to choose the latter. "He was tall, sir, taller than me. And big. He had blond hair."

"Did he have a beard?"

"No. I just saw the hair under his cap, sir. He was wearing a telephone company uniform and he had identification and a work order. It had your name on it."

"My name's getting on a lot of things."

"I don't know what you mean, sir."

"That's okay. What else?" Chinsky kept the distance between them to a minimum. It was all that was needed to keep the words flowing.

"That's all, sir. He looked like"—Albert groped for just the right word. He smiled more from relief than humor as he found it—"like a workman."

Chinsky's lids narrowed, his eyes rolled ever so slightly into his head. He almost grabbed Albert's lapels, but restrained himself. Albert would become indignant if manhandled. "What else, Albert? What else? Think!" Chinsky was on his tiptoes, his nose a half inch from Albert's. Albert was very uncomfortable.

"That's all I can remember. He was big and tall and blond. A workman." Albert paused. "Wait. There was something else. He had a snake tattooed on the back of his hand. I noticed it when he showed me the work order."

"Which hand?"

Albert looked at his hands to remind himself. "His right hand."

"What else? What did he look like? His face. What can you remember of his face?"

"It was a normal face. I can't describe it." Albert was at the end of his information. He hadn't given Chinsky much, but the tattoo would be helpful. It would be hard to hide.

"Albert, don't let anyone else in my apartment. I'm conducting some experiments up there, and the materials are toxic. If someone were to knock over a bottle, even by accident, the fumes could kill them. So don't let anyone in, regardless of what they say." It was a lie, but it would focus Albert's attention on following his orders.

Albert was relieved. Both for the extra breathing space and because he now understood the situation. There was, after all, a logical explanation for the doctor's strange behavior. It put his world back into perspective.

Had he been less eager to find a reason, he would have questioned the plausibility of a home laboratory.

Chinsky turned to Brenda and Jerzy, who had

stood mute during the interrogation. "Let's go," he said, as he moved toward his car.

"Where did you learn to intimidate people like that?" Jerzy asked.

"In medical school. We practiced on nurses."

■

As the small caravan pulled away from the apartment building, the Buick across the street started up. Duke drove with his right hand at the top of the wheel, the flat-headed cobra staring up at him. Led by the little red foreign car, they were easy to follow. Especially since he knew where they were going. The bug he had installed in the bathroom was—like the others—the best available. A little shower water couldn't dull its hearing. Imagine, the brunette a cop. A woman! And small too. They didn't care who they took nowadays. No matter. He didn't have a contract on her and there were no freebies in this business.

He lagged a half mile behind as they led him to Brenda's apartment. He circled the lot, found their cars, and pulled out. No sense being visible. He smiled. This job was getting easier. He wouldn't have to keep track of the hippie; he could just watch the car. He smiled again. The redhead was a looker. Maybe he'd work it so he could spend some time with her. The guy he would take out tomorrow.

■

"I think I should call this in," said Jerzy. "I can have your whole place swept in less than an hour."

"No," said Chinsky. "I need to sort this out. If we pull those bugs we won't know who's behind them."

"Luke, that's ridiculous. Flo is right. Let's get them out and let the police handle this. They can watch the apartment and if anyone tries to bug it again, they'll nab them."

"No," he said firmly. His tendency to act alone, to rely on his innate individualism, asserted itself. "I need time to look at this stuff." He pushed the printouts toward them. "If I get the police involved in this, there's a chance that they'll wind up with the data and I'll be back where I was. I need to find out what I can about the cure."

"I disagree," said Jerzy. "But what do I know? I only got the stuff out of the computer. I'll tell you, though, you're going to have to make up your mind fast, 'cause I'm beat. I can't stick around to argue about this."

"You're right." Chinsky agreed more to buy time than out of conviction. "But give me the night to think this through." He looked at Brenda. "Assuming I can stay."

"Wouldn't have it any other way, sport."

■

The redhead's apartment building was not as fancy as the hippie's. No canopy, no doorman, and far less glass. The building was dirty redbrick with four stories of picture windows, a clone of unpretentious, durable, moderately priced buildings in Skokie, Duluth, or St. Louis. Without having set foot inside, Duke had been in and out of this building a dozen times.

The vestibule would be just big enough for two eleva-tors and some mailboxes; the stairwell, tucked into a corner with a red-and-white exit sign over the door. There would be a back entry leading to the parking lot. Whether the building had carpeting would de-pend upon if it had been upgraded—so rents could be raised. Duke guessed it would have carpeting. Yup-pies paid extra for that.

After sitting out front for a half hour, Duke eased the Buick back into the parking lot. The cop had left. He was glad he hadn't waited in the lot.

Slowly, eyes darting from one opaque windshield to another, he drove around the lot to make sure no one—not lovers, not thieves—occupied the cars. The Porsche was still there, next to the Pontiac. He parked at the end of the lot, farthest from the entryway. Five minutes passed and nothing other than the lumines-cent eyes of a prowling tomcat moved. He was alone. He eased the door of the Buick open, taking care not to make a sound.

Staying in the shadow of a hemlock hedge border-ing the lot, he made his way to the rear entrance of the building. It wasn't locked, which surprised him. Security must not be a problem around here.

Once in, he could see straight through, down the blue-carpeted passageway, to the front door. To his right was the rear stairwell. He opened the door a crack. A sixty-watt bulb gave dim light to the well. Some of these buildings, as a security measure, had one-way locks on the stairwell doors. You could get in but it took a key to get out. The brushed-aluminum hardware of the door fixture was the nonlocking type.

He slipped into the stairwell and walked up one flight. Again, no lock. He assumed that the remaining floors would mirror the first two. Tracing his path back to the first floor he reentered the main corridor.

He was momentarily startled by a young couple, talking animatedly, heading toward the parking lot door. They paid no attention to him. He avoided looking at them directly, but saw it wasn't Chinsky or the redhead. A moment later he heard the growl of an engine turning over, then the Doppler of the withdrawing car.

It was quiet again. The bright, bluish glare of the recessed fluorescents bothered him. Too much light.

He walked the corridor to the front door. As he suspected, another stairwell flanked the entry. He looked inside. Except for carpeting and papered walls, it was the same as the rear well.

He went over to the mailbox. There were four apartments on each floor. From the size of the building, the apartments were decent sized, probably three bedrooms. Duke looked at the names. Byrne was in 4B. He smirked. The penthouse.

Walking back to his car, looking up at the building, he tried to visualize the layout of the rooms. The placement of the kitchen and bathrooms were obvious from the shape of the windows. The bedrooms would be in the corners, and of course, the oversize window gave the living room its view. A simple layout, easy to remember.

He unlocked the trunk and took out what looked like a leather toolbox. To avoid the noise of a slam, he left the trunk slightly ajar. Inside the Buick, he snapped the brass catch of the toolbox and pulled the leather case open. A dozen or more compartments, each with a different gadget, revealed themselves. The silent craftsman took out a folded suede cloth, little bigger than a handkerchief, and spread it on the seat next to himself, forming a lint-free workplace. Again he dipped into the toolbox; this time he took out a plastic bag. Gingerly, he opened the bag. In it was what looked like a portable radio. It was, in fact, very similar to a radio, but it only received a specific frequency.

On its face was a set of tuning knobs and two LCD, or liquid crystal display, windows. A strip of Velcro covered its back. On the side was a small black switch that changed its function from receiver to transmitter. Nothing on the device was labeled. It was a custom-made tool, and Duke knew all its characteristics. He had designed and commissioned it. He laid the radio on the cloth and reached into the bag again. This time he took out a number of hard plastic disks, each about the size of an Eisenhower dollar, but thicker.

He selected one and put the rest back.

The disk unscrewed to reveal the workings of a small transmitter. Duke fished a nickel cadmium battery the size of a dime out of the toolbox and slipped it into the transmitter. The LCD of the receiver immediately lit up. The top window read CENTER, the bottom 00.00. He switched the receiver off. He looked for some metal on the interior of the Buick to test the small electromagnet on the back of the transmitter. It stuck to the steering column. He gave it a sharp hit from the side; it moved but stayed attached. It was engineered to stay attached to the underside of a fender when a car hit an eight-inch pothole at ninety miles per hour. The axle or tire would usually fail before the magnet let loose.

He laid the transmitter next to the receiver.

Off to one side of the toolbox were three small boxes, similar in size to cigarette packs. Duke took one out and slid back the top end of the box—the end where the cigarette pack would open. Inside was explosive plastique and space for an electronically controlled detonator. There was enough explosive force in the little device to rearrange the frame of a two-ton truck while gutting its insides with a fireball. Duke glanced at the LCD of the receiver to confirm it was off. It wouldn't have mattered if it wasn't. The detonator had an automatic cutout to prevent detonation when the distance on the bottom LCD display was less than .1 mile.

Nonetheless, Duke liked to be cautious. He checked the magnet on the box. It held. Like a surgeon selecting a scalpel, he drew a stainless steel toothpick-size electronic detonator from the toolbox and pressed it into the plastic explosive, leaving the pick exposed a sixteenth of an inch.

The last thing he took out of the leather toolbox was a harness for the receiver. He attached it to the dashboard with high-adhesion double-sided tape. He mounted the receiver on the harness. The Velcro held it firmly. He sat back in his seat and adjusted its position, so he could see the displays while driving. He gave the receiver a whack with his hand. It stayed

in place. He lifted it slightly and the Velcro let loose.
With a red wax crayon he marked a C on the matte
plastic case. He put it back on the suede cloth with
the sigh of satisfaction a good craftsman gives when
admiring an exceptional tool. He then repeated the
entire process with another set of little boxes. These
he marked B.

Duke closed the toolbox and put it on the floor.

His initial preparations complete, he drove out of
the parking lot and around the block. The drive relieved some of the tension he always felt after putting
a device together.

Approaching from the opposite direction, he
pulled back into the parking lot. As he entered, he
looked slowly around. He made a quick visual check
of the back door to the apartment building. It was
closed.

He casually pulled next to the red Porsche and
parked.

In less than ten seconds he had opened his door,
slid the transmitter and black box marked with a C
under the rear fender of the Porsche, and tested each
to see that it was firmly attached. To a casual observer, he could have been a driver who stopped to
retrieve a dropped coin.

He looked around again. Seeing nothing out of the
ordinary, he walked around to the Pontiac and attached the B device. Then he went back to the running Buick and drove out of the parking lot, heading
north. Two blocks away, he stopped and parked.

He reached over to the B receiver and switched it
on. The LCD immediately lit up. The top window

displayed SOUTH, the bottom 00.20. He pushed the switch on the C receiver. It mirrored B. Duke smiled and decided to go back to the Ramada.

Chinsky and the girl were in good hands.

CHAPTER
15

THERE WAS LESS here than he thought.

Crumpled balls of yellow notepad paper littered the floor. Chinsky's notes were scattered over her desk. Apparently Rathbone had set up five groups of patients and had administered a different agent to each. One of the five showed remarkable improvement. Other than that, his nightlong analysis had yielded little. He'd known almost as much when they'd left the lab.

It was five o'clock. The bitter taste of coffee soured his mouth. He felt the weight of fatigue drawing a felt curtain across the stage of his mind. Only will held back the curtain. Brenda, still dressed, a wisp of auburn hair cloaking her cheek, lay asleep on her couch. She had tried to help, but a waspish comment or two from him had driven her away. He went it alone and he had gone nowhere. His brain refused commands. Simple connections became complex. He needed rest.

■

Chinsky wasn't in yet. Were they that efficient? He hadn't heard anything on the news, nor had there been a call from the police. But if he wasn't dead, why wasn't he here, at work, where he was supposed to be? Damn! Murcheson wasn't here either, so he couldn't ask her to track his young research chief down. He wanted to know Chinsky's status, but it wouldn't do to be obvious about it.

He leaned over to his desk phone and dialed Chinsky's office again. Mary answered.

"Dr. Chinsky." The name was a command.

"I'm afraid he's not in yet, Mr. Snell." She was expected to recognize the voice.

"I want to speak with him as soon as he gets in."

"Yes, sir. I'll tell him."

Maybe, thought Snell as he hung up, they were more efficient than he gave them credit for.

■

She awoke to find Chinsky stretched across her bed, covered only by a thin sheet. He slept through the rush of water that signaled her shower, the bubbling of brewing coffee, and the drone of morning TV news. From the volume of yellow balls dotting the carpet around her desk, he had worked late. The bastard had a sharp tongue when things didn't go his way. Her ego still felt the pricks left by his verbal darts. Brenda didn't understand him. His work isolated him. Made him insensitive. They needed to talk. But not now.

Brenda found an extra set of door keys and left them atop her note. Then she left.

■

More than three miles away, Duke lay snoring on the Ramada Inn's king-size bed.

Taped to the mirror above the credenza was a thirty-six-inch-square map of the city. The scale was precisely two miles per inch. A faint-blue plastic grid of quarter-inch squares overlayed it. A black dot marked the location of the Ramada at coordinate zero zero. Chinsky's and Brenda's apartments were marked by red dots, as was Croft.

Though Duke slept, the receivers didn't. "C" pulsed steady with no change in the message displayed on its face. The LCD display of "B" reconfigured every few seconds, adjusting for Brenda's change in direction and distance. A cord ran from each receiver to a printer about the size of a paperback book. Every fifteen seconds the "B" receiver sent out a tiny surge of electricity. The tiny hammer within the printer hit the continuous loop of the character set and typed out the time, direction, and distance from the base. One hundred and twenty-three lines after she eased out of her parking lot, the printer went into a stable pattern lasting for sixteen lines. The computer in the printer summarized the movements and printed the coordinates where the transmitter rested. It then shut down to await the next series of movements. Brenda at coordinate 11.25E, 11.50S had arrived at the *Free Press*.

■

The light blinked Morse code signals over his eyelids. He threw an arm across them to stop the dash-

dash-dot-dot-dot flashes. Through an opened slit he looked for the source of the irritation and found it in the partially opened venetian blind. An erratic wind flowed through the slightly opened window. Guarding his eyes, he took in his surroundings. The room was a restful beige accented with black. The four-poster bed lacked a canopy. It wasn't his bed, but it was familiar. He knew why. It was her room. It was an uncomfortable bed. The posts restricted activity and bruised errant thighs or arms. Why am I here, he wondered? Where's Brenda? Last night's work slowly rolled over his emerging consciousness. The printouts. He snapped to a sitting position, awake, alert, anxious to make sure it had not been a dream. Slipping on his Levi's, he hobbled out to the small study, where he remembered working.

Balls of discarded paper, like kernels of popcorn, lead to the stack of printouts on the small Queen Anne desk. No dream. They were there. So were his notes. And the frustration of finding little the night before.

Where was Brenda? Drawn by the aroma of fresh-brewed coffee, he made his way to the kitchen. The note on the table was a series of neatly printed lines.

Luke

> *Good morning.*
> *You were out for the*
> *count when I left.*
> *Hope you slept well.*

> *Gone to work.*
> *I'll call you later.*
>
> *Brenda*
>
> *P.S. The keys are for you.*

Two door keys were linked together by the chin-strap of a miniature Lions' football helmet. He pocketed the keys.

My God, what time was it? 10:00. He was late for work. They could do without him for a morning.

He poured a cup of coffee and went back to the small desk.

What next?

Time to get organized, to make use of those superb analytical skills you're so proud of. Time to make sense of this. He pulled a yellow legal pad in front of him. *What do I know?* he asked himself, then wrote it at the top of the page in bold block letters with a heavy underline. *Start with what you know.* That was the basic rule. He knew about Rathbone, Charlie, and the trials.

The yellow pencils were all worn down to the wood. He picked up a small handful and sharpened them. Then he sat down and went to work.

WHAT DO I KNOW?

Listing the facts helped him focus his attention. Once down, he could manipulate them until they formed a coherent pattern. Where to start? With Rathbone, of course. He started his list.

1. Rathbone was conducting human trials, perhaps illegally.

No speculation at this point, he told himself, and crossed out the last two words. Unless the records are phony and Charlie is a shill, the fact of the human trials is established. Given the trouble I had getting the records, I'm going to assume they're authentic. If they are, then:

2. *All test subjects had HIV infections.*

The charts were clear on that. He had checked the white blood cell counts as well as the lymphocytes. They all fit the infection profile. For a while he had speculated that there was another group, an uninfected control group. But then he realized that was unnecessary. One of the infected groups could be the control group. What he did know was that:

3. *One group*, segregated in their own file, *showed significant improvement in white blood cell count.*

Could be, he thought, that each file group was receiving a different agent. Maybe a different dosage of the same agent. Maybe a combination. His mind was clear now, all traces of tiredness obliterated by rest. He could feel the quickening of his pulse as his thoughts raced. He picked up a chart and studied it again. Most of the codes were self-explanatory. There were no entries that resembled dosages or pharmaceuticals. The codes in the two right-hand columns, however, were unintelligible, a series of numbers.

The left-hand column on the record repeated the same number. That could be the code for the treatment. He checked the other files in the group. Some of the code numbers were the same, but not all. The variation was only in the last two digits: 307616 versus 307632. Odd. The progression between last two digits in this group was geometric. He sorted the charts. Yes. There were two charts for every term: 01, 02, 04, and so on. It's the dose, he thought. He doubled the dose. The first four numbers were his treatment code, the last two the dose.

Chinsky leaned back, pleased with himself. That sly old fox. It was so obvious, most analysts would look right past it. Last night, muddled, he had done exactly that. *Now is the time to press on, find out what I can.* Rathbone was obvious. A million bucks says he was also consistent. Chinsky dove into the other piles and sorted them. Each followed a similar, but not duplicate, pattern.

Group 2212, particularly those with doses above 30, showed improvement. The progression here was in tens. Charlie was 221260. He was ready to write it down on the list when he caught himself. "I'm speculating," he said out loud. "No room for speculation yet. Just the facts, ma'am," he said, parodying the *Dragnet* cop. "Just the facts."

Spurred on by success, he turned his attention to the next-to-last column, a series of four-, five-, and six-digit numbers.

29622
2971
29741
29703
2981

They all started with the same two digits, 29, except for some of the longer charts, which started with 09, then progressed to 29.

It was the 09's that gave it to him. Why start with a zero? They're dates, he realized with a flash of insight. Mirror images of dates. 192121 is 12 December 1991—12/12/91 reversed. 1981 is 1 August 1991—1/8/91. He emitted a self-satisfied sigh. So, he had the treatment codes and the dates. "Thank you, Dr. Rathbone," he said to the emptiness. He hadn't been trying to hide anything. The organization, the methodology, was there. Security was there, too, but not in the form of archaic indecipherable codes. Rathbone was not the one trying to hide his work. What remained covered was the treatment agent. With it, he would be in business.

No time for kudos. He whipped his attention back to the listing. Tentatively he wrote:

4. *Rathbone had a cure for the viral infection.*

That wasn't speculation. It was there in the white blood cell counts. Now he even had a name for it: 2212. Even if he didn't know what that meant.

Curious that Rathbone had deleted the clinic files on Saturday—before his death. Was it part of his own security procedure? Snell gave the impression that *he* had removed the files. But not until Monday. By then, they were already gone. It didn't fit. In any case, the office files were the key to the cure. And they were gone.

5. *All Rathbone's files were missing—office and clinic.*

He now had the clinic computer files and some of the office files. But there was more he didn't have. Rathbone's work logs, including the meaning of the code, were still missing. If the formula was anywhere, it was in the work logs. Formula 2212. At least there was a cure. Rathbone, for all his talk of teamwork, must have worked alone.

A team would have left a paper trail three miles wide. Maybe with a team there would be paper, but no cure. Then again, sometimes, not often, you needed people. Brenda had helped find Jerzy. Together the three of them had unlocked the computer files. He couldn't have done it alone. It was an unsettling thought. He wouldn't have needed them, though, if Snell hadn't sequestered the records. Yes. Snell.

6. *Snell is somehow involved.*

It was a weak statement and he knew it, but it was true. The phony call to security. The return of part of the records at Snell's instruction. More than coincidence. Something was being covered up.

But if Snell was trying to cover up something, why appoint him to monitor Rathbone's projects? Snell must have known that eventually the fact that Rathbone's records were missing would surface. The incident with Charlie made it sooner rather than later, but it was inevitable. Or was it? Were they to be suppressed forever? Snell said the records were destroyed. But they weren't. The clinic computer records proved that. What if Snell was bluffing? What if he didn't know about the clinic records—just as he hadn't known of the lab records? He was involved, but to what extent? And why? Perhaps it was, as Snell said himself, the protection of the company. Or maybe it was more. For instance, did Snell have the apartment bugged? He recalled the intrusive look of the tiny transmitter and recorded his next fact.

7. *My apartment was bugged.*

That's for damned sure. It could be coincidence, a nosy competitor going to unscrupulous lengths. He'd heard stories like that. But he didn't think so. Why would anyone take the trouble to bug his apartment? Could it be the police? Didn't they need a permit or something? Did they have to tell him if they were going to listen in? Of course not. The way that detective, Washington, acted, he was a suspect. Is that why they were bugging him? Drugs. Someone, Brenda, said one of their theories was that Rathbone's killing was connected to drugs. Did they think that he, Chinsky, was dealing drugs? He rejected the notion, then recanted. From their perspective, it was plausible. It would explain the bugging. He didn't know how far the police were allowed to go in the solution of a murder, but he suspected that the violation of a suspect's rights wouldn't be a major obstacle in the pursuit of a killer.

8. *Rathbone is dead.*

A fact, clearly. Perhaps the key fact, but he was beginning to think otherwise. Rathbone dead left a cure hidden. Who would benefit from a suppressed discovery? Not Croft—and that meant Snell. Both the man and the company would reap enormous profit from an AIDS cure. Certainly not the patients. A competitor? Perhaps, but unlikely. If we in the company didn't know he was onto something, how would they? Even so, what would they gain? Croft's gain was not their loss. His death could be a coincidence. From the patient charts it was clear that Rathbone was dealing with hard-core addicts. Who knows what they would do? Maybe one got high and killed him. Maybe he was supplying heroin as a quid pro quo for their cooperation—and stopped because he no longer needed them. Maybe. Speculation. The salient fact was a dead Rathbone.

This is it, he thought. *This is what I know.* He looked at the list again.

Not enough to answer the key questions of why this was happening and who was behind it. Not enough even to make a credible hypothesis. He studied the list again. The first three facts lead to the fourth, an inevitable conclusion that a cure existed. The only element missing was its nature. The last four statements dealt with circumstances surrounding the cure. The chronology is wrong, he thought, and drew an arrow from the last statement—*Rathbone is dead*—inserting it before the fifth—*All Rathbone's files were missing*. He rearranged the list in his mind. Rathbone dead; files missing; Snell involved; apartment bugged. Blinking at the yellow paper a new thought began to emerge, first slowly then in rifle shots that ricocheted off one another. Maybe they don't want to suppress it. Maybe they don't know what it is, either. Maybe they're trying to find out the nature of the cure. Maybe Rathbone's death had nothing to do with the cure. Maybe he blanked the computer files as a routine security measure. Maybe Snell took the files, trying to find out what Rathbone knew. Maybe competitors were also onto the fact that Rathbone had a cure. Maybe they were involved.

Maybe they bugged his apartment because they thought he could lead them to the cure. In his mind it began to make sense.

Rathbone took an important secret with him when he died. Now someone was trying to ferret it out. Once again, if he knew the cure, would he know who the someone was? Probably. The sinister fog cloaked around the situation began to evaporate.

■

Duke was shaving as receiver "C" came alive. Coming out of the bathroom he noticed the tongue of paper sticking out of the small printer. He went to the map and plotted the coordinates. The hippie was going north. Probably to Croft. About time. Duke was beginning to think he would never leave. The redhead was still downtown.

For the next ten minutes the "C" track followed I-75. No doubt about it, he was gone. Time to get to work. Duke slipped the receivers in his pockets, picked up his tool kit, and hummed "My Way" as he left the motel suite.

CHAPTER
16

IT WOULD NOT be easy. Proxy had seen people confront Snell. Once or twice, Snell had backed down. It was a matter of leverage. If someone came to the confrontation with better facts, Snell would listen. Or if the opponent showed Snell he had more to gain by conceding than fighting, he conceded. Usually Snell knew the pressure points before entering a conflict. If the odds were against him, he avoided it. "You can't lose if you don't fight," was a favorite saying of his. Proxy had the leverage of their long relationship. It was worth a concession or two. But the real leverage was in the file box, hidden in the apartment. If he guessed right, Snell didn't want the cure to surface. But Proxy realized just how weak his position was. Right now, he was the *only* thing that stood between Snell and the box. That needed to change.

As it now stood, three things protected him: Snell still trusted him, Snell didn't know where the files were, and Snell didn't know he knew. When he faced Snell, two of his three advantages would evaporate like water on a hot stove, leaving him with only the location of the files for leverage. Not much of a lever if Snell didn't want the records, just wanted them suppressed. He didn't need to know where the records were. Not if by getting rid of the one who knew would keep them submerged. Would he do that? He shivered. Ask Rathbone, he thought.

Why not go to the police? Or the newspapers? Then the confrontation with Snell would be avoided, the information made public. But there were other risks in that course. At this point all he had was well-founded suspicion—and, of course, the files. Snell would deny everything, as he had done with Roger years ago. In the next breath he would brand him, Proxy, a gay psychotic dissatisfied with Croft's lack of progress on a cure. Snell would drag out the old police record, and him out of the closet with it. It would be enough to slow the authorities down. Were the computer records he had trashed recoverable? He didn't know. If they were, they would verify his allegation. With warning, though, Snell would find a way to further eliminate all internal trace of the tests. There were probably other Proxys he didn't know about who licked at Snell's boot. A week ago he wouldn't have believed it. Now, he was sure of it. Snell's bidding was done too quickly, too efficiently. His mentor might also find a way to implicate him in Rathbone's death. After all, he had the files. Going public was not the answer.

Nor was confronting Snell—until he increased the odds of his survival.

■

Mary was fidgeting, unable to contain herself.

"Mr. Snell called three times. Do you want me to call him?"

"That's okay, Mary. I won't be able to see him today."

"But, Dr. Chinsky, he's well, he's the president."

Chinsky nodded sympathetically, reassuringly. "Yes, I know. But he'll have to wait. Can you get me Nurse Stanton over at the clinic?"

Maybe he should call Snell. But what would he say? I was here last night and cracked the computer records that you lied to me about. And then I stole them. And this morning I cracked Rathbone's computer code. Did Snell really want to hear that? Did he really want Snell to know? Snell has been throwing up roadblocks all along. Better to wait, find the last piece, the formula for the cure, before anyone else can muck up the situation.

Mary buzzed him from the outer office. "Miss Stanton is on the line."

"Thanks, Mary." He pushed the lighted button to make the connection. "Ms. Stanton? Dr. Chinsky. What's happening?" He had called her from Brenda's and left instructions that she was to get contact information on any patient who came in, particularly their social security number, and draw a blood sample.

"Two more came in."

"Did you draw blood?"

"On both of them. But only one remembered his social security number. The other one will call in with it."

They needed that number.

"Good. Anything else?"

"No. It's been pretty quiet."

"Okay. I'll be over with Dr. Paxton in pathology for a while. If any more come in, call me there."

Herb Paxton was one of the best pathologists in the business. Before he joined Croft he had spent five years as associate director of the University of Michigan Hospital laboratory. Trained at Stanford with an internship at Mass General, he was young for a chief of pathology at Croft; but his track record warranted it.

In many ways he was much like Chinsky: young, bright, independent, with sharp analytical skills. On occasion, he and Chinsky had gone drinking, even double-dated. But they had never become close friends. Not close enough to share confidences. Perhaps it was something neither of them was capable of.

Chinsky sat in Paxton's office, the patient charts piled in front of him. "Herb," the researcher said, "over the past few months you've been running some tests for David Rathbone." He patted the stack of charts.

"Yeah," the pathologist agreed congenially. "Every once in a while. Nothing too complicated. He first talked to me about it more than a year ago. Said it was for some independent research he was conducting, to back up a paper he was planning for the *Journal*."

"You know that I'm picking up some of his projects?"

"Right. Nice move for you. Congratulations. Too bad about the circumstances, though."

Chinsky agreed. "I need some information on

some of those patients. I've developed a list from the charts." He handed a list of names and the code numbers Rathbone used to Paxton. "For some reason the files on these patients are minimal. I'm trying to reconstruct certain aspects of them. Any chance you can give me a complete lab report on each of them?"

"Whew." Paxton whistled as he looked at the list. "Sure, we can get it, but it'll be a little work. As I recall, the tests on these patients were comprehensive and redundant. The records are stored in a number of files based on which analyzer we used. Rathbone was supposed to keep the master record on his computer.

"There were a lot of tests. The entire presymptomatic virus screening panel plus the autoimmune panel and, of course, the comprehensive screen."

"I'd appreciate it if you could reconstruct the reports." Chinsky hesitated a second. "There's something else I need, Herb."

Paxton looked at him quizzically.

"I'd like to get an analysis of the composition of agents that have been ingested by certain of these patients."

"You mean comparative chemistry?"

"Yes."

"Patient to patient or across patients?"

"Which can you do?"

"Both, if we have samples. I assume you can get current samples."

Chinsky nodded. "It may take some time, but they can be had."

"Then we can do it."

■

Brenda called at four o'clock.

"I tried the apartment. No answer, so I figured you were at Croft. Get my note?"

"Yes. Thanks for the keys."

"You're welcome." She hesitated, afraid to raise the issue. "Have you thought about going to the police?"

"I've thought about it," he said noncommittally. "I still have a few things to do. Then we'll see."

"I'd like to break the story when you talk to them. Could I do that?"

There was a long pause.

"Look," she said, "you don't have to commit now. I'd like to talk to you—I've had a very interesting day —but tonight I have to earn my keep. Feel like a ball game?"

"Business or pleasure?"

"My business, your pleasure. You can sit with me in the press box."

"I really should do more work on this thing."

"You need a break. I'll throw in dinner." She was not to be refused. Besides, the idea of putting this all away for a few hours appealed. Especially if she were part of the package.

"Sounds good," he said. "Where should I meet you?"

"How about the Press Club? Know where it is?"

"No."

She told him.

"See you at six," she said, and hung up.

■

The lavender metropolitan cab pulled into the one-way drive of the Press Club's lot just as he got his parking ticket.

"Leave it," she yelled from the cab's rolled-down window. "Let's take this over to the ballpark. It's a lot easier." He shrugged his shoulders and joined her in the cab.

She was in a chatty mood, filled with news that she had to share. "What a day!" she said as he got in. "I've talked to both Anne Rathbone and Detective Washington. Rathbone was a strange duck."

"Where's your car?"

"I left it at my apartment. I'll drive back with you. We usually take cabs on assignment. Gives us more mobility. Anyway, did you know that the Rathbones didn't have any kids? He didn't want any. Thought he had bad genes. His father and grandfather both died young—cancer." Chinsky nodded. This was something he knew already. Rathbone always talked about how he would never have his threescore years and ten. The gene that had truncated his life, though, was lead-coated. Brenda tumbled on with her story. "Anne Rathbone is very nice, but really distraught. He was her whole life—but it's strange, she didn't know anything about his work, I guess. I don't mean his latest projects, I mean about the company and his responsibilities, things wives and husbands usually talk about. She's wrapped up in the country club and her charity work. He was her entry to that world and with him dead she's not sure she'll be accepted."

"That sounds crass."

"Doesn't it?" she said, surprised. "It sounded crass to me too. But that's how she came off. It took me a few minutes to get into the interview. At first she was bereaved. But the more we talked, the less love I felt between them."

"Researchers are like that," he said.

"Are they?" she asked archly.

"It's the nature of the work. Makes you a cynic. Nothing is taken for granted. Everything needs to be checked. Romanticism and emotions are suspect."

"Are you like that?"

He looked at her and tugged his beard. "A bit. No, more than a bit, a lot."

"You don't seem like that to me."

"You don't know me." He moved the conversation away from him. "Did you get anything you can use for your article?"

"Quite a bit, actually. Some insight into the fervor Rathbone brought to his work. The way I figure it, he was so into his work that he didn't have the patience to bring her along. I guess he was pretty driven."

"He was a perfectionist."

"I sensed that. Mrs. Rathbone said he became upset with disorder." She shook her head. "But it was more than that. I could feel a tenseness when she talked of things out of place, as if he would find out and disapprove. He must have been compulsive."

Chinsky could attest to that. Look how neatly Rathbone had organized the computer data.

"Anyway, I have enough to do a profile on both of them, but it would be useful if you told me about the technical importance of some of the things Rathbone did. We can do that later. Let me tell you about Washington, though. What a character. He's convinced Rathbone's death is somehow connected to drugs. Talk about cynics. He's the champ!"

"Sure he's not just leading you on?"

"I don't think so. If he is, he's pretty damn good. Anyway, why should he?"

"Why should he tell you anything? Seems to me he has nothing to gain by talking to you and a lot to lose. You could print something that blows his case."

"That's exactly why he needs us. If he keeps quiet, we print anything we can get our hands on. If he's not onto it already, it makes the cops look dumb. Maybe, as you suggest, it blows the case. They don't like that. So they cooperate and we keep the stuff they want held back out of the paper. It's a two-way street."

"How do you know so much? You're a sportswriter." As soon as the words were out, he regretted them. She was beginning to see herself as a hard-news reporter doing temporary duty on the sports beat.

Her eyes tightened a bit as her customary retort died in her throat. With a dignified coolness she said, "Billy told me how it works." Flaunting her restraint, she gave him a self-satisfied smile. "Anyway, Washington's second theory is that someone inside of Croft had something to do with it. He's looking for a motive." She paused and looked at her lap. "I think you're one of the suspects."

He nodded. "I thought he might be leaning in that

direction. It's ridiculous, but he gave me that impression when we talked. I think he sees everyone as a suspect. What did he say?"

"He brought up the argument you had with Rathbone before he died as an example of how someone within Croft might be involved. I don't think he gives it much weight, but it's on his mind."

"I've been thinking that it might have been the police who planted the bugs in my apartment. It'd be easy for them to get a telephone work order. If I'm a suspect, it fits. Maybe I'd better talk to him?"

"What would you say?"

"I don't know. Just that I had nothing to do with it."

"And if he asks about the research?"

"Why would he?"

"What if he found out about it later? It would seem as if you were holding something back."

She was right. Why did he always think he was the only one who could be right? "You're right," he said. "What else did he have to say?"

"He has word out through the DPD that he's looking for information about anyone on the street who knows about Rathbone. I suspect that sooner or later a junkie with AIDS who was a test subject is going to show up. Then Washington will be coming around to talk to you."

"He already has two men inside Croft. One of them was down to see me about drug requisitions."

"I know, but according to Washington, they haven't come up with anything yet. He may not be telling me everything, though."

"What about your deal?"

"It works on his terms."

Before he had a chance to tell her of his progress, the white bulk of Tiger Stadium ended their conversation.

Chinsky had to admire her style. She waded right in with the boys and played their game, maybe even beat them at it. She gave him a press badge and told him to stay close. He did. He had only been to a half dozen or so baseball games in his life and never so near the action. Nor had he realized so much was going on.

Before the game, she interviewed the manager, Punky Lemon, along with three of his players. She tried to goad them into indiscretions with some provocative questions. They stayed discreet. After a few tries, she took a few good-natured gibes from her peers. They used banter to keep tensions manageable. Still, to the outsider, the camaraderie between reporter and player was obvious. As they went up to the press box, she confided that the interview wasn't very productive. He thought it was fascinating.

Brenda kept up a line of chatter through most of the game, only breaking the flow to make a few notes. Mainly she talked about analogies: how a characteristic of this player or that situation compared to a usually famous player or some obscure situation of the past. She knew the sport well enough to impress him.

The visiting White Sox scored seven runs in the first inning. From there it was downhill. Brenda told him that Yogi Berra had said, "It ain't over till it's over." By the third inning, with the score thirteen to nothing, she concluded it was over. Still, she couldn't leave. What if Yogi was right? The fans paid her to tell them about it. They also paid her to stick out the agony, so they could go home and read about it tomorrow. She passed on that bit of philosophy in the bottom of the seventh. The final score was fourteen to four.

They went down to talk with the team.

Chinsky tagged along on her heels as she walked into the locker room. Gray metal lockers flanked varnished oak benches. It looked just like all the high school and college locker rooms he had ever used. The smell of sweat—mingled with the fresh, clean heat of the clothes dryer and seasoned with Ben-Gay —produced that universal locker room odor. Only the sitz baths and Nautilus equipment gave it professionalism.

While shoes, socks, and shirts came off, revealing bunioned toes and an impressive array of torsos, modesty prevailed. It wouldn't last long. After a game like this, the players just wanted to shower and go home. Brenda, along with the male members of the press, had thirty minutes to ask questions and get out. It was organized baseball's concession to equal rights.

Chinsky was awed at this proximity to celebrity. The boys were in a bad mood, but not depressed. As more than one player observed, it was just one game. Tomorrow they'd bounce back. Brenda cornered slugger Delbert Maskera and asked him if he still thought they had a chance at the pennant.

"Yeah," he had said. "If we keep within six games

by the end of the road trip." She reminded him that a week ago the number had been five. "Five, six, what's the difference?" he said. "As long as we're close."

Chinsky thought it made sense. Brenda didn't.

She kept needling Maskera until he snapped a wet towel at her. She jumped out of the way in time to avoid a smart nip that would have left a purple bruise by morning.

"Strike one," she taunted. Those who had been watching piped in with catcalls and ribald comments aimed at both Maskera and Brenda. She gave them a grin and the finger.

It took another half hour on the laptop computer to write her column. She hooked up a modem to the public phone and zapped it in. Then they left.

The novelty of the evening had taken his mind off his problem. "You're really pretty good," he said as they headed back toward her apartment in his Porsche. "I was surprised at the way you handled those guys."

"Thanks. I think." She smiled. "That was a compliment, wasn't it?"

He could only catch the highlights of her face in the shadows.

"Sometimes I think being a woman makes it easier to get stories. The novelty makes it easier for me to approach the players. They're not used to being interviewed by a woman. On the other hand, I think they're very superficial with me. Unless I decided to have an affair with one of them, I don't think I could get them to talk with me on a heart-to-heart basis. They seem to think they have to amuse me. All I really ask is that they level and tell me what they're thinking. My readers don't care if I'm a man or a woman. All they want is some insight into their heroes. They want to know why things are the way they are. Some good analysis, some decent character sketches, some laughs, some pathos, and a first-place team keeps the readers happy. That, as they say, is the whole ball game."

"Maybe it's the patter."

"The what?"

"The patter. Maybe the player's don't take you seriously because of all the sports patter. I really noticed it tonight. Every time you said something, you threw in a sports twist—like you were trying to be one of the boys."

She pulled her chin in as she considered his words. "Maybe I am," she said at last. "I guess I started doing that to show everyone I knew what I was talking about."

"You seem to do it more than most of the men writers."

"Do I?"

"Uh-huh," he confirmed, giving his shaggy head a nod. "I think it may get in the way."

"Does it get in the way with you?"

"Sometimes it's a bit much."

It was her turn to nod understanding. "I can see how it might. But it's become such a habit that I don't even think about it, especially when I'm nervous."

"Like when you're talking to the players?"

She smiled. "Yeah. And like when I'm talking to you."

"Don't be nervous with me. I'm safe."

There was an awkward pause as both of them searched for something to say. Chinsky found words first. "How did you get into this?" he asked. It was enough to restart the conversation.

"Just lucky, I guess. I was something of a tomboy. Mom signed me up for girls' softball and lacrosse and soccer and tennis and any other sport that would keep me out of her hair. It worked; she had the straightest hair in town. By high school, though, I had dropped out of most organized sports.

"I got interested in boys and the fascination of how much there was to be learned. There just wasn't time to do everything, and sports lost out.

"It came back, in a way, though.

"The guy I was going with was editor of the year-book; he needed a sports editor. None of the boys could write as well as I could, so I took the job. For one blissful year it kept us together. Then we broke up, but I was still sports editor.

"The same thing happened in college. Only, that time it was the newspaper instead of the yearbook.

"I was the first girl—I was still a girl then—sports reporter who wanted to cover men's varsity sports. But they wouldn't let me in the locker room. So, I had to catch the guys before they went in. I thought it was unfair, and I wrote columns about it, one a week for a year. It worked. By the time I was a senior, I had access to the men's locker room. It's like being in a men's club where all the business is conducted over the urinal. You've got to hang out in the right places."

Chinsky gave her a pained look out of the corner of his eye, but she kept on with the chatter.

"If you're not there you don't get in on the action. Or so I thought. What I found out was that the stories were pretty much the same, but the environment was a lot smellier." Chinsky liked the way she talked, casual, comfortable with life. But he also noted that there was a defensiveness. She carried a chip on her shoulder that a strong breeze could knock off.

"After I got out of school, I applied for writing jobs at all of the big dailies. No offers, though. So I took a job at a weekly in Pittsburgh doing high school sports and home living features. I met a lot of nice kids. I think most of their mothers thought I was after the bodies of their young boys. At least, there were enough snide letters to the editor."

"You're kidding."

"No, it's true. Those mothers were very protective. But they should have been protecting me instead of some of those young studs. High school athletes are probably the horniest animals in the world. I had to work at staying pure. Anyway, I kept on applying for jobs with the dailies and after two years on the Pittsburgh farm team the *Free Press* called me up to the majors. Whoops. Sorry. They offered me a job," she corrected herself. "That was five years ago, and here I am.

"Now you know all about me."

Chinsky didn't say anything. He wanted to hear her talk more about herself, but he also wanted to talk about his analysis and conclusions. He knew no graceful way to change the subject. As if by instinct, she made it easy for him.

"I've been a magpie. You haven't said a word all evening. Have you figured out anything from the records?"

"I was just thinking the same thing," he said. The rest of the way he told her about his list, conclusions, and the search Paxton was doing.

■

Duke's monitor told him Chinsky's car was on the move. Christ, it was about time. He was beginning to worry that the hippie had found the transmitter and dumped the car. Maybe they would go to the broad's flat and make his job easy. Sometimes you got lucky.

■

The elevator reached her floor. They got off and went to her doorway. She fumbled for the key. The light wasn't much better up here than it was downstairs.

She found the key and had it halfway in the lock when Chinsky remembered to look for his match. He had trapped a match between the jamb and the door as he was leaving in the morning: just like in the detective novels. At the time, he'd felt foolish. He would feel even more foolish now if he forgot to check his little security system.

He saw the match. It was on the floor. Someone had opened the door while they were gone.

He grabbed her hand before she could turn the

knob. His other hand flew up to his face, and one finger crossed his lips as he gave her the sign to be still. He pointed down to the match and then picked it up for her to see. "Do you have a cleaning service, or anyone else who might have come in while we were gone?" he asked in a whisper.

She shook her head. "I have a service, but this isn't their day." She was barely audible. He nodded in understanding. He moved her away from the door and took the key and knob in his hand. Standing out of the doorway, he threw open the door with one swift motion.

The inside knob crashed against the wall and bounced the door back toward him. He caught the door with his foot and eased it back open. This time it stayed.

Chinsky waited for thirty seconds. There was no movement inside the apartment that they could hear. He reached around and felt for the light switch. The light came on. He couldn't see anything out of the ordinary from this angle. Crossing the hall, he darted to the other side of the doorway. He eased his way back slowly to see into the apartment.

Brenda, across the hall, stood silent. She had pinned him with her eyes.

Cautiously, he went in. Everything seemed normal. He motioned her in and at the same time looked for an object that he could use as a weapon. Nothing seemed right. There were no long pokers or letter openers handy. He took a cloisonné vase by its skinny neck. It had some heft. Brenda closed her eyes, then opened them as if to say she would sacrifice the vase for their safety. He motioned her to the opposite side of the room and moved slowly toward the study. He could feel his muscles tightening, tensing for action. The blood rushed through his body, sharpening his senses. He flicked on another light. That room was empty. In succession, he went through the bedroom and kitchen, giving up the vase on the way and replacing it with a sturdy knife. All the main rooms were empty. Brenda kept far enough away so that the two of them couldn't be grabbed by the same arm.

"It seems empty," he said, still speaking softly. "Let's check the bathrooms and closets." They, too, were empty. Only then did he go over and close the front door. There was a bolt above the lock. He rammed it home and latched the chain lock.

He quickly went to the phone and unscrewed the mouthpiece. There were no extra parts. At least, as far as he could tell. Taking her cue from him, Brenda checked the phone in her office.

"Are there others?" he asked.

There weren't.

He was wet. The relief of finding no one opened the dam that had held back the sweat.

He went into the kitchen and put the knife on the counter. His hand was trembling. He could see that Brenda was trembling too. He reached for her; she came into his arms. The tension of the search transformed itself into passion as she found his lips and opened her mouth on his. He held her close and returned the kiss. Neither opened their eyes. They stood together, not daring to let go, for a long time.

"Someone was here," he said. He could feel her

trembling in his arms. He pressed her gently toward him. "It's okay," he said. She was pushing away. The tremble he realized was not fear, but mirth.

"It was me," she said, unable to hold back the peal of laughter. Pushing away from him she doubled up. "Oh, my God! I feel so stupid. It was me! I came home before the game to drop off my car and take a shower."

He stood there with a sheepish grin on his face. It was funny. His clumsy precaution and their melodramatic search were out of a grade-B movie. He wasn't sure whether to be serious or to join her in laughter. Brenda solved the problem by taking his hand and leading him to the bedroom.

■

Duke wanted to know what was going on.

The bugs he had placed required him to tap into the phone line or catch the sound in a parabolic receiver. The tiny, freestanding transmitter only had a transmission range of one block. Even then, he would have to catch their voices in an aluminum-coated umbrellalike device and amplify them into earphones. It took him fifteen minutes to drive to her apartment, another three to focus the umbrella and tune in on the conversation. There was none. He checked the power indicator. The center light glowed red. It was flanked by two unblinking green lights. He was tuned for maximum reception.

A shrill shriek followed by rasping sounds confirmed his tuning. The random sounds continued: wheezing, gasps, shrieks, then a clear "Luke. Oh,

Luke!" followed by what he deciphered as heavy breathing. He leaned back in the front seat of the Buick and grinned. It was the bedroom mike. The hippie doctor was fucking the redhead and he got to listen in. The girl moaned, then let out a series of sounds followed by a muffled cry and gasp after gasp after gasp.

Duke felt himself getting hard as he sat with his legs spread in front of him. He knew she was coming. He closed his eyes and imagined himself in Chinsky's place.

Chinsky let out a throaty moan, then sucked in his breath. She gave a sharp cry, then an unlikely purr that trailed off into hoarse breathing.

Duke was damp between his legs. He moved his legs together to hide the stain spreading over his crotch. Only indistinguishable murmurs came through the earphones. He strained to hear what was going on. An occasional giggle, but no words. After a while, there was no sound at all. Then came what Duke took for a snore, and another like it. They were asleep.

As much as he would like to go up there and take care of Chinsky, he knew it was a poor plan. Still, if he could figure a way to take him out, he'd get dibs at the broad. That would be good. But it wouldn't work, and Duke was a craftsman first and cocksman second. He snapped off the snoring sounds and packed his gear.

Halfway back to his motel a plan started forming in Duke's mind. It wouldn't be as much fun as killing the hippie while she watched, but it was almost as good.

■

It was three-thirty when Brenda's phone rang. She reached over Luke's furry chest to make it stop ringing. She felt warm and wet and good. He took a little nip at her breast with his lips just as she picked up the handset. She let out a little noise that must have surprised the caller. Then she said, "Hello?" She took the receiver from her ear and looked at it, then at Chinsky. "It's for you," she said, handing him the handset.

"Chinsky?" the hard, controlled voice on the other end asked.

"Yes?" said Luke, still not quite awake. Even with the sleep on him, though, he knew that he should not be getting a call at this place at this time.

"Was she a good fuck?" the voice asked.

Chinsky was instantly awake. His first reaction was that this was some kind of obscene call. Almost as quickly, he knew it wasn't. "Who is this?"

"Never mind. I've got your records. Would you like them back? Would you like to trade them for that red pussy you've been banging?"

Chinsky looked at Brenda, alarm covering his face. He looked away again. "Who is this, what do you want?" he repeated.

"It's not what I want, hippie, it's what you want. Do you want your records? If you do, be at your apartment in an hour. Alone. I'll be watching. If I see anyone with you, anyone, your records are gone forever. One hour. Your apartment. Alone." Click. The phone went dead.

For the first time in his life, Chinsky was truly frightened.

CHAPTER
17

LUKE CHINSKY was momentarily blinded as Brenda turned on the bedroom light.

"What is it, Luke?"

He didn't want to talk to her. Whoever called could hear them. Besides, he was afraid his voice would betray his fear.

"It's okay. I have to go."

"Go? Go where?"

"My apartment."

"What? Why?" She bolted to a sitting position.

"I just have to go there. You stay here."

She wrapped the top bedsheet around herself like a brown paisley toga. He had his jockey briefs back on and was scanning the carpet for his other argyle sock.

"You can't go there. That's why you're here." He didn't want to tell her that this place was as bad. It would frighten her. Right now he had all the fright he could handle. He had an unreasonable belief that she was safe—safer—here. The voice had said come alone and he intended to.

"The man on the phone said he has Rathbone's records," said Luke as he sat on the edge of the bed.

"Is that what the phone call was about?" she asked as she came over and sat next to him. He could feel her heat through the thin sheet. His body threw off an involuntary shiver. The room was warm: he was cold. Her warmth didn't change his temperature. She hugged his bare arm and put her head on his shoulder. The toga slipped off her shoulder, allowing her warm breasts to cradle his arm. "Luke, I don't think you should go."

He shivered again. He didn't look at her or even feel her body next to his. But he knew she was wrong; he had to go.

"I have to," he said with resignation. What he didn't say was that from the tone of the voice on the other end of the phone, it was evident that if he didn't go to his apartment, the voice would come to him. It knew he was here. It knew Brenda was with him, and that they had just made love. It was as if it was watching them, could see into their souls, if not all the way in, at least far enough to find the place where fear lurked.

He gently removed his arm from hers and reached for the errant sock. He put it on. Absentmindedly he walked over to the phone and unscrewed the mouthpiece. Still no bug. He needed to find it. At least, he thought, the voice couldn't see them. Even so, he felt violated. His privacy had been stolen, then used to bludgeon him.

The emotion of relief that had led them into wild, passionate lovemaking had dulled their vigilance. After the bugging of his apartment, they should have made a more thorough search. It was naive to think that because the phones were clean, there were no other devices. A wry smile crossed his face. Passion had its price, he thought. It was not a price he'd expected. But then, was it ever? Love was trusting someone, getting too close, then being hurt because of it. He should have known better.

Brenda was uncharacteristically quiet as he moved from place to place, acting the exterminator. Finally, under a table, he found it. In anger he threw the tiny transmitter to the floor, then kicked it. Not satisfied, he found one of Brenda's stiletto-heeled shoes and beat the bug until it was quite dead. Then he picked up the pieces and threw them into the bathroom wastebasket.

She had put on a robe and watched, leaning against the door jamb, as he splashed water in his face.

"I'm going with you," she said.

He pulled a towel off the rack and wiped his face, then turned and walked to her. He took her in his burly arms and pressed her close to his chest. Now he could feel her. She felt like someone he wanted to keep in this position for a long time, even though he knew to do so would ultimately cause him pain, great pain. "I'm afraid you can't," he said softly, knowing he was about to get an argument. She pulled back away from him, but he didn't yield. Against her will, struggling, she stayed pressed against him.

"Let go of me," she said through clenched jaws. He let her back a little, so he could see her face. She continued to push away.

"It's important that you stay here. I need you to do something for me," he whispered. The struggling diminished. As it did, he gradually let loose of her. His hands rested on her hips and she looked him in the eye.

"What?" she asked. The tone wasn't quite belligerent, but it was close. He knew she thought whatever he was about to say was a ploy to keep her away from his apartment. In a way, it was. He drew her in again.

He continued to whisper, "Remember I told you I thought all this was happening because someone was using me to track down the cure?"

She nodded.

"I'm not so sure I was right." His voice, barely audible, was flat, emotionless. "Whoever was on the phone said he had the records, Rathbone's records. If they have them, they don't need me to find them. And if they're not looking for the records, they're trying to suppress them. It could be a bluff. It could be real. At this point I don't know. The only way to find out is to go and see what they have."

"Luke," she interrupted, shaking her head, "don't go. It's not worth it."

He shook his head back at her. "Listen to me. I *have* to go. You're my backup. If anything should happen, you need to know what to do." She was listening intently. "You have to take charge of those patient charts and the other data I've collected. It's the only evidence I have that a cure exists. If anything happens to me"—he stilled her before she could get her objection out—"no, no, listen to me. I don't think it will, but if anything happens to me, see that they get into the right hands. It may be my only protection." He went back into the bedroom and found his trousers.

"If I'm not back here by eight-thirty, I want you to call the police and send them to my apartment. Tell them you just got a call from me, and I'm threatening to commit suicide or something. Say anything, but get them to move fast. Then, get the notebooks into your editor's hands and convince him to publish the story. If he won't print it, take them to the FBI or anyone who will take them seriously and make them public. Tell them to talk to Renee Stanton at the clinic and Herb Paxton in pathology. Write that down, okay?"

"Luke, I still think I should go with you. Look. I'm used to being around roughhousing guys. If anything happens, there'll be two of us. We can make other arrangements for the records. I can leave the key with a neighbor."

"No, damn it! Look." He raised his voice for the first time. "I don't want you with me." His temper flashed. Then, in a gentler tone, again whispering, "I need you to do this. Besides, this is my problem. I don't want anything to happen to you—even by accident. If you're with me, I'd feel responsible for you, it'd distract me. Please, for me? Stay here. I need someone to cover my back, and you're the only person who can do it."

"You'll be more exposed alone than if I'm with you. Why don't we just call the police and tell them someone's in your apartment?"

"He may not be there. He told me to come alone. He'll be watching. If he sees the police, the records may be gone forever."

"I doubt it. The cure is worth millions. No one's

going to destroy the records." She was implacable. He disliked arguing.

"Brenda, this is tough enough without my worrying about you. Will you please do as I ask and stop arguing?"

She stood directly in front of him, looking up the inch or so needed to face him head-on. He could see the next thrust coming from that storehouse of objections she kept in her brain. Her mouth tightened, started to pucker, then relaxed. Her eyes closed, she swallowed and nodded her head. "Okay. I'll do it your way. I don't like it, but I'll do it, commissioner." It was as close as she could get to accepting authority. He took her head in his hands, kissed her on the forehead and then the mouth. He felt the backbone melt from her body.

"One more thing," he said. "Don't answer the phone. If I need to call you I'll let it ring twice, wait a few seconds, and call back."

She nodded but wouldn't look him in the eye. He wasn't sure whether the nod indicated agreement or just understanding.

"I'm going." Now that she agreed to stay, he wanted to move quickly. A long good-bye might weaken his resolve.

"Please be careful." Her eyes pleaded more than her voice.

"I will," he said. "I'll be back before eight." Neither of their smiles was natural.

■

In the Croft executive suite the heavy drapes were drawn. Lights out, Snell sat at his desk. His eyes were open, but the blackness of the room allowed no image to register on his retinas. Through the night he had sat, brooding. The Scotch had had little effect. He was neither drunk nor drowsy.

Why didn't Weisel call? It was seven o'clock in Germany. He should have called by now.

Chinsky hadn't answered his call either. All day he had tried to call the researcher. He was in. Paxton in pathology had confirmed that. And he was onto something. Paxton said something about tracking tests on Rathbone's patients. He had to be stopped. Naming Chinsky to replace Rathbone had been an error, but that mistake should have been rectified by now. Why hadn't Weisel's man handled him? Were all of these people incompetent? Was Weisel playing him for a fool? Thinking that if the cure came out, he, Snell, would be ruined and taken out of the picture? There was no money in it for Weisel that way. But what if he wasn't after money? What if he was after control of Croft? Weisel's kind would do it, of that he had no doubt.

They were, he knew, conspiring to stop him. First Rathbone, now Chinsky, and perhaps Weisel. Was Chinsky still alive, out there Somewhere? Working to ruin his plan. There was no one he could trust. Not even Proxy. Gay Proxy. Gay Proxy, whom he had counted on. As soon as Proxy learned the facts, his loyalty would be suspect. He might continue to follow orders. Then again, he might not. Snell had the desperate feeling of a man whom fate had conspired against. He was alone.

Alone with his vision. Others mouthed encouragement, but he gave the plan substance. He despised the timid little people of the world. Yet it wasn't their fault. It was his responsibility to lead them, show them the way. He needed to be strong. They, the nameless rest of them, would watch him fail or succeed. Either way, once the outcome was known, they would waddle in, vultures at the feast. Dead body, live body, it mattered little to them. Weisel would be at the head of the line. His good friend Weisel. His trusted associate. The German would lead the pack that would peck and tear at the spoils until they were gone. Then they would starve until the next leader came their way. The next Snell.

It would have been so much easier for them if they would just listen to him, do as they were told. What fools! In the end, his genius would prevail. They would be rich—or dead. He would be richer—and alive.

But first, he needed to rid himself of that meddlesome researcher, Chinsky. The name soured his mouth. Chinsky, so proud of himself for unraveling threads that shrouded secrets that should have died with Rathbone. Rathbone had been of the same ilk. He had probed and probed until he had pierced the veil of the mystery covering the God-sent disease. Chinsky and Rathbone. Both had the effrontery to offend God and Snell. It was hard to know which offense was greater. Rathbone, now Chinsky, was bent on saving the sinners of modern Sodom. They

were contemptible. Snell would like to tell him that
and watch him cringe. Perhaps he would. Then he
would turn him to salt.

Why didn't Weisel call and tell him that Chinsky
and the reporter were dead?

■

The orange glow of the lamp cast its soft shadows
over the bedroom. Proxy sat, still fully clothed, nurs-
ing a fine champagne cognac. He had sorted through
the alternatives, then gone over them again, and yet
again. His best bet was Chinsky. The researcher was
young but tough. Snell had made a mistake assigning
him to cover Rathbone's cases. The stubborn, determined individualism that made Chinsky a good researcher would also make him dog the cure once he
was onto it. Look how he had tracked down the fact
that some of Rathbone's files were missing. It shook
Snell. At the time it had shaken him too. The researcher had done that without even knowing what
he was looking for. Given the data in those boxes,
Chinsky would pursue the cure and make it public.

Exactly what Proxy needed.

Unless Snell got to him first.

It would be his own job to take care of Snell, to
make sure he didn't interfere until it was too late.

He took a long draft of cognac. It warmed him.
Chinsky, Chinsky, Chinsky, he thought, *you have no
idea how we all count on you. Please be equal to the
task. We need you.*

The LED display of his bedside clock pulsed 4:07.
He would call first thing in the morning. Now it was

time to get a little rest. Tomorrow—no, today—planned to be busy. He walked over and flicked the switch of the clock alarm, then collapsed onto the waterbed.

■

Duke watched the monitor record Chinsky's journey. It would be a simple thing to detonate the explosive under the car. Then he could get to the girl. It would be easy, but not right. They wanted this one to look natural. Fat chance. Still, they were paying for the job, and he would give them what they paid for.

■

Chinsky slowly circled his apartment building, trying to pick out his windows. Only two or three in the building were lit up, none in the area of his apartment. He was surprised at the amount of traffic. A whole society functioned while others slept.

He drove down the ramp of the building's underground garage and parked in his spot. He opened the trunk of the Porsche and fished out the jack. It was bound together with a metal spring band. He flipped the latch of the band and extracted the jack handle from the center of the assorted metal parts. Chinsky hefted the slim black rod, assessing its destructive power. He estimated its weight at about four pounds. One end had a right-angled bend, ending in a socket. In a practiced hand, it had the potential to maim or kill. In his hand, Chinsky thought ruefully, he would swing it and break his own kneecap.

It was four twenty-five when he turned the key in

the elevator lock and punched the button for his floor, the jack handle in his left hand. The elevator had never moved more quickly. He reached his floor sooner than he wanted to. The corridor was empty, unnaturally quiet, he thought. It was never noisy, but this morning he could even hear the echo of his own heartbeat as he slowly walked toward his apartment.

He stood looking at the door for a full minute before putting the key in the lock. Sweat dripped down the small of his back. He felt the wet on his forehead. Inside, blood surged through his veins in pounding throbs. It felt as though his temples would burst from the pressure. He switched the jack handle to his right hand and turned the knob with his left. The door opened easily, silently. He pushed it all the way open, not going in, just standing there. His plan was to be in the apartment when whoever it was showed up. His fear was that he was too late.

He was.

He stepped across the threshold and reached for the light switch.

"Leave it off," the telephone voice said from somewhere in the dark. "And drop the iron."

Chinsky was reluctant to let go of his security. It was virtually all he had.

"Drop the fuckin' iron or I'll blow your fuckin' head off," the voice said in a more menacing tone.

The jack handle thumped to the floor.

Rage burned in Chinsky. Heat flamed in his cheeks. He fought to keep his temper in control. His shoulders twitched in little flexes, getting ready to hit anything that moved. But no target was to be seen.

His eyes were adapting to the dark. A sliver of moonlight came in through the living room window and gave the foyer a faint glow. Most of the light, though, was from the hallway.

"Now shut the door, asshole."

Without turning around, he pushed the door closed. Everything became darker.

Chinsky felt helpless. Why had he been stupid enough to come here? Brenda had been right, after all. With the force of a hammer, insight told him Rathbone's records were not part of the voice's deal. With bravado he asked, "Where are the records? Who are you?"

"Shut your fucking mouth. Come here."

Chinsky didn't move. He didn't know where here was.

"Where?" he asked.

"Don't play games with me, hippie. I can see every move you make. Right now I want you to move toward me, slowly. In the living room, hippie."

Chinsky took a tentative step toward the moonlit living room. His eyes were fully adjusted now. As he passed out of the foyer the outline of a man emerged from the shadow. The light was strong enough to reflect sparkling highlights from the barrel of a pistol.

Chinsky knew he was in trouble. He was also glad he had dropped the tire iron. It was no match for a gun.

His senses searched for an advantage, something to give him an edge, in this unfair contest. He took the two steps down into the living room and advanced slowly toward the voice.

"Who are you?" he asked again. He could make out what looked like goggles covering the man's face. As he realized what they were, a flash of fear returned, accompanied by an overwhelming sense of resignation to disaster. The voice wore infrared glasses. The voice could see in the dark. The voice was a professional.

"I told you to shut up. You must be hard of hearing, hippie. Stop right there."

Chinsky stopped. The fear was gone. Or he was too numb to feel it. The resignation still lingered, though. He fought to overcome it, to get his adrenaline pumping. He was determined not to appear intimidated.

"I came here for the records. Where are they?"

The man laughed.

"I didn't think that would work. You sure are a dumb son of a bitch. There are no records, asshole." Chinsky could see the big, chunky body jiggling with suppressed laughter. "I just told you that to get you here."

The words infuriated Chinsky. His eyes glossed over with a hot red color. He started to lunge toward the voice.

An overlong snout of a Walther P-38 barrel snapped up and pointed straight into Chinsky's face. He froze. He was now close enough to see that the pistol barrel went on forever. It was long, almost too long, too thick to be a handgun. It was, he realized, a silencer that made it so long.

The barrel tip of the pistol started moving around in tight little circles, its aim never straying far from the center of Chinsky's head. The orbital movement of the gun was hypnotic. He wanted it to stop, yet was fascinated by the even regularity of the circles. He stood transfixed, bathed in the wash of moonlight cascading through the window.

"Unbuckle your pants and drop 'em."

Chinsky did as he was told. He started to step out of the leg holes. "Keep your feet in there," the voice growled. "Now drop your shorts." Once again Chinsky obeyed. He shook his legs to make his shorts fall to his ankles. This time, though, he made no attempt to shed the clothes.

The pistol barrel moved slowly down, toward his genitals. He shivered. Somehow the gesture was more threatening than staring down the barrel.

"You sure got a puny pecker," the voice chortled. "I bet that redhead would like to see what a real cock looks like."

Chinsky flushed. He wasn't embarrassed by exposing himself. But knowing that this slimebag had listened to them in their most intimate moment started his adrenaline pumping.

"You're sick," Chinsky said. "You probably can't even get it up unless you're hurting some poor bastard."

The tight little circles stopped. "Click" went the pistol hammer. The gun was poised to emasculate him.

The barrel moved up sharply, motioning him to move. "Walk over to the wall. Keep your pants on."

Chinsky let out an inaudible breath. He thought

he had lost it. He also noticed that when confronted, the man backed down. This guy was a bully.

Unfortunately, he was also clearly in command.

As Chinsky shuffled toward the wall, he kept looking for a weapon. In the sleek, sparsely decorated room none was apparent.

As he reached the wall the voice barked out, "Put your hands up, over your head."

He did.

"Lean against the wall."

He did.

"Keep your hands on the wall and move your feet away."

It was awkward moving his feet back, constrained as they were by his trousers, but he did it.

Sounds signaled the man getting up from the chair and moving toward him. The barrel of the pistol felt cold and slick as it came to rest just touching his right temple. A hand came down and gripped the top of his right arm while a foot slammed against his instep. His feet moved six inches farther from the wall. The foot kicked again, this time to spread his ankles. Another kick and the shorts were a rubber band linking the angled pillars of his legs.

The pistol moved away from his temple and the hand let go of his arm. He was precariously balanced against the wall. One more kick would have put him on his face.

He felt the hand grip the side of his neck and squeeze. The last thing he thought of before he went blank was the cobra tattooed on the back of the hand that had held his arm.

CHAPTER
18

THE NOISE in his ears wouldn't stop—not for long. The bee came back every few minutes, buzzing with monotonous regularity.

Rinnng.

Pause.

Rinnng.

Pause.

Rinnng.

It sounded like a telephone. He wished someone would answer it. His head hurt. The pain was a dull, hot knife poking against the tender tissue of his right temple. It seared with each ring. Slowly, the sound forced an unwanted consciousness on him. Some primeval sixth sense deep inside his brain told him not to move or make a noise. He eased his eyelid open an eighth of an inch, not enough to be noticed but enough to see where he was.

A desert of nubby carpet stretched before him. His mouth was arid; all moisture was being wicked away by the tiny wool fibers that twined over his lip. He pushed his tongue around in his mouth, searching for wetness. It tripped and stumbled on the dry interior until a spurt of saliva gave him lubrication. God, how he hurt. What was wrong with him? *Rinnng.* Pause.

Not enough light was getting through to his eye for him to see. He struggled to open the lid another fraction. The only visible movement was a tiny flutter of his lash. A bright white flash of reflected light pierced his iris, momentarily blinding him. The lid snapped shut, then, after a moment, worked its way open again. The blinding flash was gone, but the hard, sharp object from which it ricocheted slowly came into focus. Smooth, silver, it rose imperiously from the gray desert. A chrome leg. Of a chair. His chair. He shifted his eyeball. Fabric and color confirmed his conclusion. *Rinnng.* Pause. *Rinnng.*

He was at home. Why was he on the floor? Why did his head hurt so much? Why did the phone keep ringing? Instinct choked a groan. Slowly the nerve ends of consciousness crept down to his neck, shoulders, belly, and thighs.

He itched. The fibers of the carpet were invading his groin. The almost imperceptible pressure of the tiny strands felt like a hundred ant legs—all exploring the sensitive skin of his groin. He realized that he was naked from the waist down.

He wanted to scratch. To move his pelvis. Anything to stop the itch. The hidden hand of his psyche held him in check. The image of a cobra lurking in a meadow of hairs passed through his head.

His eye still focused on the chrome of the chair. The fuzziness of the image was resolving itself. The cobra was in his mind. He remembered the hand and almost started.

The phone stopped ringing.

Slowly, he moved his eye around his field of vision.

The strands of carpet looked like an endless microscopic slide of a bacillus colony. He could see no movement, but he could hear it. Muffled, distant, something was being scraped.

He shifted his head a bit. By forcing his eye to the edge of its socket, he could see the darkened square of the window. The first glow of morning cast a warm light on the gray of the night. A reflection in the chrome chair leg flashed a shadow to his eye. Something in the room was moving. He eased his lid shut a sixteenth of an inch and kept perfectly still.

The memory of the recent past floated back to him. He remembered the voice. And the gun.

■

Duke, stripped to his shirt, pushed the dining room table into a corner of the room. The glacierlike movement of the table toppled a chair. The goddamned phone had finally stopped ringing.

This was a good plan, he told himself again. Spangler wouldn't believe it. But shit, it was good. It had come to him after the hippie passed out. Son of a bitch never knew what hit him. He'd be out for another hour. Until he saw the punk laying there, bare-assed, he didn't know how he'd do it.

One way could have been the bathtub. Put the sucker in the water, then throw in a radio or hair dryer. Moist cooking, he called it. All the outlets were on the other side of the bathroom, though. It wouldn't look natural, like an accident.

Another way would be to sit him up in a chair, put his fingers around the gun, shove the barrel in his mouth, and force the trigger till the round blew. Two problems with that. He'd have to take the silencer off the Walther to make it look natural. Without the silencer, even muffled by the guy's mouth, the Walther made a lot of noise. Good chance someone would come running. No big problem, but he wanted to get away clean—without anyone noticing. The second problem was that he'd have to leave the Walther. And he liked the piece.

He moved all the chairs but one to the walls of the room. Yeah. It was really good.

■

His eye was closed too far; not enough light came through the slit to see. He risked opening it another sliver to capture more moonbeam. It made his right cheek hurt. With each small movement he could feel the pressure of the wall against the top of his head. He remembered the wall—standing, leaning, arms outstretched, when the world went dim. He must have fallen straight down and knocked his cheekbone against something—the baseboard? Whatever it was, it felt like it had gone halfway through his arachnoid membrane, the delicate, lacelike middle layer of the brain's protectors.

Footsteps, muffled by the carpet, moved across the room. He could actually hear the carpet fibers bending, springing back, bending with each step. His senses seemed to be overcompensating for the lack of sight. The chrome flashed again, then again. Someone, probably the voice, was dragging something heavy through the room.

Chinsky gave an imperceptible flex to his trapezius and deltoid muscles. He sent messages across and down his body, checking the feedback from his pectorals, triceps, biceps, glutei maximi, and quadriceps. The feedback was positive. He could feel their willingness to respond. His adrenaline began to flow again. The last time he had met Cobra-man he had been surprised. This time surprise would be on his side.

He guessed that Cobra-man was in the dining room.

Ever so slowly he turned his head to get a better view of the room. Though his eyes were now fully accustomed to the dark, the increasing morning light helped. He could almost see across the entire carpet, except that portion of the room blocked by the sofa. His pants were a problem. Any attempt to get up, to run, would be hampered by the cotton shackles. Carefully, both to gain more leverage for a spring and to see if he could slip out of his pants, he pulled his knees toward his chest. The drag of his tennis shoe on the rug reminded him how difficult it was getting jeans off with shoes on. He wiggled his foot enough to loosen the heel. The first shoe came off, then the other.

Cobra-man walked into the living room again. This time Chinsky could see thick rubber-soled shoes as they crossed from the dining room to the bedroom and back. What was Cobra-man doing?

A click in the foyer caught his ear.

His eyes rolled in their sockets, trying to find the source of the noise. Only an edge of the foyer's travertine wall was visible. He heard, rather than saw, the door open. The muffled noises from the dining room continued, uninterrupted. Had Cobra-man heard the noise? He wasn't reacting. Someone had unlocked the door. No one had the key to his apartment. Except Cobra. He had gotten in twice. This could be an accomplice. Chinsky felt the resolve drain out of him. He could never overcome two of them.

The intruder left the door open, and the light from the hallway illuminated the foyer. Spilling into the living room, it created an aura around Brenda, who appeared in the doorway like an avenging angel.

The soft luminescence of dawn absorbed the harshness of the hallway light. She was crouched like a cat burglar, ready to pounce. He watched as she made exaggerated, slow-motion movements. Cautiously, quietly, she moved forward, as if aware of the danger. This was the time to make his move. He tensed his muscles to push himself up from the floor.

■

One more cord, Duke thought. There should be a lamp cord in the living room. It would do. Better yet, there was a small nylon rope in with all that camping stuff in the hippie's closet. That would be better, more realistic. He stepped down from the dining room chair placed under the ceiling hole. Thin black-and-white insulated electrical wires snaked their way out of the metal junction box. Their ends were carefully turned to avoid contact with each other. The chandelier that had once hung from it lay discarded against the wall.

The box was strong enough. Duke had tried his weight on it, and it had held. Chinsky was a lot lighter; there would be no problem.

Let's get it over with, he said to himself. *Then I can go have some fun with the broad.* She would still be there in her apartment, waiting for him. A wide grin graced his face as he anticipated the pleasure. He turned to get the rope from the bedroom closet.

■

There was a thump from the dining room and the heavy footsteps got louder. Freeze! His brain screamed, putting a brake on his reflexes. Cobra-man was coming toward him from the dining room. Chinsky, eyes now wide open, could see both Brenda and Cobra. Brenda, he was sure, couldn't see Cobra-man. Nor could Cobra-man see her, yet.

Forcing his eyeballs to the top of their sockets, he caught a glimpse of Cobra's face. In that brief glance, he saw more than he wanted to. The face invited violence. The eyes squinted out from puffy cheeks. Sometime in its history, the straight Flemish nose had taken an iron pipe across its bridge. The pipe had left more of a crook than a dent in its slope. But it was the mouth, a cruel mouth, that dominated the face. A fleshy underlip pushed itself up, creating a perpetual sneer. On the left side, his lips—instead of joining—came apart where they should have met, baring his canines. The strong jaw could drive the teeth deep into muscle and tear meat from bone. An animal, thought Chinsky, lurked just below the surface.

Brenda made a scraping sound.

Cobra's head snapped toward the foyer. As it turned, he stopped in mid-stride and hunched into a fighting stance. He couldn't see her. She couldn't see him. But he knew someone was there. The faint glow of the light had alerted him. Chinsky, reflexively reacting to the glance Cobra threw his way, snapped his eyes shut. A half second later he eased them open again. Cobra's arm reached to the small of his back and started to draw his pistol. In that one motion Chinsky realized that as soon as Brenda stepped through the doorway, she was dead.

The image of Cobra's hand—swinging back, fingers uncurling, forming a mitt to cradle the gun—moved in slow motion across his consciousness. In real time the action was a split second. In Chinsky's perception the movement was like the slow, steady swing of a giant pendulum. In that fraction of time, Chinsky rolled his body toward a chair and yelled, "Killer!"

The last thing he saw before he ducked behind the chair was Brenda's legs go out from under her while her hands, locked together in prayer at the ends of outstretched arms, flew in front of her face.

All any of them heard was a spit and thud as the silenced gun delivered its first missile. Cobra's first shot pierced the wall six inches above the floor where Chinsky's head had been a second before.

The chair was stylish and comfortable to sit in, but lacked the bulk to stop a bullet. It offered, however, sufficient cover to let Chinsky slip out of his trousers and shorts. Except for three sets of lungs pumping air, the room was silent. Six ears listened for clues about the movement of the others. Chinsky decided to break the impasse.

"He has a gun," he shouted, and immediately dove away from the marker left by his voice. A fresh bullet ripped through the back of the chair two feet from his head.

"So have I," Brenda shouted. "Hang in there, Luke. I'll get the son of a bastard." It was life and death, he thought, and she was playing her cute-woman games.

As if to make her point, an unsilenced shot exploded from the foyer. The bullet pinged off metal. To avoid the cross fire, he crouched as close to the wall as he could. The silencer spit out two more rounds. Then it was quiet again.

He could hear Cobra moving around to get a better firing angle on her. He reached out his arm to pull his trousers toward him. Some coins in his pocket clinked. A thud accented another hole punched in the back of the chair not two inches above his outstretched arm. He jerked his arm back as if it had been touched with a hot poker. He closed his eyes, feeling it would make him invisible, then, realizing his foolishness, opened them and tried again. This time the trousers slid noiselessly.

Chinsky's ears were like sonar. Every nuance of sound signaled position, distance, movement. Cobra was still moving. Toward Brenda. There was no sound from the foyer.

He found the pocket with the coins and muffled them with one hand as he slipped his leather belt out of its loops.

■

What the fuck was going on here? Where did this broad come from? It must be the redhead. Shit. He thought she'd be waiting for him back at her place. This would make it tough. She was screwing up his plan. No way now he could make it look like suicide. Christ, there were bullet holes all over the place. Best thing to do is to take them both and get the fuck out.

And he'd better do it fast. The noise of that cannon she's using is going to attract some attention.

The hippie was awake, but he wasn't going anywhere. Without a gun he was no threat. Leave him until the redhead's taken care of. Shit, he thought again, this wasn't how he intended to drill her. What a mess.

Spangler's going to be pissed.

■

He could feel Cobra moving along the opposite wall. His fingers crawled up the back of the end table next to the chair, searching for an ashtray he knew was there. He touched it, lifted it silently, and brought it down to his stomach.

Cobra was between him and the dining room. Unless he was standing, which Chinsky doubted, the chairs would block his view of Chinsky's moves. Only noise would give him away. If he could distract Cobra, he had a clear shot at making a dash for the bedroom wing. The critical point would come as he hit the bedroom doorway. In that instant, Cobra would have a clear alley to blow a hole in him.

Like an athlete, he mentally walked through every motion he would make, once, then again, and again. Every muscle felt its flex. He pictured each piece of furniture and felt himself bouncing off their edges as he made his dash. In a few seconds, he made the short journey a half dozen times. He was ready.

With one hand, he looped the belt around the leg of the chair farthest from the foyer. Moving very quietly, he crawled as far as he could toward the entryway while still retaining cover. The belt trailed in his hand until it would reach no farther. He took a deep breath and tossed the ashtray at the picture window. It crashed into the safety glass with the bong of a mallet on a cymbal. In the same movement he jerked the belt, upsetting the chair. Like a domino falling, it sent a floor lamp crashing to the floor. The lampshade jumped in a high graceful arc, then rolled. The sudden, unexpected noise was volcanic in the tense stillness.

In the chaos of eruption he was up. Two quick steps were all he needed before he dove into the bedroom doorway, away from the noise. He heard the silencer spit two times. As far as he could tell, neither shot was in his direction. Brenda's shot rang out to answer Cobra's. He wasn't sure if she knew who she was shooting at.

"I'm okay," he shouted to her. "I'm in the bedroom. He's on the other side of the living room, by the dining room." If she really knew how to use that gun, they had Cobra-man trapped. "He can't get out without crossing your line of fire. If you see anything move, shoot. It won't be me." As he said the last word, a shot cracked. At least, by the sound of it, Brenda was doing the shooting.

Chinsky looked around the bedroom for a weapon. The approaching dawn made it easier to see. Nothing that caught his eye looked lethal—let alone ominous. He remembered his camping gear stashed in the closet. In one swift motion he slid the closet door open and reached for a duffel bag stored on the top shelf. Upending it, the contents cascaded to the floor. A canteen, a first aid kit, a flashlight, a couple of blankets, and a little hatchet in a leather case tumbled out. He grabbed the hatchet and threw off its case. It was dull, but it was a weapon. He wasn't sure he was going to be of much help.

He pushed the bed away from the wall so that its edge was about three feet from the door opening, then pulled the mirror that hung above the chest of drawers off the wall and leaned it against the side of the bed. He adjusted the angle until he had a clear view of the alley between the foyer and the living room furniture. Brenda was in a prone position with her pistol stretched out in front of her. He could just make out Cobra's head peeking from behind his blind. His pistol, cocked close to his ear, was at the ready.

"He's behind the chairs next to the dining room," Chinsky said in the most conversational tone he had used thus far. "I can see both of you." Then to Cobra, he added, "The game's over, asshole." The vulgarity was said with the same contempt Cobra had used last night. "Throw out your gun and you may get out of this alive."

The answer was a spit and a thud that left a spiderweb in the mirror. A spring twanged, followed by the rasping sound of metal against metal. Cobra had shoved in a new clip.

Chinsky strained to see movement in the living room. He couldn't. He knew Cobra couldn't get any closer to him without exposing himself to Brenda. Where was he?

"You're pretty smart, hippie," Duke growled. "Now that you're out of the way, I can pick off your little girlfriend. With such a good seat you're gonna get to watch it all." Despite the words, Duke didn't like the way the hippie had been able to slip into the bedroom. Was there a door in there that led outside? He didn't think so. Still, there was no way for him to take care of Chinsky until he took care of the girl.

It had probably been two minutes since the start of the action, but to Duke it seemed much longer. Time was on their side. Sooner or later the shots were going to attract a crowd. It would take them a little while to rouse themselves, then track down the source of the commotion, but eventually it would happen. They converge like flies on ripe fruit. Once people started looking out doors, filling the hallways, it would make his escape more difficult. Not that he couldn't handle it. A shot or two and they'd pull their turtle heads back into their shells. Trouble was, they'd talk: to the newspapers, to the TV, to the police. Nothing would come of it, but it would create noise. Unwanted noise.

Time to change the flow. Regain control. Show that redheaded bitch and her hippie boyfriend how a pro worked. It was time for another kind of noise. He twisted the silencer off the Walther P-38.

■

Chinsky saw and heard him coming at the same instant.

Cobra vaulted over the back of the chair, twisting in the air and landing directly in Brenda's line of fire. While still in the air, his first shot cracked out. His motion, and the unexpected noise of the blast, caught Brenda by surprise. She recoiled from the sudden threat, trying to focus on the whirling mass in front of her. Too late.

Chinsky's reflexes were quicker than hers. As soon as he saw Cobra coming over the top of the chair, he knew the tempo of the action had changed. He was on his feet, out the door, hatchet raised above his head. To make his shot at Brenda, Cobra had turned his back to Chinsky. Chinsky's legs pumped, driving to gain momentum. He didn't have much time. In a second Cobra would be on Brenda. Instinctively he knew she was no match for him. Just as certainly he knew that once Brenda was disarmed it would take but a slight twist of Cobra's body to bring that ominous black gun to bear on him. As he took his first step he saw Brenda cower at the bulk of Cobra. The shot missed her, but not by much.

Chinsky drove his trail-hardened legs into the floor, looking for leverage to move him faster. His face distorted itself, both from the intensity of the effort to gain ground and the emotion of the fate that was about to meet him. If he didn't get there, she was dead. As he pushed off from his second step, he swung the little hatchet back to the end of its arc. He was still in midair, a full six feet from Cobra, when the bullet hit Brenda.

■

The bitch was hit. But not seriously. She still had the gun and maybe enough stomach to use it this close up. From the corner of his eye he could see the hippie running toward him. Should he spin and plug the hippie or finish off the broad? The decision took but a fraction of a second. There was no way the hippie could hurt him, but the broad had a gun. Finish her first. He raised the Walther to catch her full in the face. It was a fast decision, the result of years of training in this kind of work, but fast as it was, it took too long.

■

Brenda, hit by Cobra's bullet, pirouetted. She struggled to come back, to bring the gun to bear on the gunman. Too slowly. Cobra hesitated a moment, then his gun moved to the center of her body. Chinsky gave a last powerful lunge, hurtling himself through the space that separated him from the killer. The hatchet traveled the full curve of the arc allowed by his arm. Every millisecond it gained in momentum and force until at its apex it became a lethal steel-tipped club. The insignificant Boy Scout hatchet raced down in a swift, brutal arc that ended by slicing into the right side of Cobra's neck. The dull blade ripped deep.

The momentum of his jump was arrested in the force of the blow. The hatchet feeding on the meat of Cobra's neck took on a life of its own and escaped his hand.

Cobra, on his knees when he had been axed, tumbled like a gnarled, old oak. The hatchet was still in his neck as he hit the carpet. The impact with the floor loosened it, and blood pumped out, splattering the carpet in a wide red fan. The spurts grew feeble as life ebbed from the assassin. Chinsky had no doubt; he was dead.

Without stopping to inspect the body, he leapt up the two steps to the foyer. Brenda was on her back, struggling to get up. The cloth of the beige blouse covering her left arm was a spreading pattern of red. From the rate at which the patch was expanding, Chinsky knew that the bullet had taken a chunk from her arm. He was over her in a second. Gently holding her wounded limb, he eased her slowly back down to the floor.

"It's okay," he said. "It's over. You've got a nasty wound. Let me take a look at it." He quickly glanced at her eyes for signs of shock. They looked normal and he thought she was all right until she broke out into what he thought was hysterical laughter.

To calm the hysteria, he reassured her in soft, warm tones. "It's okay. It's okay. It's just a flesh wound. I'll take care of it for you." She shook off his words by tossing her head from side to side. Barely regaining her composure, she said, "No. I'm okay. It's just that you looked so funny"—she choked back another laugh—"flying through the air with your genitals flapping."

Involuntarily, his head snapped down to look between his legs. She was right. His pants were still on the other side of the room.

■

It took less than five minutes for him to bind the wound and immobilize the arm. It didn't look too bad. The hole was clean. The bullet had passed through the lateral head of the triceps, just below the deltoid. The hole was well away from the humerus, the long bone of the upper arm. There was more blood than damage. The arm would be sore for a week or so and tender for another two. Considering the situation, she had come out of it pretty well. He caught himself. Hell, it was his situation and she had taken the bullet. He was the one who had come out pretty well.

Brenda was weak from the loss of blood and latent shock. "Rest here a minute," he said as he gently leaned her against the wall. She looked into his eyes, as if to say thanks, and gave a slight nod. Her eyelids flickered, then closed. Exhaustion was overtaking her. He covered her with a blanket from the bedroom.

Cobra was lying in a fetal position at the foot of the stairs. Chinsky walked over to the body and leaned down to inspect it. As he suspected, death had been immediate. The hatchet had sliced into the trapezius and severed the occipital artery. The dull blade had torn the skin rather than cut it cleanly, yet the depth of the cut was impressive. It had taken more strength than he thought he had. The skin was split from the middle of the hairline almost to the front of the throat. It appeared that the sternomastoid muscle was severed. It must have been the angle at which the blow was delivered, he thought clinically. Cobra's face was pushed down into the plush carpet, hiding the features, but Chinsky could remember the violence they displayed. They matched the ugliness of the gash.

A momentary flash of anger rose in Chinsky. He was glad Cobra was dead. But alive, he could have found out something about him. Who was he? Why was he here? In a petty way, the source of his hate was not the frustration of ignorance: it was the eavesdropping the killer had committed at a very private moment. Rationally, Chinsky knew it was a shallow reason for homicide, but for him, at this moment, it was enough. As quickly as it came, the anger passed.

He was alive. From the way the encounter had started, he was lucky. No. Not lucky. It wasn't luck that had saved him. It was Brenda. He had told her to stay at the apartment. He, as always, was going to handle it himself. Alone. But he hadn't. He had needed her. She had come through for him, against his advice and admonition. Alone, he would now be dead.

It was not a thought he was comfortable with. He shook his head to clear it, then looked again at the dead Cobra. Let's see who you are, fella.

He fished the dead man's wallet from his pocket. Nothing in it but cash, a lot of it. Chinsky didn't stop to count the bills, but threw the wallet on the floor to start what would become a small pile. Roughly, without respect for the dead, his hands emptied Cobra's pockets.

A couple of clips of ammunition, a number of keys —one group linked together by a paperclip—the assorted accoutrements of daily life were all there. But no clue as to who this hulk was. Or to the bigger question: why he was there, lying dead on Chinsky's floor, in the first place. On the corpse's belt was a leather pouch with what looked like an electronic device in it. Chinsky unclipped the pouch from the belt and put it in a pile next to the body, along with the keys and money.

His eyes caught the back of the dead man's hand. The cobra stared at him. He felt an unaccountable chill. The blue, inky eyes held him hypnotized. It was a look he would not soon forget.

Chinsky stood up and looked around. Sunlight streamed through the windows. The long night was over. He walked to his first hiding place behind the chairs. His pants were lying there, legs intertwined with shorts. It took a second to sort out the leg holes, but he untangled the clothes and put them on. Deanna, his cleaning lady, was really going to be pissed, he thought, as he looked around the room. The decorator, on the other hand, would be delighted.

He walked to the dining room. This is where Cobra had been when he had awakened.

It took him a minute to figure out the scene. The heavy plate-glass table with its chrome base had been shoved to one side. That must have been the muffled, scraping sound he had heard. Chairs were stacked and tossed against the walls. Except for one, which was positioned in the center of the room. Above it, the guts had been torn from what had been his chandelier. Hanging down from the opening, casting an ominous shadow against the far wall, was a black electrical wire twelve inches long. Its end was carefully twisted into the form of a miniature noose. Then he understood. Cobra was going to hang him. Why? He began to nod his head. It was to have been a suicide. It was beginning to come together. Somewhere in the apartment, there would be a rifle, the one that had killed Rathbone. He was sure his lifeless fingers would have been all over it before the night was out. The deranged scientist had gone berserk and killed his boss after a heated argument. Either in remorse or as a continuation of the dementia, he takes his own life. Case closed. Rathbone and Chinsky are out of the way.

But it still didn't make sense. What could be in it for anyone? If it had to do with Snell and Croft, the motive was wrong. The pieces didn't fit together. Either he had the wrong pieces or the wrong puzzle.

He walked to the bedroom and picked up his knapsack from the floor. He loaded the small pile of Cobra's belongings into the bag. Chinsky wished he knew the man's name, although Cobra, or just plain "him," seemed to fit. Still, he'd like to know who it was he had killed. The police would ask. There was no question but to call them in now. Well, he

wouldn't have an answer. Cobra was the best he
could do. It would have to be enough.

Brenda moaned and called out. "Luke, where are
you? Luke!" A tinge of hysteria grew in her voice.

"I'm here," he called, moving toward her. He could
see her relax. "It's okay. I'm here."

"Thank God. I guess I fell asleep. I saw him coming toward me, grinning, pointing that ugly gun. I was
terrified." She wanted to keep on talking, but he put
a finger over her lips.

"Shhh. We can talk about it in a minute. Rest."

She shook her head. "I'm all right. What happened?" She had thrown the blanket off and started
to push herself up. He pressed gently on her good
shoulder to keep her in place.

"Listen to me. I'm the doctor. You rest a few minutes, then we'll decide what to do." He gave her a
look that would brook no argument. It was the best
bedside manner he could muster.

"The guy with the gun is dead. I killed him with a
little ax." A chill shivered his spine. It was the first
time he had said it out loud, and it terrified him. "I
think he's the guy who killed Rathbone." He paused
for emphasis. "And I think he was going to kill me.
He was getting ready to rig a noose in the dining
room. If you hadn't shown up, I'd be swinging from it
now. You saved my life."

Confusion covered her face. She began to mouth
the same question he had asked.

"I don't know why," he said, before she could get it
out. "I'm certain it's tied in with the cure, but I don't
know why. It doesn't make sense."

The ring of the phone interrupted him. He remembered that it was an insistent ring that had awakened him. "Stay here," he said as he walked across the room to answer it.

"Hello."

"Dr. Chinsky?" asked a vaguely familiar voice.

"Yes, this is Dr. Chinsky."

"Thank God, I reached you. This is Ben Proxy. I work for Croft. I need to talk with you. I have Dr. Rathbone's records."

Chinsky could feel the blood drain from his head, down through his trunk to the very tip of his toes. The room slowly began to spin around him, first to the right and then to the left. Was it him or was it the room. What was real? Where was stability? Where was the bedrock he had known? A few short hours ago he had listened to the lie and believed it. "Do you want your records?" Cobra had asked. "Be at your apartment," Cobra had said. He had been through this scene already. The voice came out of the fog, distant, menacing. "Dr. Chinsky, did you hear me? I've got the records. They're safe. You can have them."

"Do you want your records?" Cobra had asked. Cobra was dead. Brenda was bleeding. His life had been a cord's length from death. What did they want of him? Whatever it was, it was too much.

Trancelike, the hand dropped from his ear. The phone slipped from his fingers back into its cradle. Dazed, he walked over to Brenda and started to wrap the blanket around her.

"Luke, Luke, what's the matter?"

He picked her up and started toward the door. "We have to leave," he said, as the phone started ringing again.

CHAPTER 19

PROXY STARED at the handset. Chinsky had hung up on him. The crazy bastard! It was as if he didn't hear him—or didn't understand. Why would he hang up?

He redialed the number. No answer.

This was crazy. It had taken him all night to reach the conclusion that Chinsky was part of the solution to his problem. Now the guy hangs up on him. It was as if the researcher didn't comprehend what he was talking about. He was giving Chinsky a medical breakthrough. Chinsky could help him wipe out not only the virus, but the lie being forced upon him and his fellow travelers. He needed Chinsky. Chinsky, although he may not yet know it, needed him. By God, Chinsky was going to get those records whether he recognized their importance or not.

■

Still no word.

Snell felt the weight of the sleepless night. His tired eyes burned and his mouth was bitter from the Scotch residue. The vigil had been a waste; Weisel hadn't called. Something was wrong.

From the sounds in the outer office, the staff had begun to arrive.

He pushed himself up from his chair and went into his private washroom. The face that stared back from the mirror had shadows under its eyes and the drawn look of a drained man. He needed a shave. He turned the water on until it ran hot, then drenched a washcloth and applied it to his face. He could feel the pores suck in the moisture. It helped. The eyes were less red and some of the tiredness was washed away.

Something was wrong, or Weisel would have called.

Should he call the German? No. That would show apprehension. Letting Weisel know his concern would only undermine the authority he was trying to build. But if Chinsky and the reporter had not been handled, Weisel had failed. On the other hand, maybe Weisel's people had been successful. It would be like Weisel not to call, to try to create uncertainty, to see if he, Snell, would react. It was better not to call. But he had to find out what had happened. And without being obvious.

He walked back to his desk and picked up the phone. "Get me Jake Salley at the *Free Press*," he told the secretary who answered.

"Jake, this is Brad Snell," he said when the editor came on the line. "One of your reporters has been pressing me for an interview."

"Hell, Brad, that's their job," Salley said. "Right now your company is news."

"No problem. I'm willing to do the interview."

"Good. So what can I do for you?"

"I'd like you to assign a particular reporter to the interview."

"Who?"

"Brenda Byrne."

"I'll be damned," Jake Salley said.

■

Chinsky drove to Brenda's apartment in something of a daze. Brenda, weakened by trauma and blood loss, slept. In disconnected spurts he replayed the encounter with Cobra. He tried to focus on reality, but the remembered fear obscured his vision. Cobra's menacing voice, the charade with the gun, seeing Brenda—thinking her doomed, the wounding shot, and the call, the last call that brought the unreasonable fear to the center of his soul and blinded him with panic. What did this Proxy want of him?

The bright morning sunlight, the task of getting Brenda upstairs and dressing the wound, brought him back. Loss of blood was minimal, but he wished he had remembered to bring some of his equipment and supplies. He made do with some cotton swabs, hydrogen peroxide, gauze, and ace bandages. She sat across from him, feet pulled up under her, shoulders wrapped in a warm wool blanket as the morning sun brought fire to her hair. She looked a lot better than a woman with a hole in her arm should.

Her eyes opened and focused. He could see her puzzling over the sling, blankets, and locale.

"We're home," he said.

"What happened?"

"You were shot saving my life. It's going to be all right."

She struggled to form her thoughts. "The man—"

"He's dead."

She shuddered. "I remember. You . . ." Her voice trailed off.

"How do you feel?"

"Tired."

"Your arm?"

"It aches, but not much. Oh, Luke, are you okay?"

"Me? Yeah. I'm okay, thanks to you. I'm glad you're not good at following orders. You saved my life."

"I couldn't let you punt without protection," she explained. "So I gave you an hour's head start, then followed."

"I'm pretty sure he was going to hang me, make it look like suicide. That would wrap up Rathbone's murder and get me out of the way. Everyone would attribute the whole affair to a high-strung researcher gone batty. He would have succeeded if you hadn't popped in like Annie Oakley. Where did you get the gun?"

"I've always had it, ever since I moved to the city. Dad taught me how to shoot when I was a kid. He said it was one of the basic skills necessary for survival in modern society," she said ruefully. "Until this morning, I thought he was just being a cynical curmudgeon.

"When you left, I was so frightened for you that I couldn't just sit here and wait. I knew you'd be angry if I followed you, but I figured that was better than letting you get hurt. I used your underground pass to get in." The coded card allowed access to the resident's garage and private elevator. He had forgotten he gave it to her. "If anything had happened to you and I had just sat here, I would have never forgiven myself. As it turned out, you wound up saving me."

"Don't kid yourself. If you hadn't shown up it would have been over for me. You, and whoever that was on the phone, saved my life.

"Phone?"

"Just before you opened the door, the phone started ringing. I think it woke me up. The guy, Cobra, knocked me out."

"Ohh." It was a small, sympathetic moan.

"Then you came."

"What are we doing here? What happened to the man you—?"

"He's still there. There was another phone call, from someone named Proxy. He said something that scared me, so I bundled you up and left."

"What did he say?"

"He said he had Rathbone's records."

There was momentary confusion on her face. "That was the same thing the other man said."

"I know. That's what unnerved me. I felt like the nightmare was going to start again. I just wanted to get away from there. I picked you up and came here."

"Do you know this Proxy?"

"He said he works for Croft. His voice sounded vaguely familiar. Seems to me I remember a vice president named Proxy—sales, marketing, something like that. But I don't remember ever meeting him. He used the same line Cobra used. I wonder if they're in it together? I'll bet Proxy didn't know Cobra already used the line about the records to get me back to my apartment."

"Why do you call him Cobra?"

"The tattoo. Remember Albert said the guy who bugged my place had a tattoo of a snake on his hand? He was the one. The snake was a cobra."

"You think he and this Proxy—?"

"I don't know. If they were together, why would they use the same line?"

She frowned. "Sounds bush league. But not Cobra. If he killed Rathbone, he's big time, a professional— that was no amateur job."

"You're right. It was awesome, the way he took me out. I went into the apartment with a tire iron in my hand."

"I know, I saw it when I came in. I wondered what it was doing there."

"It was the only weapon I could think of. I never believed that anyone would be waiting for me or that he'd have a gun. I don't play in that league." Her sports clichés were infecting his speech.

"Why was he there? Why did he want to kill you?"

He shook his head. Good questions. No answers. "I don't know," he said. "Things happened so fast I haven't had time to piece them together. For instance, two days ago we were practically the only ones who knew Rathbone's records were missing. Now two guys use it as bait."

"Flo knew. But I can't believe she had anything to do with this."

"Yeah." He started recounting the people who knew—or at least had an inkling. "And Stanton at

the clinic, Charlie Brown, Snell, the security guard—
Knowles. Lord knows who they told. Maybe more
people know about this than I thought. But, Christ!
What's in there that would cause someone to kill?
I'm looking for a cure. Why would anyone kill for a
cure?"

"You don't have the cure," she reminded him.

"You're right. Why would anyone kill to keep me
from finding the cure?"

"I don't know," she said, grimacing. "Luke, I don't
mean to be a burden, but my arm's beginning to
hurt."

"Let me see if I can find something. Where do you
keep your painkillers?"

"I don't have that many; I don't normally use
them. If there are any, they'd be in the medicine
cabinet." He got up to get them, once again damning
himself for not having the foresight to bring his kit.
He could write a prescription, but then he would
have to go out and fill it. He didn't want to leave her
alone, not just yet.

While he rummaged through the cabinet, the
phone rang. The sound froze him. Before he could
react, Brenda answered it. "Who is it?" he called,
apprehension coating the cry, knowing that somehow
Proxy had found them.

"It's okay," she answered. "It's for me."

The words calmed him. He had thought he was
over it, but he wasn't. He was like Pavlov's dog, sali-
vating fear at the sound of a bell. She was still talking
when he came back.

"I'd love to do it! You just wrote yourself a ticket to

the play-offs. But, Jake, there's one problem. I hurt my arm last night and I'm feeling really rotten right now. Can I start on this tomorrow?" She listened to the answer, then said, "Okay. But can you set it up for later tonight? Give me a little time to nurse this arm." He said something. "No, I just got clumsy and hurt it. It'll be all right in a while, but right now it really hurts. Jake, I really want to do this." She listened. "That's great. Set it up for later tonight. I promise. No home games tonight. You can count on me, Jake. And Jake"—she turned her sweetness on— "thanks again. I really appreciate this." She was beaming as Chinsky walked over to her.

"You don't look as if you need these," he said, as he handed her three Tylenols and a glass of water. "I'll get you something more powerful later."

"Oh, Luke," she said, the pain seemingly suppressed by her obvious delight. "Jake is arranging for me to interview Snell. He liked my work on Anne Rathbone and Washington. Says my piece on Washington was better than he could have done. For Jake, that's high praise. Isn't that great?" She popped the pills into her mouth and took a slug of water to wash them down. "I told you, I've always wanted to do hard news. Who knows, if this story works I may get assigned to the city room. But," she teased, "I would hate to give up sportswriting. I'd miss seeing all those cute little buns." At the surprise on his face, she said, "Well, they're not as cute as yours, but they are cute." She was, obviously, feeling better. Not well enough, though, to be prancing about on a story.

"The way things are developing, this story could become a career."

She gave a weak laugh. "You're right. Even if the Cobra thing hadn't happened, we can milk these things forever—or until the next item breaks—between character profiles on all of the principals, and a piece or two on how this will affect the fortune of the company. If the police nail a suspect, there's the arraignment, the indictment, jury selection, the trial, the verdict, sentencing, and on and on. As long as the readers want to read about this, it'll be news."

"That's not what I meant."

The downturned lips showed he had a bitter taste in his mouth. They both had narrowly escaped disaster and she was milking the situation. "I think you ought to slow down. Pay attention to that hole in your arm. Maybe you should pass on the interview with Snell." It was blunter than he intended, yet expressed his feeling.

"I'm okay. You said it was just a flesh wound and I believe you. Besides, it feels better now. Luke, is something else wrong? Don't you want me on this? Why shouldn't I interview Snell?"

"I'm worried. I guess there's nothing wrong with it. But I'm scared, for me and for you. I have a feeling I can't shake that Snell's involved in this. Logically, it makes no sense for him to be, but he's done so many things—taking the records, that phony call. I just have this feeling."

"Do you think he had something to do with Cobra following us?"

"I don't know. I have no hard evidence. Call it a sixth sense. I guess I'm a little edgy."

"I can understand that, but Cobra's dead. The police will pick it up from here and we'll be out of it—personally, anyway," she added.

"I'm not so sure," he said precognitively. "I'd like you out of it. I'm not sure whether I'm a news subject to you, or someone special."

"What does that mean?" she asked with genuine surprise.

"When I hold you, when we make love, I don't want to feel as though I'm being interviewed."

"Is that what you think? That the only reason we made love is so I could use the material? What an ass! You are insufferable."

"I didn't say that," he protested.

"You implied it. Look. If this means that much to you, I'll choose between you and the story right now." The anger in her was getting the upper hand. "And, for your information, I'll take you. Let someone else do the story."

He was startled. It was not the choice he would have predicted.

A tear wandered down her cheek, curved around her nose, and found the edge of her mouth. He was sorry he had raised the subject. Now he did feel like an ass. He wanted to kiss the tear away.

He walked over to her and tried to give her a gentle hug; she shrugged him off. "I'm sorry," he said. "Whenever someone gets too close, I push them away."

"Why?"

"Probably to keep from being hurt."

Her face looked sad, as if she understood. "I won't hurt you. Besides, you feel good to me. Don't you have that same feeling?"

"It feels good now. But I don't trust emotions. Something will happen. Something terrible. Something that will be more painful than all the good feeling of love, and it will all hit at once and leave a wound that aches forever."

"It doesn't always work that way. You can have feelings and still be logical. People do it all the time. Give it a chance, Luke."

"You're right. I was letting my emotions get in the way of my head. I think you should do the story. If you don't do it, someone else will. And while this thing is still developing, it'll be good to have someone on the inside."

"Luke, that's not what I meant. You're more important than the story. Look, this may sound trite, but it's not. I've been a loner all my life. And I haven't really minded. Probably, like you, I haven't trusted people. Not because they hurt me, but because if I trusted them, liked them, then I couldn't use them. I need people to get what I want. For whatever reason, they made relationships, my using them, easy. Anything that's too easy doesn't have a lot of value. These past few days have been special for me. I really care about you. I don't know if what I'm feeling will last—I think it will—but I don't want to let go of you. At least, not until we give it a chance."

He knew what he felt for her was more than a casual infatuation.

"I know. I feel the same way. Besides," he said with a smile, now completely out of the melancholy that had gripped him, "you own me. You saved my life. Now I'm your responsibility, forever." He could feel her face muscles stretch into an answering smile, acknowledging her ownership. Neither of them said anything for a long while. Eventually, her soft snoring told him she was asleep. He just sat there, not moving, not risking the chance of waking her.

As he sat there, the enormity of the danger he had faced confronted him, full on, for the first time. Someone was out to kill him and he didn't know why. They had almost succeeded. But who would want to kill him? Had Rathbone asked that same question? Cobra was dead, but he knew that didn't end the danger. Someone had put him up to it. Who? Why? He needed answers.

He looked at his watch. It was five after nine.

Chinsky eased out of the seat without disturbing Brenda and went over to her dining room table. The knapsack sat there, filled with Cobra's trappings. He emptied it on the table's piano-varnish finish. He had not looked closely at any of the items until now. He had been holding the bag when Proxy's call came in. In his shock he had unthinkingly held on to it while he carried Brenda to the car. His own money clip mingled with the things he had taken from Cobra's pockets: wallet, cash, handkerchief, comb, keys. He picked up the transmitter that he had mistaken for a radio, and turned it over in his hand. He couldn't immediately gauge its function. He put it down. He would come back to it later.

He opened the wallet and dumped the money on the table. He had been through the billfold before, but now he searched it thoroughly. In one compartment was a neatly folded piece of paper. Chinsky's name, address, and phone number were written on it. The letters were simple and uncomplicated, written by a laboring hand unsure of the art of pencil manipulation. A second piece of paper, folded as neatly, contained the same information about Brenda. There was nothing else in the wallet: no driver's license, no credit cards, nothing. Chinsky picked up the wad of bills and counted them. One thousand two hundred and twenty-seven dollars, arranged in ascending order. The bills were all turned so that green showed from one side, black from the other. The heads all pointed in the same direction. Cobra was an orderly man.

Chinsky picked up his own money clip and put it back in his pocket. What was left was Cobra's. There were two sets of keys connected by the paper clip and a crumpled note, presumably written in Cobra's hand. It was Brenda's telephone number again. This paper, though, came from a Ramada Inn in Southfield.

On a hunch, he walked over to the phone and dialed the Ramada's number. He asked for room 435, the number stamped on the key.

The phone started ringing.

After ten rings, the operator informed him that no one was answering. He thanked her and hung up. No way of telling if Cobra's room was empty. He still had the keys in his hand. One set was to a rental car, the other to the room at the Ramada.

He went back to the instrument that looked like a Walkman radio. A crude "C" in crayon marked the face. The dials on the front turned easily. Nothing happened. He pushed the buttons in. There was a click as the right one was pressed and released, but the device gave no other indication that it was being tampered with. Chinsky turned it over in his hand, looking for something that would turn it on.

Although Chinsky had no way of knowing it, it was, in fact, on at that very moment. The device was in the transmitting mode, sending signals to a detonator encased in a stainless-steel box lodged under the fender of his car. The tenth-of-a-mile safety cutout on the detonator had saved Chinsky the price of a new car. He found the sliding switch on the side and pushed it. The LCD lit up with a reading of 00.03 in the bottom window and EAST in the top. It didn't mean anything to Chinsky. He held the device up to his ear to see if it made noise. There was no sound. He tried clicking and turning the buttons again. Nothing changed. He flicked it off and set it back down on the table.

Chinsky looked in on Brenda. She was still asleep. It was nine twenty-three. The Ramada was ten minutes from here, just up Northwestern at Telegraph. He decided to give it a go.

■

It was 7:00 P.M. in Hamburg. The sun leapfrogged clouds; the high temperature and humidity made the day uncomfortable. In spells like these, the burghers escaped to the parks. The green of the trees and the crisp grass cooled their bodies.

Ernst Weisel would have liked to join them in a stroll, perhaps through the Alsterpark along the shore of the Aussenalster. Though one of the richest men in Hamburg, indeed Germany, he took pleasure in the simple, natural pursuits of life. He liked the city and its people. The abundant greenbelts accented the newness of the buildings. The robust, cheerful citizens were always polite and friendly. He found pleasure in walking his city. Now, instead of joining his poorer neighbors along the walks, he sat in his modern, sterile, air-conditioned office, pondering the problem Spangler had given him an hour ago.

Ernst had still been in the office when his *Untergebene* called. The tycoon believed in getting to work early, staying late, setting the example. At first, he was irritated; he liked to do the calling on his schedule. As Spangler told his reason, Weisel's annoyance ripened to disgust. The good nature he had felt earlier in the day dissipated.

Throughout his life, people had brought him their problems, and he solved them. He had an ability to clear the ambiguity surrounding an issue, to find the core. Then, he was quick to take action. Swift, persistent—if necessary, ruthless—pursuit of the solution generally resulted in huge profits to Weisel, profits that escaped less clear-sighted or determined men. He was just as aggressive in aborting an operation turned sour or strategy gone awry. He was, therefore, one of those rare individuals who enjoyed many successes and few absolute failures.

Herr Weisel was also an amoral, greedy man—but a cautious one. The brake that restrained lesser men from action often revolved around morality, concern for the well-being of—the effect on—fellow man. Not so for Ernst. Even though he enjoyed being with and interacting with people, high and low, he could discard their opinions, or even them, if they stood between him and money.

Weisel had applauded Snell's direct, decisive action in the AIDS matter. Snell had shown leadership quality. His opinion of Snell was further buttressed when Snell proposed neutralizing the troublesome researchers. Scientists were good at solving problems, but not very good at business. Too often, they became distracted with intellectual or theoretical glass baubles and lost sight of the gemstone, profit. Scientists could be trained, thus replaced. They were expendable. He gave Snell credit for astute analysis and decisive action.

But Spangler's news was disquieting. Weisel did not like the botched job Spangler's hireling had left or Snell's—according to Spangler—loss of control. It was Snell's operation; it was up to Snell to detail the arrangements he wanted executed—the pun amused Ernst—and then ensure they were carried out. That, in Weisel's mind, was the function of an executive. If the project failed, the executive failed. It was then appropriate to sweep both out of the way and make room for the next project, as he liked to say. Snell had allowed his *Untergebene*, Proxy, to get out of control.

The German's instruction to Spangler had been terse, final. *"Machen Sie es wieder gut und dann los!"* Fix it and get out.

Now Weisel grappled with the problem of securing the profit from the cure in Snell's wake. Again he laughed at the pun. To do that, he needed the formula for this cure. More importantly, he needed to make sure it fell into no hands but his. The large head nodded ponderously as the elements of the problem came into focus. Clearly, he would have to give Horst new instructions. But first, the details must be worked out. Always the details.

As he looked through the penthouse window, he could see the setting sun break through the clouds. The sun didn't shine in Weisel's office.

The problem would take thought. Perhaps the fresh evening air would clear his mind. Weisel hefted his three hundred and forty pounds out of his oversize desk chair, donned his homburg, and went out for a stroll.

■

He stood there in his pressed blue suit, starched collar, white shirt, and conservative blue-and-gray rep tie. A minute change of reflected color told him someone was looking through the tiny peephole built into the door. Apparently satisfied that he was safe, the peeper opened the door.

"Miss Murcheson?" Spangler asked as the door swung open to reveal an attractive woman. Proxy was right. She was a stunner.

"Yes?" Alice Murcheson answered, a question mark

in her tone. She was obviously curious as to what this well-groomed gentleman wanted of her.

"Miss Alice Murcheson, secretary to Mr. Bradley Snell of the Croft company?" Spangler asked, for clarification. He did not want the wrong one.

"Yes," she said again.

"I," Spangler said in the most officious voice he could imagine, "am Bertrand Gottlieb of the law firm Brady, Boone, and Carmichael." He had appropriated the names from a business card pilfered from a restaurant's prize bowl. To complete the impression, he handed her the card.

She looked at it. As if the card were an identification badge, she opened the door a little wider. "Yes, Mr. Gottlieb, what can I do for you?"

Spangler raised the slim briefcase he held in his left hand a tad. "I have a matter to discuss with you. May I come in?"

"Yes, of course," she said, stepping out of the way to allow him entry. She motioned him to a chair in the living room. He waited for her to sit before he took his seat and placed the briefcase on the marble-topped coffee table that separated them.

"I tried to reach you at your office," he said. "They told me you were ill. I hope it is nothing too serious and that my visit is not an inconvenience."

She shook her head. "I have been indisposed," she said politely, "but at the moment, I am quite all right. What is it you have to discuss with me?"

Spangler snapped the locks of the briefcase and opened the lid.

"This may take some time," he said. "If you have guests, I can come back later."

"No, now is quite all right." She was beginning to show some irritation. Her reply, though, told him what he wanted to know. She was alone.

As if he were retrieving papers, he reached down and curled his fingers around a 9mm Intratec autopistol, silencer fitted on its threaded barrel. The thirty-six-shot magazine was already loaded. With a slight movement of his thumb, the safety was noiselessly switched off. In all, the weapon weighed over six pounds, but he raised it effortlessly, shielded by the top of the briefcase, then pointed it directly at Alice Murcheson's face. Shock registered on her face, but she froze, not daring to move.

"I would like to talk to you about some tapes you stole from Mr. Snell," he said.

■

Chinsky replaced the Ramada's house phone on its switchhook. No one answered the phone in room 435. Chances were, the room was empty.

He pushed the elevator button for the fourth floor. The elevator opened on a well-lighted but narrow hallway lined with numbered doors. 435 was to the right. Cleaning women were starting their morning rounds. He avoided them.

Chinsky found 435. A Do Not Disturb sign hung from the doorknob. He ignored the sign and knocked. No answer. The key slid in easily and turned. With a slight push, the door opened. There was no sound from inside. A quick glance in the bedroom and bath told him the room was empty. He heard the door click shut behind him. The bed was rumpled, but the sheets had not been turned back.

A map was taped to the mirror above the built-in desk. A black dot marked the Ramada; his apartment, Croft, Brenda's apartment, and the *Free Press* were also marked. Yesterday's itinerary flashed before him. With a finger he followed a line marked by a yellow highlighter starting at his apartment. It traced the faint yellow line that mimicked the route he had taken the previous day. Every turn, every stop was marked. He wondered how Cobra had been able to follow him and trace the map at the same time. He had probably done it later, after he returned to the room. But if he could recall the route with that degree of precision, why bother tracing it? A better explanation was that he traced it in the room while he, Chinsky, was en route. That meant that some type of transmitter had been planted on his car. Neat trick. He picked up the microprinter. The numbers and letters on the printout protruding from the machine meant nothing to him. He set it down again. Next to it was another small box, like the one on Cobra's belt. This one had a "B" printed on its front. He flicked the switch. SOUTH 03.23 appeared on the screen. "B" for Byrne. "C" for Chinsky. This thing tracks a car. Neat trick. He flicked the switch again and tossed the box on the bed.

A brown leather suitcase took up most of the rest of the top of the Formica-topped credenza. The suitcase looked more expensive than the piece of furniture. He opened it. Inside were shirts, socks, under-

wear and a .357 Magnum Colt Python revolver.
Chinsky picked up the gun. It had weight. The design
reminded him of six-shooters he had seen in west-
erns. Although he was no judge, it looked destructive
to him. He placed it gently on the bed and continued
looking through the suitcase. On the bottom, under
all the clothes, was an address book. Its brown plastic
cover was worn, as were its thumbed-over pages. The
book was about six by eight inches in size and an inch
and a half thick. He flipped through the pages. It was
filled with names and addresses, none of which he
recognized. He looked under C for Chinsky. His
name wasn't there. He hadn't made the book. Maybe
that was good. With a flick of his wrist, the book
joined the gun on the bed. There would be time
enough to study it later.

A leather envelope held three driver's licenses and
a half dozen credit cards. Voila! Chinsky said to himself. Now we find out who you are. The licenses were
in the names of George Padre, Robert Sensal, and
Willem Van Allen. The one from Illinois, Van Allen's,
had Cobra's picture on it. Not a good likeness. None
of the menace showed through, just the beefiness,
crooked nose, and hint of cruelty in the mouth. He
lived on Halstead in Chicago Heights. Chinsky knew
the town; it was a rough neighborhood. The signature
on the license was in Cobra's childlike hand. "So
that's who you are," Chinsky said out loud. It was a
small triumph to have established this one bit of information. Chinsky looked at the other two licenses.
Neither had a picture, although both were signed in
Cobra's handwriting. Well, maybe I don't know who

you are. The killer could be any one of the three—or none. So what. In his mind the killer was Cobra, or if need be, Van Allen.

The suitcase held nothing else of interest. He opened the closet. It contained a hanging garment bag and a suit on a hanger. On the floor was a small leather bag. It was unlike most leather bags Chinsky had seen. Its shape was not that of a briefcase, satchel, or medical bag. Instead, it was rectangular, much like a toolbox. He lifted it off the floor and put it on the table by the window. Inside, he found a number of devices, some wrapped in plastic. Most seemed to be electronic gadgets. He couldn't figure out the purpose of any of the devices.

He opened a stainless-steel box about the size of a cigarette case. In it was a pliant substance the consistency of soft putty. It came to him that this could very well be explosive plastique. He had never seen it, but it was mentioned in all the spy novels. He smiled at his melodrama. Rummaging further, he came across a set of slender rods, each about the size of a cigarette. These, he thought, must be the detonators. In a flash, it came to him. The gadget in Brenda's apartment wasn't a tracker. It was a transmitter to set these things off electronically.

He pulled the hanging bag out of the closet and emptied its contents on the floor. It yielded nothing other than an assortment of toiletries. No labels in the suit.

The drawers in the credenza were empty, except for a Bible and phone book. He looked under the bed.

There was no under; the box springs were fastened to planks that extended to the floor.

There were no more places to look.

Disappointment cloaked him. No records. Cobra didn't have the records. It had all been a ruse. What a fool they had played him for.

He packed the Magnum, transmitter, printer, and address book in the leather box. The map he rolled into a tube.

One last look around. He went over to the desk and picked up the phone. Under it was a small stack of Ramada Inn notepaper identical to the one he had found in Cobra's pocket.

"What a detective I am," he chided himself, as he looked over the scribblings. He had almost missed them. Some of these notes had doodles on them. The word *Duke* had been written dozens of times in a half dozen styles; there were also daggers dripping blood and what Chinsky took to be airplanes. Each sheet contained what appeared to be a single phone number. On some, around the border of the notepaper, he apparently had doodled his name. Duke was a more appropriate name for Van Allen. Only one of the papers had a name on it, *Spangler*, right over a phone number with an extension. Chinsky wondered who Spangler was.

■

The reporter was still alive; either that or her ghost was to interview him at eight tonight. Weisel's man had failed in at least part of his assignment. Maybe it was time to call Weisel to task, to let him know that he wasn't as good as he thought he was, to begin the changing of the guard. Weisel had had a good run setting up the cartel. It had made millions for all of them. Now, though, it was time for younger, fresher, more imaginative men to take over. Like Bradley Snell. Given the riches that would flow from the AIDS cure, the others would defer to him. With Weisel discredited, he was the natural leader. Perhaps this slip on Weisel's part was the beginning of the end for the fat old German.

Snell pulled the phone closer and dialed Weisel's Hamburg number.

■

Brenda awoke feeling much better. She washed her face and called out for Luke. No answer. She wandered from room to room looking for him. In the kitchen, taped on the refrigerator door, she found a large note that read:

> Gone to do some detective work.
> Be back at 9:30.
> Take care of yourself—I'm
> getting attached to you!
>
> Luke

She smiled. It was a commitment. More than she asked for. Certainly more than she hoped for.

She had had flings before. Most of them were over before they started. This, though, felt different. When he touched her, held her, there was a tenderness. It wasn't raw sex. She enjoyed sex, but she wanted more. That's probably why she had such a hard time finding anyone worth settling down with. Men, it seemed, were more interested in satisfying themselves than building relationships. But Luke seemed different. She could talk to him. God! It wasn't all their fault. She wasn't an easy person to get through to. Yet she opened up to Luke.

At times, she hid behind her tough sportswriter image, but she knew he was more comfortable when she let down the facade. It would be hard; her tomboy pose had saved her from a lot of scrapes—mostly with men.

She knew she was smart. That, too, got in the way of some of her relationships. She liked to talk to her companions about ideas. Most just wanted to talk about things. Luke reveled in discussing ideas. Yes, he was a keeper.

■

Chinsky made it to the lobby without being seen. As he walked toward the Porsche, his mind wrestled with the problem of the transmitter. It would have to be hidden somewhere out of sight, perhaps in the engine compartment or on the underbody. He tossed the bag and map on the seat next to him and started up the car.

Curiosity took hold and he decided to give the Porsche a quick once over. He turned off the ignition, got out, and popped the hood. slowly he scanned the compartment, but nothing seemed out of the ordinary. He dropped the hood; it caught with a solid, reassuring thud. Every time he heard that noise, he reminded himself of what a fantastic machine this was: well engineered, good to look at, pleasant to the touch—like a sensuous woman.

Dropping to one knee, he looked under the front fender on the driver's side. Shadows made it hard to see. He pulled a flashlight out of the glove compartment. As far as he could tell, which wasn't all that far, nothing was under the front end. He could get on his back and scan the whole underbody of the car. No, it would be easier to get the thing to a garage and put it on a hoist. Checking the fenders would do for now. Making his way around the car, he hit pay dirt under the right rear fender. There, firmly attached to the frame, were two foreign devices, one a small, round cylinder, the other similar to the stainless-steel boxes in the leather kit. It took all his strength to pry the stainless-steel box loose. It was impossible to get the disk free; his fingers couldn't find enough leverage.

Taking his prize, he got back into the car. Turning the cigarette-size box over and over in his hands, he inspected it thoroughly. He was about to open it, when he thought better of the idea. What if it was booby-trapped? My God, he thought. It could have been booby-trapped when I took it off the car. Anxiety pricked his nerves and the car suddenly became hot. What if the gadget back at Brenda's is really a transmitter instead of a receiver? He froze. A transmitter set to blow this device. All of a sudden, the innocent silvery box became ominous. Jesus! If it *was* a transmitter, and Brenda messes with it, all hell could break loose.

He bolted from the car, intent on getting to a

phone to warn her not to touch the little radiolike
device sitting on her polished dining room table.

■

Brenda saw Duke's belongings on the table. The
sleek black transmitter attracted her attention. She
picked it up and flicked the switch on the side. The
LCD windows displayed NORTH and 03.23. What, she
wondered, does that mean? She turned the front
knobs just as Chinsky had. And, as when Chinsky
tried it, nothing happened. Bored with the device,
she switched it off—or more accurately, from receive
to transmit. As she set it back down on the table, she
felt some give in one of the knobs. She pressed it
once, then again. Each time there was a click. Still,
nothing happened.

At least, not as far as she could tell.

CHAPTER
20

THE BLAST HIT just as he opened the rear exit door of the Ramada.

Chinsky felt his body being pushed—hurled—into the hallway, flipping in a perfect somersault. The first crash of noise was followed by the crackling roar of oxygen being sucked into the vortex of the fireball. The pressure of the sound expanding in his head felt like it would pop his eyeballs. He landed on his hands and knees, head pointed toward the now-glassless door through which he had almost just passed.

Outside, a brilliant red-orange-white ball of flame filled the spot once occupied by his brilliant-red Porsche. Fiery fenders, tires, bumpers, and segments of the thousands of precision components that go into an expensive, modern European sports car rained from heaven.

Chinsky was awed by their leisurely descent. Burning pieces shot up from the blazing fireball and gracefully arced back to the asphalt, where they bounced, creating miniature arches outlined in black smoke. From his sheepdog position, Chinsky, motionless, watched his car disintegrate. The sacrilegious words "Jesus fucking Christ" formed on his lips and tumbled out of their own accord.

It was the most impressive fireworks display he had ever seen. The fluorescent flames shrank in size and intensity, while the burning rubber and oil gave it a billowy black backdrop.

People poured down the hallway to see what had happened. A maid was the first to reach him. "What happened?" she asked in an awe-filled voice. She was uncertain whether it was more appropriate to help Chinsky, kneeling in a pool of shattered glass, or to look outside at the compelling beauty of the roasting car. The car won.

She, too, became religious. "Mother of God," he heard her repeat at least a half dozen times.

Others, following the maid, resisted the temptation to rush outside and bent to help him. He was all right. Aside from a bruised knee, he felt no ill effects from the blast. Except for the car, his beautiful car. Hands helped him up, brushed him off, and checked his body. It was almost as if, by doing so, they could reassure themselves of their own safety.

The spicy-sweet smell of burning rubber wafted through the air. All hope of anonymity lost, he pushed through the crowd to watch the car burn. The shower of miscellaneous Porsche parts had slowed to a drizzle. The flame, however, continued to consume what fuel it could find.

In their need for conversation—explanation—the early arrivals pointed to him and whispered to late-comers that he had been there first; he had seen it all. More than one person asked him, "What happened?" There was no answer that would make sense to them, so he waved them off. He was pointed out to the manager, who was beginning to take charge of the situation. An interrogation, he knew, was about to happen. He searched for a way to avoid it. It was one thing to lose anonymity, another to gain celebrity. He needed to get away from here. He shook off the manager without explanation.

His watch said ten fifteen. What a morning.

Pushing his way through the small crowd of gawkers, he was back in the hotel, searching for a phone. As he dialed Brenda, three thoughts ran through his mind: the irony of her blowing up his car, the tragedy of his beautiful machine being barbecued, and the narrowness by which he had escaped the same fate. He was somewhat surprised by his lack of anger at the situation. Perhaps it was because he was still alive. Maybe the pattern was changing and things were beginning to turn his way. Given his situation, it was the height of optimism.

The phone kept ringing. No answer. Then he remembered the code. He hung up and dialed again, letting it ring twice, then pushed down the switchhook. He dialed again.

This time Brenda answered immediately. "Hi," he said, "this is Luke. How are you feeling?"

"I'm fine," she said. "I woke up about fifteen minutes ago and saw your note. You should have wakened me." He smiled at the irony of the comment.

"In retrospect, I agree. Did you happen to see some things I left on the dining room table?"

"Yes, I was trying to figure out what they were. One looked like a radio, but I couldn't make it work."

"I wouldn't be so sure," he said with a hint of

humor in his voice. At least he had confirmed the relationship between the transmitter and his bright-red—now charcoal-black—car. "Tell me exactly what you did with that gadget."

"Nothing much. I picked it up, turned a few dials, pushed a few buttons. I couldn't figure it out."

"Apparently, it's a transmitter that triggers an explosive device. Unfortunately, the device it triggered was planted on the underside of my Porsche. I think you owe me a new car."

"Oh, my God." She let the out words slowly, one at a time. Then again, "Oh, my God!" Concern rushed in. "Are you all right? Of course you are; you're talking to me on the phone. You must be. Are you?"

"I'm all right." He didn't feel the need to tell her how close it had been. "I'll tell you all about it when I see you, but now I need your help. Do you feel up to moving around?"

"Tell me what you need."

"How's the arm?"

"It's good, not bothering me at all. The sleep really helped. What do you need?"

"A ride. Can you drive over to the Ramada on Telegraph and pick me up?"

"I'm on my way."

"Brenda," he shouted before she could hang up.

"I'm still here."

"Don't mess with any of the other stuff, okay?"

"Okay," she said sheepishly.

■

Albert was quick to spot him coming and held the door open. Proxy felt awkward carrying the file box. It lacked the dignity that went with his usual elegance. The situation, he reminded himself, called for unusual measures. This was one of them.

"Can I ring someone for you, sir?" Albert asked.

"Dr. Chinsky, please." Proxy rested the box on Albert's reception stand.

"No one seems to be answering, sir. Is he expecting you?"

"No, he's not, but I just spoke to him a while ago. I wanted to drop off this box."

"I'm afraid he isn't home, sir." Proxy's good grooming, impeccable dress, and vintage Mercedes made a positive impression on the doorman.

"Can I just take this up and put it in his apartment? I'm sure you have a key."

Albert was instantly wary. Fine appearance or no, he wasn't about to let anyone into Chinsky's apartment after the incident with the phone repairman. "I'm afraid that's not allowed, sir. No one is permitted in the apartments without permission."

"I don't want to go in, I just want to leave this box in there. You can come with me."

"I'm afraid not, sir. You can, however, leave it with me."

Proxy had no intention of leaving the files in the hands of a doorman. He was reluctant enough to leave the material in Chinsky's apartment without talking to the researcher, but, to prove good faith, he would. Once Chinsky saw the contents he was sure to talk.

"Look," he said impatiently, "is there somebody around in charge? A manager or someone who can authorize me to drop this off at Dr. Chinsky's?"

"There's the super." Albert liked the idea of getting the superintendent involved; it took him off the hook. "I'll call him for you."

It took only a few minutes for Mr. Kadus to make his way to the foyer. Kadus, with his gray shirt and jeans, looked more like a service man than a manager. Albert explained the situation, not mentioning the incident with the phone repairman. "I didn't feel I could let him in," he said. "If you want to, that's your business. You're the boss." The admission of the super's superiority was a concession that Albert seldom made.

"All I want to do is leave off this box."

"What's in it?" Kadus asked.

Proxy felt it was none of his business and was about to say so when he caught himself. "Just some papers. It's important that Dr. Chinsky get them."

"Why can't you leave them here with Albert?"

"That's what I asked him," Albert said defensively.

"The papers are valuable. I'd feel more comfortable if they were locked in Dr. Chinsky's apartment."

"Well, I don't see nothin' wrong with it. I'll take you up," the super conceded.

Proxy took the file box and followed Kadus.

Outside Chinsky's door, the superintendent fumbled with his keys. Before using the master, he knocked loudly on the door to confirm that Chinsky was out, then swung it open for Proxy.

Proxy was immediately hit by the salty-sweet, ripe

smell of drying blood. There was ample light for him to see Duke's body, still crouched in a fetal position, at the bottom of the step. "My God!" escaped him in a gasp. The super, anxious to see the cause of the reaction, pushed passed Proxy. The jolt was enough to knock the file box from Proxy's startled grip.

"Holy shit," Kadus said as he saw the body. "What the hell is going on here?"

They approached the corpse tentatively, as if afraid it might rise and attack them. The superintendent gagged as he saw the gash in the side of Duke's neck, but managed to hold his breakfast down. Hands over his mouth, he pushed back into the hallway.

Proxy, momentarily unmindful of the overturned box of files, knelt down to get a closer look at the body. In and out of hospitals, he had seen corpses before. But none like this. The clotting blood made the gash look artificial, surreal, like puffy Styrofoam painted red-brown. The little hatchet lay next to the body. He could see the dead man's profile. The eyes were still open. A spittle of blood ran down his chin. "You sure are a mean-looking bastard," he said aloud.

Kadus was on the phone. First he called the police, then Albert. "Get up here," he told the doorman. "There's a dead man in Dr. Chinsky's apartment." Albert said something and Kadus replied, "I dunno. We ain't looked around. I called the police."

Proxy took his cue from what he imagined was Albert's question and started to look through the rest of the apartment. Clearly there had been a fight. In the bedroom he saw the bed pulled over and the bullet-scarred mirror, along with a couple more bullet holes.

This was not the place for him to be, he thought. Not now and not with the records. The police would ask too many questions. He moved to the dining room and saw the pushed-back furniture and the wire noose dangling from the light outlet. No sign of Chinsky. The kitchen was clean, the only untouched room in the apartment. Where was Chinsky? Who was the stiff?

Albert stood looking over the body. "It's the phone company guy," he said.

"What?" asked Proxy.

"It's the phone company guy. The guy who came in here a few days ago to fix Dr. Chinsky's phone. Dr. Chinsky was very upset. I let him in while Dr. Chinsky was out. That's why I wouldn't let you in today. Dr. Chinsky made it clear that no one was to go in his apartment alone."

"How can you be sure?" Proxy probed.

"Because he told me. Put his face right into mine and said, no one goes into my apartment. I understood."

Proxy shook his head. "No. I mean, how can you be sure it's the same person, the phone repairman? He's not dressed like one."

"I remember his face. He had a mean face. Still does. Besides, there's the tattoo. The cobra." He pointed. "On his hand."

Neither Proxy nor Kadus had noticed the tattoo, but Albert was right. It was a tattoo of a malevolent cobra.

"Don't touch anything until the police get here," Kadus warned. He had regained his composure completely, but Proxy noticed he avoided looking at the body.

"That's probably what the noise was," the super said.

"What noise?" asked Proxy.

"The noise last night. Some residents called. They complained about loud popping noises on this floor. I thought it might be the air ducts contracting in the heat. I told them that, but I came up to check it out. Didn't find nothin'. Forgot about it until now. It was probably the gunshots."

"Probably," Proxy agreed as he bent to pick up his file box. One edge was split, but it was still serviceable. "I'm going to take these back down to my car. I don't want to leave them here. They're too important to mix up in something like this."

"I should go with him," Albert said. "To let the police in."

"I'll be right back," Proxy said, although he had no such intention. "Why don't you stay here with Mr. Kadus. When I get back, you can go down."

"Sounds good to me," said the super, as Proxy left.

As Proxy got into his car, he heard the shrill whine of an approaching siren. As nonchalantly as his nerves would allow, he drove off.

■

"I—I don't know what you're talking about," Alice Murcheson stammered. "I don't have any of Mr. Snell's tapes."

The autopistol transcribed a short arc so that the barrel pointed just to the left of her right ear. With a delicate touch Spangler squeezed the hair trigger and the *phffft* of the escaping round flew past her ear, shattering a small crystal vase across the room. Her hands flew to her mouth in alarm as she stifled a cry. Before they got there, the pistol was again aimed at a point precisely between her eyes.

"Please, Miss Murcheson, do not lie to me. And do not play games. You know the tapes I am talking about. While it is true that they are copies, they are the ones I am after." He could tell that his even, patient voice was making her agitated. It always happened like that. The longer you talked, the more time you gave them to think, the easier it was to convince them to cooperate. "It is true that, technically, you own the tapes. But the information on them belongs to Mr. Snell and it is that information that I seek. If you give them to me, I assure you, you will suffer no harm. Otherwise, I shall have to use whatever means are at my disposal to persuade you to cooperate."

Alice Murcheson was no heroine. She was tough when it came to the civilized world of corporate warfare. But she had never looked into the barrel of a loaded gun. Spangler stared encouragingly at her.

"They're in my closet," she said.

"Fine. I am glad you have decided to cooperate. Now, just so you do not become nervous and do a foolish thing, let me tell you what is going to happen next."

She nodded.

"I," Spangler continued, "shall get to my feet. Then you will get up and take me to where you keep the tapes. I will be in back of you. Should you attempt any sudden movement, I will shoot off a piece of your arm. Not enough to stop you from cooperating, but very painful. Do you understand?"

Again she nodded. He knew it was all she could do. He had prepared her properly. She was so frightened that words failed her. He stood up.

She took him into her bedroom. An attractive room. Too bad he had so much to do or he would have liked to dally here. Cautiously, with exaggerated movements, she went to her closet and pulled out a shoe box. She tried to speak, but the words wouldn't come. He helped her by saying, "Yes, I understand. The tapes are in this box. Good. Take it to the bed and empty it so that I can see them."

She did.

The shoes, tapes, and her typed notes dropped to the bedspread noiselessly. He motioned her away with a flick of the pistol and reached to retrieve all but the shoes. "Do you have a tape player?"

"Yes," she croaked, regaining her voice. "In the kitchen."

"Let us go there," he said.

She led him to the kitchen, and he tossed one tape on the Formica counter. It bounced off the tiny clock radio with a built-in tape recorder. "Play it," he commanded. She obeyed.

Snell's voice came over the tiny speaker, confirming these were the tapes Spangler wanted. "Thank you, Miss Murcheson. You have been very cooperative. Now tell me, who has the other copies of these tapes?"

"There—there are no other copies," she stammered.

"Come now, Miss Murcheson, we know you gave a copy to Mr. Proxy."

She shook her head violently, as if to deny it. "There are no other tapes. This is what I gave to Mr. Proxy."

Spangler walked closer to her. She stood transfixed in terror. He eased the long gray barrel of the pistol forward until it touched her lips. Slowly he moved it up, to rest on her top lip, then down to brush the bottom one. Her breathing was rapid, on the point of hyperventilation. "I don't believe you, Miss Murcheson," he said, peering deep into her eyes. "I think you made another tape for yourself, just in case." The words were soft, silky. He made a quick flick of his wrist and the silencer withdrew three inches from her lips then reversed course and crashed back into her mouth. Crimson juice squirted from her battered lip. "I want the other tapes," he said sharply; the silk was gone from his voice.

Murcheson's knees buckled at the blow. It was all she could do to keep from falling to the floor. She threw her hands forward against the countertop to brace herself. Tears welled in her eyes. Her voice was small and trembling. "There are no other tapes. I only made one. I gave it to Mr. Proxy, but he gave it back to me. Please believe me. Please."

Spangler took a step back. "Miss Murcheson"—his voice was once again soft and soothing—"you must understand that I have no wish to hurt you. But I do have a job to do. I must have the other tapes. If not, I will have to harm you. I do not want to do that. Please cooperate and give me the tapes."

She shook her head in desperation. The groan of a tiny, frightened, trapped animal escaped from her lips. "There are no others," she said between the noises. "Please believe me."

"I will have to think about this," Spangler said. "In the meantime, if you will take that tape out of the player and place it on the counter, I would appreciate it." She did as she was told.

"Miss Murcheson," he said after a moment, "I have decided to believe you. I do not think you have other tapes." He gave her a reassuring smile. He could see the relief flow through her body. Her beautiful eyes closed, then, as she sighed, opened again. She was very attractive. "But Miss Murcheson," Spangler continued, "I have a confession to make. Earlier I said that if you cooperated, no harm would come to you. I am afraid I lied." The terror was complete. He could see her knees give way and her body begin its fall to the floor. Not fast enough, though, to avoid the bullet he sent speeding to her head.

∎

Brenda was appalled at Chinsky's appearance. He had a few minor abrasions on his face, and the flying glass had left cuts on his hands. His rugged corduroy trousers were torn at the knees and the white of a makeshift bandage showed through the holes. When she saw the charred, smoldering remains of the Porsche, all she could think of to say was, "Oh, my."

The Southfield police were still there. Chinsky had

avoided giving them a report of ownership and, for reasons still unclear, denied any knowledge of why this should have occurred. It would have been easy to tell them everything. He didn't think about it. They had his address. They would contact him if they needed more information. Did he need a ride to the hospital or home? No, he had one. He took Brenda's arm and led her to her car. He wanted out of there.

Chinsky pulled into the parking lot of the Tel-Twelve Mall just down the street from the Ramada. By unspoken common consent, neither he nor Brenda had said a word.

The place he selected to park was clear of cars. He turned off the ignition and started the conversation. "Cobra's room was an arsenal. I found a bag of explosives and electronic gadgets, plus a gun. I thought the gadget in your apartment was some kind of homing device. When I got outside, I checked under my car and found another device attached to the underbody. That's how he was able to keep track of me. This guy was a real pro. I also found an explosive charge. As soon as I realized what it was, I ran to call you. That probably saved my life."

Her hands were at her mouth, stifling a moan of horror, as she realized what she had done. "It blew just as I got to the motel door. All the stuff I found in his room was in the car, including what looked like some identification. There was a driver's license with his picture on it—actually there were three licenses, but only one had a picture. I think his name was Van Allen, Willem Van Allen. It fits; he looked Dutch.

There were also some credit cards. They're gone now. They blew with the car."

"Oh, Luke. I'm sorry," Brenda said, genuinely contrite.

"Not your fault. But I have to admit, I thought I saw a ray of hope for a second. At the time, I thought I could use the stuff I found—the explosives, multiple ID's, and everything—to prove that a killer was after me. Now it just looks like there's a dead guy in my apartment. One that I killed."

"Oh, Luke, that's terrible. I didn't mean to do it. I was just wondering what it was. It looked so harmless."

"It's not your fault" he repeated. And he knew it really wasn't. "I did the same thing earlier. I thought I had turned and twisted every combination of buttons on that gadget and nothing happened. I wonder why it didn't blow up my car then?"

"Thank God, you weren't in it. I never would have forgiven myself."

"Nor would I," he said with a wry smile. It didn't, however, take the pain out of her eyes.

"I need to search your car, to make sure that it's clean. There might be an explosive on it. That's why I pulled in here. I want to do it before we go too far," he said as he opened the door.

He walked around to her door and opened it. "I'd like you to get out and wait for me here. I'm going to drive over there and take a look."

"Luke, are you crazy? You don't know anything about explosives."

"When I played around with the one under my car,

nothing happened." Tactfully, he didn't say, unless someone pushes the wrong button. "I don't think they go off unless someone detonates them. There were detonators in his room."

"You don't happen to have another girl somewhere with one of those gadgets do you?"

He turned sharply.

"Just kidding," she said.

He parked the car a hundred yards from Brenda in a relatively deserted section. Luckily business wasn't better, he thought, or this would be tougher. He went directly to the left rear fender and got down on his back. Gripping the fender, he pulled himself under. Nothing there. He scooted out and did the same on the other side. There they were, just as he remembered from his Porsche. Carefully, he pulled at one. It wouldn't move. He pushed himself out and looked in her trunk for a prying tool. A screwdriver proved adequate to the task. With a little pry, the magnet gave and the device dropped to the ground. Chinsky caught his breath, waiting for something to happen. When nothing did, he pried the other one loose.

As Brenda got in the car, he showed her the round plastic-looking device about the size of an Eisenhower dollar and another, hard metal one, shaped like a cigarette case. "These are the same as the two that were under my car. I think they're held on by magnets."

"What are you going to do with them?"

"I thought I'd toss them in Gilbert Lake," he said, starting up the car.

The plastic dollar sailed out fifty yards or so before

it hit the water. The box fell a bit shorter. He was glad to be rid of both. "I almost forgot," he said, "I also found some notes, written by the killer. I recognized the handwriting from the stuff we took out of his pockets. They were mainly phone numbers, but one had a name on it."

"Did they get blown up too?"

He pushed his hand into his pocket, searching for the papers. "No, I think I have them. If so, it may be something to go on." The wad of notes he pulled out of his pocket was folded and crumpled, but there on top was the one with the name *Spangler* circled by Duke's doodles. "I think he called himself Duke."

"What are you going to do?"

"I'm going to call this Spangler."

CHAPTER
21

PROXY DROVE NORTH on Crooks Road past Rochester, then turned west. A dozen miles later he turned southeast on Dixie Highway. He drove aimlessly in a wide circle around the outlying northern suburbs.

No wonder Chinsky wouldn't talk to him. Christ, that guy must have tried to kill him. He must have discovered something on his own and tipped Snell off. Proxy was beginning to believe in an omniscient, omnipresent Snell, one who could strike his adversaries with the dispatch of a thunderbolt. Now, more than ever, he needed to safeguard the files, put them in the right place, get them in Chinsky's hands.

Dixie Highway turned into Woodward Avenue. It was a straight shot in to the Renaissance Center. Horst kept a room there, at the Westin. He eased the gas pedal down and began passing cars.

■

Gene Brazik, a data analyst with the Southfield Police Department, matched the alert bulletin put out for Dr. Luke Chinsky, assumed to be driving a red 1988 Porsche 911 Turbo, Michigan plate number VDS 443, with the explosion of a similar vehicle in the parking lot of the Ramada Inn. The Porsche's license plate had been vaporized in the blast. But a check of the registration—using the charred vehicle identification number found above the car's firewall —through the Secretary of State's office confirmed Chinsky as the owner. He filed a correction deleting Chinsky's assumed vehicle from the state police department's interagency electronic bulletin board. The electronic program controlling the bulletin board automatically paired the messages to make it easier for readers to make data connections.

Brady tore the printout from the machine and walked it over to Cal Washington.

"Look what came over the wire." Although the network had long since stopped using wire communication, habit died hard. He handed over the paper.

Washington studied the printout. About halfway through, his jaw started its rhythmical dance. "Looks like our Dr. Chinsky is into something," he said. "Have you called Southfield?"

"Negative."

Washington pulled his black rotary dial desk phone over and dialed the number. After identifying himself to Brazik, and validating his interest in the case, he asked for details.

"They think some kind of plastique explosive was used, probably C-4." It was a common compound composed primarily of cyclotrimethylene, trinitramine, isomethylene, and motor oil. "It was away from the engine, so they don't think it was an ignition switch detonator, probably remote. They're still picking up the pieces. No one was in the car when it detonated."

"What about the body in the apartment?"

"No ID yet. Apparent cause of death was an ax wound to the neck."

"Jesus."

"Yeah. They're still there. Said we could come over."

"Let's go."

■

The number above Spangler's name was the Westin Hotel in downtown Detroit. Chinsky called. No Spangler was registered. Chinsky had them ring the extension written on the paper. Ten rings later, the operator came back on the line to inform him that the party was not answering. He wondered if they all went to the same school.

"Can you tell me whose room I'm calling?"

"I'm afraid we're not allowed to give out that information."

"If I came down there could I get the information?"

"I'm sorry, sir, you'll have to ask the front desk about that."

"Can you connect me to them?"

She did. They wouldn't.

Brenda sat across from him, feet curled up under her, yoga style. "Luke, why don't we just go to the police? I have Washington's number. I talked to him yesterday, he'll help out."

"I'm almost ready to." He tugged on his slightly singed beard. "There are a couple of things I'd need to work out." Then, as a quiet afterthought, he added, "By myself." Catching himself, he explained, "Rathbone was onto something important. He died because of it, of that I'm certain. I must be getting close to the same thing, so they came after me. I would hate to lose it because I went to the police."

"That's nonsense. You're acting like there's a fix on the game."

"Still, it's the way I feel. Too many times I've brought people in and we've gone off on tangents, lost the thread I was following. Two people have died here. I don't want to lose this thread. At its end is a very important cure."

She made an exasperated sigh. "Okay. Say I buy that. What's your next move?"

"I want to talk to Charlie again, maybe some of the others who have come in, find out how they were recruited, who else knew they were getting treatment at Croft."

"And then?"

"The phone call I got at my place was from Ben Proxy. He said he had Rathbone's records. I was in shock at the time; Van Allen had told me the same thing. I hung up on him. Maybe that was a mistake. I should talk to him again."

"And then?"

"Don't press." He was sorry for his brusqueness the moment the phrase escaped him. "Look," he said in a conciliatory tone, "I'll talk to Charlie today if I can get ahold of him. After that, we'll decide whether I should go to the police."

"They're probably looking for you now."

"I doubt it. You and I are the only ones who know Van Allen is dead."

"What about the car?"

"You're right. They may be tracking me because of that." He hadn't told them it was his car at the Ramada. "But I don't think they'll start a manhunt because of a car explosion."

"Maybe not, but they could have gone to your apartment."

"So what? They can't get in without a search warrant and there's no reason for them to get one."

"You're probably right, but be careful anyway. We've just made the finals and I don't want you benched because of a bad knee."

"Right."

"When are you going to see Charlie?"

"Now. First I'll check if he's home."

"Good. I have an appointment with Snell. We'll compare notes when I get back tonight. First one home starts dinner."

"Are you sure you've got to see Snell?"

"I have my threads to follow too."

■

The phone stopped ringing as Spangler came through the door. It was rare that he got a call. Very few people knew the number. It was probably Duke calling to report on the hit. The researcher and reporter were targeted for last night. He threw his jacket on the sofa. Hope it was a clean job. Now that he had iced Murcheson, all hell was going to break loose. There was no longer a point in making things

look natural. Nobody would believe three related accidental deaths. No way. Now the goal was get it over
with and get out. He could use Duke to handle some
of the load. It would speed things up. The Dutchman
would complain. He was probably tired after his
night's work. He had told him to make the girl look
like a rape case. Keep it unrelated to Chinsky. At the
time, Duke liked the idea. Well, now he would pay
for his fun.

He wished he had caught the call. It was almost
time to call the boss, and he expected answers.

The phone rang again.

"Yes," he answered with military precision.

"This is Ben. I'm downstairs. I'll be up in a minute."

■

Chinsky had called and said, "Charlie, I'm in trouble." It was enough for Charlie.

Chinsky had taken a bus to within four blocks of
Charlie's address. He had insisted Brenda take her
car. It would have been more logical for him to take a
cab, but as Brenda had reminded him, there was an
outside chance the police were looking for him. Cabs
kept records. Better to play it safe. Leaving the bus,
knapsack on his back, he hiked past derelicts—both
brick and flesh—to an ancient four-story with DEXTER
ARMS carved in granite relief above its doorway. A
more recent sign, with faded hand-painted black-and-
red letters on a peeling, once-white background read:

ROOMS, APTS.

WEEKLY OR MONTHLY RATES

Chinsky checked the address to make sure it was the right place.

The five steps leading to the front entry of the building were the regular meeting place for a pack of young blacks. "Hey, whitey," they taunted him as he climbed the stairs, dodging their outstretched legs. "You delivering the mail?" The titters at their own wisecracks were to give them courage as much as to intimidate him.

"What you got in that bag?"

"He's got a bagful of hogs."

"Naw, he's no fuckin' bagman. He not big enough."

"You gonna share your shit with us, man?"

Chinsky walked through them. Avoiding confrontation, he ignored them. Any sign of intimidation and they would tear the bag from his shoulder. It worked. Other than the taunts, they let him alone. He reached the entryway. Opening the door, he was hit with the acrid smell of ammonia. More than one person had come in out of the cold to relieve himself. The heat of August roasted the aroma. It would have been better, he thought, if they just broke the door window to let some air in. The stench made him gag. He almost went outside for air, but climbed the steps instead. The handrail had been pulled from the wall at the top and felt sticky to the touch. His initial reaction was to pull his hand back. He reminded himself that this was not a laboratory and held on. He needed the support in the dim light. Charlie had said the third door on the right. Chinsky knocked and was relieved to see Charlie's smiling face as the door cracked open. Charlie unlatched the door and welcomed him in.

"Dr. Chinsky, it's good to see you. I'm pleased you made it here without any trouble." The easy Caribbean friendship seemed out of place in this sun-deprived building. "Come in, come in."

Chinsky had not expected much. Charlie Brown's room was small, one of twenty in an apartment building built to house immigrant workers at the turn of the century. It was cheap housing then; cheaper now. Had it not been for HUD money and welfare checks, the building site would have become just another vacant lot. The smell of the room was refreshing after the hallway. Charlie had the window open, yet there was an aroma of spice.

"Charlie, I appreciate this. I don't want to mix you up in my business, but I need some more information."

"Sure, whatever you want." Charlie's smile widened. "You gave me back my life. Whatever I have" —he gestured around him—"is yours." It was an ironic enough statement. They both laughed and the initial tension between them dissipated.

"Can I get you something to drink? Then we talk. You can tell me what you want of me." Charlie gestured to an odd assortment of bottles on the drainboard of the sink. Mainly they were rums.

"I'd like some coffee, if you have some."

"Oh, sure, I have coffee. I make my own." He poured a cup from a pot warming on the hotplate.

Chinsky realized he was getting the only cup and that Charlie would have to wait until he finished. Unreasoned guilt about Charlie's poverty overtook him.

"Here, you have this," he said. "I'll wait and have mine later."

Charlie wouldn't hear of it. "No. The coffee is for you. Drink it."

Charlie sat on the bed, while Chinsky took the only chair. The television, its umbilical cord snaking to an outlet in the wall, sat on a corner of the table. The smell of the coffee solved the mystery of the fragrant spice in the air. It tasted of cinnamon. Even with very little, he reflected, the habits of the past are maintained. It was probably Charlie's only luxury.

The pleasantries over, Chinsky pulled out a notebook and a tape recorder he had borrowed from Brenda. "Charlie, I'd like you to tell me how you got to Croft, who sent you. Tell me the whole story."

Charlie did.

∎

Brenda decided to do some research on Van Allen. She had the basics, a name and a number. With computers tracking everything, digging out facts was just a matter of how much drudgery you were willing to devote to the task. Before she could get to it, though, she still owed Gus Donovan a short filler on the pennant race for the sports desk. And then she could get some background on Snell. It looked like a long day.

She began to understand the difficulty of serving two masters.

The arm pained her again. Chinsky had given her a prescription for propoxyphene to lessen the hurt. The pills made her drowsy, but when the hole in her arm became too troublesome, she could trade drowsiness for pain. Chinsky said the side effect would wear off in a couple of days as her body became used to the narcotic. A few days was too long. She needed to be alert now. She accepted the pain. No pain, she thought wryly, no gain.

By the time she finished the pennant piece, the newsroom had begun its cyclical descent into stupor. For the next few hours, there would be relative quiet. Fortunately, Chicago was in another time zone. It gave her an extra hour to cull sources. She went to the library, pulled out the Chicago phone book and took it back to her desk. It was difficult managing the four-inch-thick book with one hand, but she did it.

She called the research department of the *Chicago Tribune* and identified herself. They were very friendly, but had no information on their computer about Van Allen. Nor did the *Sun-Times*. Her two most convenient sources had been wild pitches. Left was drudgery. Maybe not. She dialed the central records section of the police department.

"Florence Jerzy, please," she asked. It took a second for Jerzy to come on the line.

"Hi, Flo, it's Brenda. I'm trying to track down a guy from Chicago. How would I go about getting into the police files there?"

"It's pretty tough unless you go down there yourself. They don't like to give out information over the phone, if they don't know who they're talking to."

"Is there any way you can help me, vouch for me, or something?"

"Naw, that wouldn't work either, they don't know who I am. I know what we can do, though. I can make a computer inquiry, data base to data base, through Polinet. It's the interlink between police departments. Would that help?" To Brenda, it seemed a perfect solution.

"Sounds great. What do I need to tell you?"

"Are you looking for information on a person or an event?" Brenda considered that. She had assumed that information was stored only by individual.

"Both, actually. I'm working on the background for the Rathbone murder and one of the trails leads to Chicago."

"Whoa. You're not starting up a separate investigation, are you? I could get my tit in a wringer by helping you on an active case."

"No, I'm just after background info, but I don't want you to do anything that will get you into trouble. If you think I'm going too far, just tell me, and I'll drop it." Brenda sensed that she had a mine of information at her fingertips. She didn't want to do something stupid and blow her source. "I'm after information on a guy named Van Allen, Willem Van Allen." Brenda, recalling the notes Chinsky had shown her, said, "He may also be known as Duke."

"Do you have any other information on him? Driver's license number? Address? Social security number?"

"I have his driver's license number." She gave it to her. "He's the only person I'm trying to track down, but it may be useful if I could get information on any unsolved assassination-type murders."

"In Chicago? Brenda, you've got to be kidding. My computer would be running for two days." Even Brenda smiled at the naive parameter she had set. "Can you get more specific?"

"Well, why don't you try assassination-type murders of businessmen. Is that narrow enough? Better yet, tie it to the pharmaceutical industry."

"You mean drugs? Come on, honey, that's as bad as no definition at all."

"No, not illegal drugs, the legitimate kind. Like the people who make aspirin and Valium."

"Let me try that. Anything else?" Brenda knew it was time to take her winnings and cut out.

"No. If you run those for me, I'd really appreciate it. Let me know if there's anything I can do, okay?"

"You've got a deal. Next time I have fifty tickets to sell for our fund-raiser, I'll expect a good turnout from your paper." Brenda vowed that, if Florence's information helped her get a page-one byline, she'd buy every one of them herself.

It was too late to contact any other outside sources. She had gone about as far as she could with Van Allen. She had a couple of hours or so to get background on Snell before the interview. Thank God it had been set up for late in the day.

She went to the newspaper morgue, where dead articles were kept. There were a couple of feature articles on Snell in the dailies and one in *Crain's*, the local business newspaper. Nothing remarkable. There were some clips of his promotion announcements, with a picture attached. Handsome dog, she thought.

She found a copy of the *Social Secretary*, the blue book of the gentry in Detroit and Michigan. It listed his Bloomfield Hills address as well as his winter home in Delray Beach, Florida. Nice neighborhoods, she thought. Brad and the Mrs. belonged to the right clubs: Bloomfield Hills Country Club, Bloomfield Open Hunt, the Detroit Club, Junior League of Birmingham. Bet they went to some swell parties. The most important fact was that they were in the book at all. Most people didn't even know it existed.

The newspaper's bio on Snell was remarkable for its brevity. He had gone to Princeton, picked up an MBA at Michigan, and then joined Croft. His progression through the company was swift. At forty he was president, by forty-five, its chief executive. He sat on the board of two other corporations, was a trustee of Crittenton Hospital and chaired a committee of the Detroit Symphony Orchestra. She recognized the file picture from one of the announcements, but also noted another later picture that showed some graying of the temples and crow's-feet around the eyes. My, you age gracefully, Mr. Snell, she thought.

She glanced at her watch. Time was getting in front of her. It was six o'clock. The interview was set for eight at Snell's house. She still had plenty of time. It would take only a half hour to cover the distance. With a few more minutes to find the place, she still had over an hour to dig.

■

Spangler sat alone, wondering how he was going to cover this. Duke had botched it and gotten himself killed for his trouble. Stupid bastard. The worst part had been the apprehension of telling the boss of the failure. But it had gone well. The man had been more interested in Snell's loss of control. A smile spread across his face. He would have to do it all himself; there was nothing the boss could do about it. If the fat man wanted it done fast, Spangler would have to handle it personally. The instruction was clear, "Do it and get out." His long purgatory in Detroit was coming to an end. He would not fail. He would act quickly. Tonight. Tomorrow, if necessary. Allow them no time to defend or to scatter. Move now, without resting until it is done. It was going to be a busy night.

Apart from the Dutchman's blunder, things were going reasonably well. Murcheson was taken care of, and he had her tapes. Proxy had given him the crucial files; that stupid cow had been so worked up he didn't realize that he had just given up the great prize. If he, Spangler, was lucky, Proxy would be at Snell's later tonight. If not—he would find his Golden. A call would bring him running.

He knew where they would all be, save Chinsky. Chances are he was with the girl. In the meantime, there was Snell to deal with.

The boss had made that clear.

CHAPTER
22

CHARLIE SAT THERE, talking, reminiscing, going on at length in answer to Chinsky's question. The man was a patient, nothing more. Chinsky felt for the poverty of his lifestyle, the desolation of his body, and the cruel trick the finger of disease had played on him. It was a far road from the idyllic remembrances the one-time bistro owner now had of Haiti.

The trip to Charlie's was a wild-goose chase. He recognized that now. What was it with him that he could never take the easy way? He always had to press on by himself even when he knew there were better—no, not better, more obvious—alternatives. The alternatives, he admitted, involved working with others. Not his style. He was too old to change, he rationalized. The result, he ruefully admitted, whether in the laboratory or in life, often left him chasing wild geese. It was time to go.

"Charlie," Chinsky interrupted, "don't think I'm rude, but I think I have everything I need. Thank you for taking the time with me."

Charlie didn't think the abrupt interruption rude. He was just talking to make the doctor happy. Besides, it felt good to talk to someone about things. It had been a long time. The road from Port-au-Prince to New York to Detroit had been south all the way.

Chinsky reached into his pocket. "Charlie, I've taken a lot of your time. Let me pay you for it."

Charlie wasn't noble. His eyes widened as Chinsky drew his money clip from the pocket. The money was covered by the notes taken from the Ramada, making the bundle seem bigger than it was. He worked two twenties from the clip and handed them to Charlie. "Here, this is for your trouble."

Charlie took the money with thanks. "Be careful," he said as Chinsky went back into the stairwell, "there's bad people out there."

Something Chinsky was newly discovering.

The toughs were gone from the steps. Outside, it looked as bleak as inside. There was little traffic, pedestrian or otherwise, on the street. Chinsky turned and walked north, toward Mack Avenue and the bus route.

He had to pay as much attention to where he was putting his feet as he did to where he was going. The sidewalk was cracked, and in places, crumbling. When he was a kid, he played a game that involved stepping carefully to avoid the cracks. If you stepped on a crack the devil would reach up and grab you, drag you down to Hell. To avoid being swallowed required very small feet. Unfortunately, for his size, Chinsky had big feet.

It was cloudy and humid. In spite of the overcast sky, the temperature was moving into the uncomfortable range. It was the kind of weather that brought people—especially those without air-conditioning—

out of doors. Yet, in this neighborhood, there were no people outside.

The dearth of beings was unnerving. It was like walking through the aftermath of a bombing. Beirut must feel like this, he thought. The sparseness of life and even of buildings depressed him. Two out of three lots were vacant, overgrown with weeds. A boarded-up brick building usually sat on the third. It was a ghost town in the middle of a metropolis. These were the homes of the winos and junkies, the dispossessed. There were no people outside because there were few people inside.

As Chinsky reached the corner, he turned left toward Woodward to where the buses ran. Besides, that direction seemed to be more built up, and the flow of occasional traffic was visible. Perhaps he should call Brenda, let her know he was all right. He looked for a store or gas station with a familiar blue phone symbol. None was in sight. Yet, he reassured himself, it was better to be outside than in. He knew that if he walked far enough, he would find civilization and its handmaiden, commerce.

Stripped-down skeletons of automobiles dotted the curbside. In one, he saw a pair of feet protruding from the open door of a backseat. The velour cushion was more comfortable than a cement or wood floor, the alternatives available to a street person. The shoes didn't match. In another neighborhood, he would have investigated the feet to see if the person attached to them was all right. Here, he suspected, any inquiry would bring abuse—not all of it verbal.

In the distance, Chinsky could make out a yellow-

and-red sign hanging from the front of a building. As he approached, he recognized the familiar Lotto logo urging everyone to play and get rich.

As he approached the windowless store, he saw people. A few young kids ran in the street, playing games, chasing each other. There were teenagers, too —though they could have been older; it was hard for Chinsky to tell. Most were male.

The boys, all young stallions, strutted to show bravado. Even in the heat of the day, some wore black silk jackets, though most were dressed for the weather. Nearly everyone held a brown paper bag containing a bottle. From their tops, the bottles looked like Pepsi or Coke. The boys stood around in different groups, huddled, laughing, talking, moving together. As on the steps of Charlie's apartment building, they made loud comments about him to each other.

He wondered if this trip had been such a good idea. A cab would have been easier, though he doubted whether it would have been quicker.

He knew showing fear would be a mistake. It would excite them to prove their manhood by provoking him. His best defense was his own bravado. He gave them what he thought were contemptuous, macho looks and walked past them into the store. Behind him, he could hear their laughter swell.

Inside, the party store was a citadel. Inch-thick Plexiglas protected the liquor, sex magazines, cigarettes, and clerks. Chinsky doubted if banks had better security. On a day-to-day basis, the banks probably didn't need it as much.

He looked around for a phone. There didn't seem to be any. Chinsky got in line behind a man buying a Lotto ticket from the barricaded cashier.

"Do you have a phone?" he asked when his turn came.

"You buying something?"

"I need a phone."

"This ain't no phone booth; this is the only phone I got," the spindly man behind the Plexiglas said. "If you want to use it you gotta buy somethin'."

Frustrated, Chinsky grabbed a newspaper from a nearby rack.

"I'll buy this."

"Gotta be five dollars."

"Then charge me five dollars for it," he said with disgust.

"You gonna make a local call?"

"Yes," said Chinsky.

"That'll be six dollars. Five for the paper and one for the phone." Chinsky paid.

The clerk slid the phone through an opening in the Plexiglas and Chinsky, dragging its long cord, moved out of line. There was no answer at Brenda's apartment. He tried her direct-dial number at the *Free Press*. After a half dozen rings, someone answered. She wasn't at her desk, he was told. He left a message that he was on his way to the apartment.

Outside, the threatening packs of youth still milled in their respective territories. As he passed the second group, one of the toughs stepped in front of him and blocked his way.

"You got any money, honkie?" The boy, if he could

be called that, was a full head taller than Chinsky and easily fifty pounds heavier. The brown sheen of his skin wrapped well-developed biceps and pectorals. He stood—hands on hips, feet spread, face pushed toward Chinsky—a linebacker waiting to decapitate a quarterback.

"None for you," Chinsky answered, looking his antagonist in the eye. He acted braver than he felt. He hoped his voice wouldn't crack. Chinsky started to step around the young giant, but the boy jumped in front of him again. He's quick, thought Chinsky, stopping again, this time a foot closer to the bulging chest of the linebacker. If they were going to start something, he might as well try to bluster his way out of it. There was nothing to lose by being bold. "Look," Chinsky said, "you're a tough guy. Now, why don't you just get out of the way and let me go."

A big grin spread over the giant's face. "Or what?" he asked. His particular pack of cronies had quieted down to watch the situation develop. Others were aware of the confrontation, but kept up their own chatter. Chinsky knew he was going to be *the* diversion for this dull, muggy, summer day. He hoped for rain and attempted to avoid the challenge.

"Or nothing. I'm not bothering you. Why don't you just let me go and pick on someone your own size?" While the words were conciliatory, they were said with enough force and determination to mask Chinsky's fear.

"I thought all you white mothafuckahs were bigger than all us black boys," the giant said, not giving an inch. Chinsky was sure he was going to lose this confrontation.

From a nearby group, one of the few girls called out, "Let him go, Leon. He ain't doin' nothin' to you." Chinsky mentally thanked the girl. Leon just continued to grin, challenging Chinsky to do something. Chinsky started to take a step to the left. Leon, with a catlike move, repositioned himself to block him.

"Let him go, Leon," the girl yelled again, this time in a more menacing voice. Chinsky felt like a trapped dog. It was not a good feeling. "If you don't let him go I'm goin' to tell your mama!" she yelled, again. This prompted a general round of hoots and catcalls.

"Watch out, Leon, your mama's gonna whup you."

"Hey, Leon, let him go or you're gonna sit in the corner."

"Leon, Leon, here comes your mama."

Chinsky, not sure whether the jeers were helping or hurting, made another move to get around Leon. This time Leon just turned with him and let him pass, making an exaggerated bow in the process. Chinsky didn't stop to acknowledge it, but walked steadily forward. As he passed other groups, he didn't attempt to avoid their eyes, but neither did he give them a challenging stare. To get out of here, without another confrontation, would be just fine with him.

At his first opportunity, Chinsky turned a corner. Along the way, he chided himself for his stupidity. In this neighborhood, his white skin was an invitation to violence. He should have called a cab. Charlie's warning rang in his ears.

He knew just how big a mistake ignoring Charlie's caution was, when Leon—and a half dozen of his chums—appeared around the side of an abandoned building. They must have sprinted ahead of him down an alley. This time there was no girl around to diffuse the situation.

"Hey man, don't I know you?" Leon asked as Chinsky approached. Chinsky ignored the question, knowing that he wasn't going to be able to walk out of this.

Leon jumped in front of him, his body in a crouch, arms spread to extend his range of action. The others flanked Chinsky, giving Leon enough room to maneuver. None came within an arm's length of him, but their positioning cut off all chance of escape. In any case, he doubted if he could outrun them.

Chinsky continued walking forward. As he did, Leon gave way. The crouch brought Leon's head below his own. Chinsky contemplated going on the attack. Fat chance, he thought, no weapon, facing a pack of trained street fighters.

"You don't talk much, honkie. Whatcha doin' around here?" He didn't have time to answer. Another boy, as muscled as Leon, but more Chinsky's height, darted from the right side and used his head to butt Chinsky in the ribs. A sharp pain shot up Chinsky's side. As he twisted around to face his assailant, another head caught him in the small of the back. He went flying toward the cement, hands outstretched to cushion the fall. The rough concrete tore skin from his palms. A foot, from Leon's direction, caught him in the ribs on his left side. He winced in pain and instinctively pulled his knees to the fetal position.

"Like that, whitey?"

"Stay outta here, you cocksucker."

"Honkie shit."

Another foot glanced off his temple while someone else landed a solid blow to his thigh.

"Mothafucker."

"That'll teach him to come 'round here."

"See if he got any money." Arms tugged at his legs, trying to straighten them, while hands squirmed their way into his pockets. "This fucker ain't cooperating." The chatter went on while they mauled him. Then a booted toe caught him in the temple and he heard no more.

■

It took most of the day for the specialists to identify Willem Van Allen. Never having been arrested or in the service of his country, no fingerprints were attached to his name. But through a number of unsolved murders there was a link to the prints. Just no name. The first break came with a positive I.D. from the assistant manager of the Ramada who had booked the man in the picture a room. His registered name was Roger Smith, the company GM. The dead man had a sense of humor. The room was a wreck. Someone had been there, unless the stiff was a pig. Clothes and toilet articles were scattered over the bed and floor. A bankbook from Harris Trust in Chicago turned up among the dead man's scattered belongings. Fortunately the corpse didn't use an alias in his financial dealings. The bank provided them with the real name and a social security number. A computer search of income tax returns led them to a Chicago address, where they found corroborating prints. They also found an arsenal of weapons, a collection of sophisticated electronic devices—mainly for eavesdropping—explosives of all types, and an extensive library of child pornography videos. An album of newspaper clippings contained stories of twenty-seven different killings. After an investigation, the police would find that twenty-four of the cases were still unsolved. None of the three people convicted for the murders had been executed. All eventually appealed—two successfully. The loop was closed. The dead man, Willem "Duke" Van Allen, was a professional killer, an assassin. It had taken three search warrants and the contributions of forty-seven people.

For Washington, the important link was the discovery of a custom-made .44 Magnum rifle in the trunk of a rented Buick in the parking lot of the Ramada. Ballistics matched the gun with the slug taken from Rathbone's body. It was beginning to come together. Van Allen had killed Rathbone. Chinsky was either a target or in on it, either way a definite link. Chinsky had killed Van Allen. His prints, seven good ones, were on the ax. The researcher had run from the scene. That pointed to his complicity. On the other hand, it could have been a flight of fear. The apartment was pretty beat-up, like a battle had been fought there. They pulled eleven slugs from two different guns out of the walls and furniture. Washington suspected ballistics would match some of them with the charred Walther found in the remains of the burned-out Porsche registered to Chinsky. Was the other gun Chinsky's? None was found in the apartment, nor was one registered in his name.

The blood was also a problem. The samples from both the foyer and phone were B negative. Van Allen was type A. Chinsky's type was O. Someone else had been here and was wounded. A check of hospital emergency room reports failed to identify any reasonable linkages.

A lot of strings had been tied up in a day. More dangled untied.

"Let's take a ride downtown," Washington said to Brady.

Washington was familiar with the DPD computer center. He had worked the city's homicide and major crimes divisions for fifteen years before taking the cushy suburban job. His immediate interest was in tracking drug-related murders. Detroit had the best computer center in the state; maybe he could make a few connections.

"Cal! How ya doin?" Jerzy shrieked as she saw him. She ran over and threw her arms around his neck, planting a moist kiss on his cheek.

"Lot better after seeing you, gal!" He held her away to get a better look. "My, you look finer every day."

"You reprobate," she said, pleased both at seeing him and the compliment.

"Remember my partner, Brady?"

"Sure. Hi, Brady, good to see you again. What

brings you guys down here? Business slow in the 'burbs?"

"Anything but," said Washington. His jaw was back in motion. "Following up on some things happening in our town. Thought you might be able to help by giving a printout on all the open cases of drug-related murders."

"Must be a popular topic. I just had another request like that a couple of hours ago."

"Anybody I know?"

"Naw. Just a reporter friend I'm helping out."

"Didn't know you were in the press business."

"Gimme a break, Cal. She's a friend and I'm helping out. She's trying to break into crime reporting. Come to think of it, the case she's following is up in your neighborhood."

"Oh?"

"Yeah. She's doing some follow-up stories on the murder out at Croft, the doctor."

"That's my case. Which paper does she work for?"

"The *Free Press*. Name's Brenda Byrne."

Washington exchanged a knowing look with Brady. "Flo, I think you better tell me what she wants to know, better yet, what you know."

■

Proxy sat at a dimly lit bar near the Pontchartrain Hotel while Ernie Swan played "Boulevard of Broken Dreams" on the baby grand house piano. An appropriate tune, he thought.

"Another one, Mr. Proxy?" Joe asked in a voice that

invited conversation. Proxy nodded his head, but passed on the conversation.

For Proxy, the stakes had increased enough to give him second thoughts about defecting from the protection of his mentor. His soul told him to fight Snell. His head told him the price would be terrible. Snell knew the right buttons to push. Two dead people would testify to that—if they could. Fear smoldered in Proxy.

Horst had helped. He didn't want to involve him, but it had poured out. Horst said his best course was to confront Snell now. Tonight. Get it all out. Easy enough for Horst to say, he was more manly. He didn't have Snell to face. He didn't know Snell.

By now the police had found the body. Were they looking for him? The doorman and the other guy certainly had given his description. That wouldn't be enough to link him, though. His appearance was distinctive: the beard, hair color, style; he was easy to describe. Just as easy to recognize. But, unless there was a full-scale search for him, it was a big city. People—even distinctive ones—were hard to find. He tried calling Chinsky again, not really expecting an answer after the morning's events. All he got was a recorded message.

"Joe," he said, just loud enough to catch the barkeep's ear.

"Yeah, Mr. Proxy?" Joe came over to him. It was a slow night. The regulars came and went, but the bar stools were mostly empty.

"What do you think of this AIDS thing?"

"You mean that gay disease?" Proxy looked Joe in

the eye for a second, then his gaze dropped. In another bar, another time, he would have challenged the generalization. Not tonight, though; he wasn't after a confrontation with this man, just some input.

"Yeah, what do you think about it?"

"Not given it a lot of thought, Mr. Proxy. Why do you ask?" The bartender, from his experience as a barroom social worker, knew the best strategy in answering an open-ended question was finding out where the customer was on the issue before committing himself.

"I work for a drug company. We're just hashing over some of the ethical issues of how to approach it," Proxy told him. "All of us in the company are too close to the situation. I thought I'd ask you, just to see what the man in the street was thinking."

"You had me worried there for a minute, Mr. Proxy." Joe's belly pulsed as he let out a short laugh. "I thought you were going to tell me you had AIDS. If you did, I'd have to be real careful when I washed the glasses." Another little laugh. Joe lit up a cigarette, something he rarely did while on duty. Talking about the disease made him uncomfortable. "I wouldn't want any of my customers to come down with that stuff. You don't have to worry, though, I hear only the queers and the junkies get it. Is that right?"

Proxy didn't take offense. It was a straight bar, and he had started the conversation.

"Kids are getting it from their mothers, too, and there are cases of people becoming infected through blood transfusions."

"I feel bad for those people, but not for the queers. They have it coming. What they do ain't natural. They're getting what they deserve." It was the opinion of middle America. Not much sympathy from the blue-collar crowd either, because it didn't touch them. Or so they thought.

"They say that by ninety-three there will be nearly two million infected people. The death rate is climbing." Proxy tried to broaden the issue.

"Is that so?" Joe said, surprised. "I didn't know that. Huh, that's a lot of queers. Maybe they'll learn to keep their dicks in their own pants." Joe laughed at his own joke. Proxy gave him a weak smile.

"What do you think the government should do about it, though?" Proxy rerouted the conversation.

"Nothing." The flatness of the response took him aback. Clearly there was little sympathy here. "Look, we waste too much money on crooks and perverts and people who would rather take a handout than work. It's about time something caught up with them. It's God's work. He knows how to handle them." Joe left his cigarette in the ashtray while he tended to another customer down the bar.

Proxy smiled at the self-righteousness of the professional alcohol dispenser. Ten times as many people were in hospitals today from smoking or booze than would ever be because of drugs or sexual preference. Yet those were acceptable vices. Public money spent on cures for lung cancer and liver transplants was not only justified but applauded.

And that was the problem. Middle America didn't give a shit. Joe didn't give a shit. They could all die and these guys would say, "Good riddance." If someone was going to fight for a cure it would have to be the people affected by it. Him. It was up to him. Only Snell stood in his way.

Horst had the records. With instructions to pass them on to Chinsky. That angle was covered. If Snell cooperated, he, Proxy, would keep mum on what he knew about the cartel and Rathbone's premature testing of the cure. If not, he would blow the whole story. Worked right, he could box Snell in a corner and get him to release the cure in a timely manner. Trouble was, Snell always managed to find a way out of the corner. Then again, he had never faced a determined Proxy. Braced by the alcohol, he was sure he could do it.

By the time Joe returned, Proxy had put a twenty on the bar to take care of the tab. He didn't want to talk to Joe anymore. Just to Snell.

■

There was dirt in his mouth when he regained consciousness. Weeds blocked his vision and his face lay on a thistle. He barely felt the touch of the sharp needles. The overwhelming sensation was fire. Each limb, as well as his trunk, sent separate signals to the pain center in his brain. Instead of canceling each other out, they amplified each other. Searing heat flashed up from his middle section as he tried to move his face away from the thistle. The pain caused him to collapse again, pushing the needles back into his cheek. He lay still, trying to hold back the involuntary tremors, hoping it would help the pain subside. It didn't. The fire was accentuated by someone pounding his temple with a tomahawk. With one huge effort, he pushed his head up from the ground and thrust his arm between his face and the thistle, then collapsed again. The needles dug into his arm, but it felt better. It was all he could do to roll over. Only then did he remember to open his eyes.

The light was beginning to fade, though it was still day. All he could see was sky. He tried to focus. There was nothing but the haze of a honey-tinged cloud in his line of sight. He closed his eyes again and remembered the attack, the beating; an involuntary flinch warded off a remembered blow. The pain of the move was as great as if the blow had landed again.

After a moment or two, he rolled over and raised himself to hands and knees. Then to knees alone. No one was around, save a dog with bared teeth twenty yards away. He was in a field, really three vacant lots, between abandoned buildings, perhaps ten yards from the sidewalk. They must have dragged him there after the beating. Or maybe he had crawled. Regardless, he was alive—and glad of it. A flash of hot pain from his kidney made him reconsider.

Pushing one foot under him, then the other, he made it to his feet and staggered to the sidewalk. His newspaper, still folded, was a few feet away. He reached down to check his pockets. One was torn out from his pant leg, the other was turned inside out. His wallet and money clip were gone, as were the notes—including the one with Spangler's name on it. As the thought struck him, Chinsky dropped to his knees. Glass left from some broken Gallo bottle bit

into his flesh. He hardly felt it. The frustration of the
missing note eclipsed all other sensation. Whatever
else happened, he knew it was now essential that he
force himself to his feet and somehow reach Proxy.
There were no other alternatives.

■

  He picked up the phone and dialed. A woman answered. "May I speak to Mr. Snell," he asked.
  "Can I tell him who it is?" The rich southern voice
was more conversational than businesslike. He had all
the information he needed. Snell was home. Spangler
hung up the phone without answering her.

CHAPTER
23

SEVEN TWO-OFFICER TEAMS patrolled the four-square-mile area designated as the Thirteenth Precinct. Many of the cops on the beat felt that the precinct, like a floor in a hotel, should be renumbered. It was an unlucky place. Five cars were assigned to patrol during both the four to midnight and midnight to eight shifts. The extra two cars were part of the "power shift" that patrolled during the high activity period of seven at night to three in the morning.

Officer Ursula Brown, riding shotgun in a power shift blue-and-white DPD scout car, motioned to her partner, Derrick Waters. Fifty yards ahead a white male walked with a slight limp, his left hand pressed against his ribs as if he were in pain. He could be in trouble, or more likely, high. What he couldn't be was left wandering in this neighborhood. White folk were not highly regarded in the Thirteenth. If this guy stayed in their precinct, they were going to handle him one way or the other: now, when things were relatively quiet, or later, after a stat call—later would also mean a run for Taylor Ambulance to the E.R. of Detroit Receiving.

Waters pulled the car over and up on the curb twenty feet in front of Chinsky. As they got out of the car, Waters made a location report to operations. Brown automatically moved her hand to the grip of her holstered service revolver. They approached Chinsky, now standing still, from different directions. A belligerent move and one of them would have the advantage of being behind him. You took no chances in the Thirteenth.

"You okay?" Brown asked.

Chinsky shook his head. "I was mugged."

"You look it." She took his right arm and moved him against the scout car. Waters gave him a quick patdown from the back. He was clean.

A couple of people came out of abandoned-looking buildings to watch the show. Brown opened the rear door of the car and guided him to the seat. "What are you doing walking around in this neighborhood?" she asked.

"I was on my way to catch a bus." He shook his head, as if that were the wrong answer. "I was visiting a friend."

"Where does he live?" He told her. "Where are you from? You live around here?" He didn't. "What's your name?" He told them. "Do you have any identification, a driver's license?" He didn't. They took everything. Waters picked up the microphone and called operations.

"Central, this is seven zero three. We've got a mugging victim, name Chinsky, C-H-I-N-S-K-Y, first name Luke. Not in bad shape. We're going to give him a ride to Receiving. Over."

"Acknowledged, seven zero three," the squawk box responded.

The police car was on St. Antoine, a half block from the emergency room entrance, when the radio crackled, "Seven zero three, this is Central. Advise if victim Chinsky is a doctor."

■

The alcohol bolstered Proxy's courage as he rang the bell to the Snell residence. Sarah, Snell's house-maid, opened the door and let him in. "Good to see you again, Mr. Proxy." He had always been a favorite of hers. "Don't you look handsome in your brown suit. It go so well with your color. I'll tell Mr. Snell you're here. He'll be glad to see you; Mrs. Snell is over at the hospital, so he don't have no company." As usual, Sarah put up a barrage of conversation. He learned more about the Snell family affairs from her than he did from the family. "You won't be able to stay long, though. Mr. Snell has an interview with a reporter in a little while." Through the chatter, she guided him to Snell's study.

She knocked and opened the door with one fluid motion. Proxy hadn't said a single word between the time he rang the bell and his greeting to Snell, and Sarah almost preempted that. "Look who's here, Mr. Snell. It's Mr. Proxy. I'll set an extra plate and you can have some company for dinner."

"Whoa, Sarah," Proxy said. "I don't think so. I won't be staying long. After I'm done I'm not sure Mr. Snell will want my company." Sarah ignored both the words and the ominous tone. In this household she made decisions about dinner.

"Don't mention it, Mr. Proxy. I'll set the place, and

if you want to stay you can. You don't have to tell me now." The words trailed after her as she exited and closed the door behind her.

Snell looked a bit off his normal dapper self. It was nothing Proxy could put a finger on—perhaps a few hairs out of place, or some wisps of stubble that a razor had missed. Snell was clearly taken aback at Proxy's presence. Instead of a greeting, he asked, "What are you doing here?"

Proxy, knowing that courage lay with attack, shot back, "We need to talk. Now."

Snell seemed distracted, at a loss for words, as if he were under severe stress. "Talk," he commanded.

There was no point in going through elaborate arguments to introduce his position. "This plan of yours is not going to work. The cure must be released. Give it up, Brad," he said in a conciliatory voice.

Snell wheeled and faced Proxy. "Listen. You don't know a goddamned thing about whether it will work or not. There are forces at play here that you are unaware of. They and I will decide whether the plan will work, not you. Do you understand that?" Snell's finger pointing at Proxy's nose punctuated his words.

Proxy was hit full force by the verbal barrage. It was a tone and hardness that he had seen Snell use on others, but rarely on him. He winced at the arrogant authority.

It took a moment for Snell to realize the significance of the information contained in Proxy's words. "Where the hell," he spat out, "did you learn about the cure?" His eyes narrowed. "Who told you?"

"Nobody had to tell me. I read Rathbone's notes. The ones you had me steal."

"Steal? They belong to me. To Croft."

"They belong to the world, not to you—or Croft. What are you trying to do here?" he snapped back.

This was not the way to deal with Snell. "Look, Brad," he said more reasonably, "what's to gain here? Why are you holding back on the cure? If we market it we'll make a fortune. There's more than enough money for everybody." Tentatively, he ventured the fearful thought that had been silently developing in him. "This has something to do with this secret group you belong to, doesn't it? The one that gave us the Priden market."

Snell stared at him as this nugget of information was tossed out. He was being stoned by his own disciple. Proxy, unaware of the effect of his words, hurled more.

"I was stupid enough to think it was our great research and marketing that gave us a monopoly on the high-blood-pressure market. But it wasn't us. It was you and your friends."

Snell, now wary, searching for clues of where Proxy was coming from, said, "Who told you about that?"

"Never mind. I've heard your tapes. I know all about you and Sunito, Wahlbanger, Tofler and all the rest." These were the leading international pharmaceutical corporations named in Murcheson's notes. "I know about Avco's nonsteroid analgesic." The drug had virtually captured the sports market. "And Wahlbanger's nicotine mint. The only reason they have a virtual monopoly is that all of you agreed not to compete." Proxy was breathing hard. "And I know you agreed not to develop an AIDS cure. 'It was decided that a cure or vaccine to bolster the immune system against opportunistic attacks is unacceptable,'" he mimicked the tape scornfully. "Do you people know what the hell you're playing with? Why are you doing this?"

"You listened to my tapes?" Snell asked incredulously. "Where did you get them? You stole them, you despicable little faggot!"

It was a rifle shot to Proxy's ego. Snell, Proxy knew, was capable of business callousness, but this went to the heart of their personal relationship. Snell had never before mentioned his sexual orientation. The venom with which it came out warned Proxy that there was no coming back from this conversation.

"It doesn't matter how I got them. What matters is that I know and others know and you're not going to get away with it. Even if you could, it doesn't make sense. Have you agreed to give the market away, Brad?" There was confusion in his voice. Giving someone else the market was a business decision, not an ethical one. If Snell had made a deal that would give them a payoff without producing and marketing the product, fine. Especially if his major concern, the availability of a cure, were not a factor.

Snell answered with a cynical laugh. "You wish.

"You fags have been praying for something like this to keep you alive, so you can go on corn-holing each other. Well, it's not going to happen. You've lived against the law of nature and God; now you'll pay the price." Snell's voice was taking on a hysterical, preaching quality. "You and the addicts shooting up dope. Now you'll all pay. Not forever. Not until you're all dead. Nooo. Just until there are enough of you dying so that you'll do anything, pay anything for a cure." A hush entered his voice. The words came out barely above a whisper. "Ben, my friend, let me tell you a secret. As much as I hate queers and prostitutes and addicts, I wouldn't hold back a cure just to spite them. Not on your life. This, Ben, is about money. Today a quarter million people are known to be infected. In three years there will be a million infected and in ten, perhaps fifty million." He was messianic, the hand of wrath reaping the harvest of sown seed gone bad. "This thing your people introduced is bigger than the plague. I kneel to that airline steward, Dugas. Don't you see? If we introduce the cure now, there are millions to be made. If we have the discipline to wait a little while, there will be billions." As he said it he majestically, slowly, spread his hands palms upward as if he were giving Proxy the world.

Without warning Snell took a step forward and grasped the blonde's lapels. "It's not too late, Ben. You can give up your filthy habit. Even if you have the disease, I can have the agent prepared. All you have to do is give your word. We've been through a lot. I need someone I can trust."

"Let go of me, Brad." Proxy gripped Snell's arms and with the force of revulsion pushed them away. But Snell's powerful fingers curled tight around the fabric and held on. Snell's eyes were hard; clear, impenetrable varnish coated them. To free himself Proxy balled his fist, ready to send a haymaker to

Snell's head. As he drew back his arm the fist involuntarily relaxed. Conditioned by the behavior of twenty years, he was not yet ready to physically fight his mentor. So he stood there, impotent, while Snell talked in his face.

As much as he hated to hear them, the words frightened him. As the terror of AIDS emerged from an obscure disease to a scourge preying on those with unconventional habits, he had feared it was the fire of Sodom, come to destroy those who violated the values of Judeo-Christian culture. Snell's words reinforced those of the bartender's, and—filled with nonsense as they were—raised the suppressed fear and guilt within him. They robbed him of his ability to fight the irrational rambling, for his thoughts were no more coherent.

"When I saved you, last time, I thought you had learned your lesson." Snell spat his words at Proxy's face. "But you didn't. And now you're afraid to pay for your sins. There is always a price, Ben. There is always a price! Those of us who have lived a clean life," he emphasized the phrase by pacing the delivery of the staccato words, "don't have to pay that price."

Proxy knew the people Snell was talking about were his old-money friends. The board room and country club set, which formed an impenetrable circle. Almost impenetrable. Proxy knew of people in Snell's circle who visited the same spots he did. But that was not the point. It was the image of things that drove Snell. The image that lied about reality. "We don't," his mentor shouted, "shove needles into our bodies or do disgusting things with other men. The only people who have to fear the virus are those who do. And most of them are drug-addicts. It serves them right, too, trying to run the country, to take over without doing any work, just stealing and killing and taking handouts." Even through his fear, Proxy was revolted by the man's ignorance piled on prejudice. Snell, he could see, was moving toward the edge of irrationality. All the hate and bigotry in him poured out—as if it could justify the crime he was perpetrating. Proxy brought his arms up and with one swift thrust found the strength to free himself from Snell's grip.

"Brad," he shouted, "you're pathetic and sick." The disgust in his voice was strong and forceful. "There are people out there dying, little boys, mothers, fathers, good people. People who have never touched dope, who are heterosexual. They're dying too." A bitter snarl distorted the even line of Proxy's sensuous lips, mirroring the distaste of bile that foamed within him at the thought of Snell's words. With pleading compassion he tried to bring Snell back. "But even if they weren't, the people who are dying are human beings. They're people who have committed no sin against humanity. They harm no other human beings. They are gentle, loving people. You may not agree with their lifestyle, or with their addiction, but you have no right to condemn them, us, to die because of your prejudice."

"Ohhh, those are such pretty words, coming from you," Snell sneered. "But I didn't invent AIDS. It was set upon you by a vengeful, wrathful God."

Where did Snell get the moral authority to inter-
pret what justice was for them? Did that, too, come
with country club membership, with private schools,
with silver spoons? The last vestige of loyalty slipped
away from Proxy. "I didn't come here to argue with
you. I've thought it over, and I'm going to release the
virus records. This cure is not going to be suppressed
by you or by anyone else."

"Don't kid yourself, Ben. I don't need you. You'll
never see the inside of Croft again. Those records are
mine and I'll use them as I see fit. Get out of here,
I'm through with you." The voice was contemptuous,
a master talking to an errant slave.

"I don't think you are. You don't have the records, I
do. They're out of Croft, and I'm the only one who
knows where they are. By tomorrow, though, everyone
will know. Then we'll see who's out at Croft."

■

The early evening light was somewhere in between
gray and black. The clouds effectively hid the stars,
yet the moon gave off a soft luminescence.

Snell's street had a rural charm to it during the
day. At night, it disappeared into a cloak of country
darkness. Long ago, in an effort to retain the farmlike
ambiance of the neighborhood, the village council
elected to forgo streetlights. The long-past decision
worked to Spangler's advantage. In spite of the dark,
the Snell house was clearly visible. Interior light
poured softly through a battery of windows and cast
an aura around the building.

The house was separated from its neighbors by

acres of land. There was little need for stealth in the lonely darkness of the outside. Nonetheless, Spangler kept in the shadows of the trees as he worked his way through the grassy terrain. Ten feet from the kitchen windows, outside the circle of light, he stopped and watched. A uniformed, ebony woman, making salad, moved back and forth across the room. After a few minutes, he walked to the penumbra of another window; there was no one in the dining room or in the great room.

The buzz of air-conditioning condensers created white noise, effectively masking the occasional crack of a twig snapping underfoot. Unless someone were intent on finding him, Spangler was as good as invisible.

Staying outside the house's aura, he made his way to the other side. A lighted pool, glowing a warm electric blue, prevented him from moving closer to the living room. It was unnecessary. The open glass walls showed him everything he would have seen on close inspection. The room was empty. The privacy of the house's setting was so pervasive that the Snells had little need to withdraw behind curtains. Spangler was pleased. His work was best done in seclusion.

Spangler shoved a shell into the shotgun, then another. The twin barrels of the 20-gauge Browning B-SS were only twelve inches long. It was Spangler's favorite weapon. The spray of pellets packed into its three-inch shell would fill a small room, tearing pockmarks in anything in their path. He smiled to himself; with a weapon like this you didn't need to be accurate, just close.

Snell, Spangler saw, was in a study in the wing opposite the kitchen. Golden was with him. Thank you, Golden, he thought, for making my job easier. He shifted the shotgun from one hand to the other. His fingers confirmed that the safety was off.

It would be easy to push the shotgun through the window and blast Snell. But there were drawbacks to such a quick solution. If he failed to deliver a killing shot, he would be on the outside, his maneuvering space cut off by walls. Snell and dear Golden would have the advantage of the house. Silently, he moved away from the study.

There were three doors, excluding the pool entry, to the living room. The kitchen seemed the easiest entry.

■

Her arm ached, and she didn't feel like driving. So far, she had explained the sling on her arm as a mishap with a step. The story had enough humor in it that people didn't feel sorry for her. After a polite inquiry, they dropped the subject, which was fine with her. She hailed a cab.

The interview with Snell would be difficult. She knew more than she was supposed to, more than the police. A wrong question could alert him that she and Chinsky were on the same team. The corporate boss was sure to be sharp and quick. He had to be—to have achieved his position in the boardroom jungle. Her interviewing technique would be critical; she had to lead him, without piquing his interest about her relationship with Luke. It was a high-risk game, but still, if she confirmed Luke's theory that Snell actually knew about Van Allen or the cure, it would be worth it. She—Luke—needed confirmation. To get it, she needed a strategy.

It was impossible to make notes with one arm in a sling, especially in the jerky backseat of a cab needing shocks. Every time she started to jot down an interview question, the steno pad would bounce off her lap. When she managed to connect pencil and paper, the writing was barely legible. This wasn't going to work. The taxi driver was unfamiliar with the semirural back roads of posh Bloomfield Hills. It didn't help that the rare street signs used gold letters on a black background, almost impossible to read without a flashlight beam directly cast on it. People around here didn't make it easy for visitors. Brenda had a map, filched from the file room, open on her lap. In the bouncing light of the cab, she tried to trace their location. Reading the arterial pattern of the map while the cab bounced over the curving road was as difficult as the writing had been.

"Why don't you pull over." she said. "I can't read this damned thing." The trip had already taken longer than she planned. A late entry would upset the tone of the interview. The last thing she needed was to be lost.

The cabbie leaned over the back of the seat. "Want me to find it?"

"No. I have it. Look," she said, turning the map so he could see. "We're right here. The house is right around the corner and down one intersection." Her fingers marked the places. He took the map from her hand and turned it to get his orientation.

"Let's go," she said impatiently. "I'm late as it is."

CHAPTER
24

SPANGLER PULLED a nylon stocking over his head. The tight fabric crushed his features into the anonymity of a Cabbage Patch Doll. He tested the knob of the door closest to the kitchen windows. It was locked. He leaned the shotgun against the wall and took a scythe-shaped piece of metal from his pocket. Exerting pressure on the knob, he slipped the thin, curved metal blade around the bolt. With a slight tug, the bolt slid back into its housing and the door opened. Easier than using a key.

He entered the dark mudroom and stood for a moment, letting his eyes adjust. Not too much time, he told himself, or you'll be blind when the light hits you. He moved quickly across the small room to the door on the opposite side. He opened it a crack and let the light contract his pupils. The maid was bending into the refrigerator. Without a sound, he shifted the shotgun to his left hand and drew the silencer-fitted autopistol from its holster. The door gave a small squeal as he eased it open.

Sarah, perhaps alerted by the noise, sensing she was not alone, straightened and turned until she was looking into the bloated cylinder Spangler pointed at her head. Her eyes opened wide. Her mouth followed course, as a scream started its way up from her lungs.

It never found the air.

Spangler squeezed the trigger. The emerging bullet passed gas as it sped from the barrel and into Sarah's open mouth.

She stood for a second, dead but still alive. Her brain was pierced, yet it functioned. The eyes continued to stare at the honey-faced intruder. The mouth still framed a silent scream.

A second puff from the pistol caught her in the left eye and spun her around as she dropped to the floor in a heap. Surprisingly little blood for so large a woman, thought Spangler. He stepped over her, not bothering to confirm her death.

■

The cab stopped at what Brenda believed to be Snell's driveway. It was hard to tell one house from another; there were no lights, other than those from the houses. "Can you point your headlights on the mailbox?" she asked the driver. He put the car in reverse and redirected the beams until they illuminated the large aluminum mailbox with a picture of flying pheasants on it. She couldn't quite make out the name. "Hold on," she said to the cab driver, as she swung the door open to get a better look. A mistake. Her purse, lodged between the seat and the door, tumbled to the ground. The sudden movement threw it open and emptied its contents on the rural road. "Shit!" she muttered under her breath as she tried to retrieve what she could. "Is everything going to go wrong tonight?" The big objects, like her bill-fold, change purse, and compact were easy to find. The lavender and orange painkiller capsules Luke had given her were visible in the dark, but too much trouble to pick up. "The hell with them," she grumbled, and left them in the dirt. Purse back on the seat, she headed for the mailbox. There was no name, but the number was right.

"This is it," she said. "There's the front door." She scooted back in as the driver started to move the cab in the direction of the porch light.

"You want me to wait for you? It's going to be tough getting a taxi out here."

"I'll probably be forty-five minutes to an hour," Brenda said, not wanting to commit herself. If she let him go, it would take an hour to get another cab. If things went badly with Snell, it could be an awkward time. Yet alone, without transportation, she would have an excuse to prolong the interview. Still, she didn't like being stranded, not in control. A recent admonition from Billy about the budget poked its way into her mind. She already owed the driver twenty-three dollars. She leaned over and read his name from the permit. "How much will it cost to wait, James?"

"I'll give you the first half hour free. After that we'll make it a dollar a minute."

"Make it forty-five minutes free and you've got a deal."

He shrugged. "Okay, lady, forty-five minutes." While they were haggling, he had crawled the car up the drive. He stopped in front of the recessed double doors and was gentleman enough to get out and open the door for her.

As she stood in the light of the entryway, she checked her tape recorder one last time. This thing had better work, she thought—writing would be impossible. It worked flawlessly. No excuse not to go in.

Proxy had ignited Snell's rage. Proxy watched the blood rush to his mentor's head as the temples throbbed and skin tightened. His rage seemed uncontainable. Proxy's eyes darted around for a weapon, something that would give him an advantage over the assault he knew was coming. Snell, he was sure, meant to kill him, if he could.

"You slimy, ungrateful bastard," Snell yelled. "You stole my records. You . . ." Snell seemed lost for words; he turned and moved toward his desk. In that instant, Proxy knew his mentor was going for a gun. He sprang to intercept Snell before he could reach it.

Spangler chose that moment to kick open the door of the study. As it swung open, Snell and Proxy both froze and stared at the stocking-faced man and the shotgun he held. It was pointed at them.

■

As Brenda raised the brass knocker on the door, a muffled blast rolled through the house. In the clear night air, she heard the tinkling of shattering glass. The sudden, unexpected noise made her flinch and she involuntarily rammed the knocker against the door with violent force. In counterpoint to the rap of the brass, a second blast shattered the air. The interval between the noises had been accented by what she thought was an agonized scream.

■

The first shower of steel pellets caught Snell full in the face as he leaned over, reaching for the desk drawer. His blood—mixed with bits of skin, muscle, and hair—splattered the fawn-colored suede wallcovering. Several closely spaced pellets entered his mouth and burst through his cheek, leaving a soggy red flap.

Proxy, a yard or so from the eye of the swarming steel, was peppered by the spray. Each tiny pellet tore through a nerve end and sent flashing purple-green pain to his brain. He screamed to relieve the agony and release the devil from his body. Spangler shifted his stance slightly and brought the shortened shotgun to bear on the writhing Proxy. "Sweet dreams, Golden," he said as he pulled the trigger. The second blast turned the blond beard orange.

Spangler broke the shotgun open and quickly ejected and replaced the spent shells. He walked over to Proxy, whose unbelieving eyes still stared at him through a bloody mane. The silenced pistol sent a round boring through the middle of his forehead. His eyes stayed open.

Spangler stepped over Proxy's body to where Snell lay dead behind the desk. With a slight sneer, he put an insurance round into what was left of the Croft president's head.

The insistent rapping of metal on metal jerked him back to the present. Spangler listened intently to

identify the nature and source of the sound. Someone was at the door, knocking. His sneer turned to a
smile.

■

Brenda pounded the brass knocker against its plate
with her good hand. She was sure the sound had been
a human scream and the noises, shots. "Let me in,"
she shouted. She continued the violent, frenzied
pounding without knowing why. A more prudent
course would have been to turn and run. When the
knocker produced no result, she started pounding the
hardwood door with her fist. The thump was muffled
but more physical.

■

Spangler knew why he was there. His job was to kill
Snell. That was done. Now it was time to leave. He
would have enjoyed another kill; the pounding door
offered that opportunity. He resisted the temptation
and jogged back through the kitchen and out the
back door into the night. In the frenzy of her pounding, Brenda cloaked whatever sound he might have
made.

CHAPTER
25

WASHINGTON SAT on the edge of the desk looking down at the seated Chinsky. A blue-brown abrasion highlighted by a yellow halo crept to the researcher's jawline. Part of his beard had been shaved to dress the abrasion. An intern at receiving had taped his ribs before they brought him downtown.

Washington was waiting for him. "Okay, Dr. Chinsky, why don't you tell me all about it, starting with what you know about Dr. Rathbone's death."

Chinsky talked for an hour. The strain of keeping it to himself had been released by the beating. He told them of his suspicion that Rathbone had developed a breakthrough cure for the AIDS virus, about the missing records and his search for them. Washington sent Brady to get Jerzy's confirmation concerning her part in the record recovery. It squared. Chinsky told them about the bugs in his apartment and the midnight call from Duke—the name had been confirmed. He told them about the return to his apartment, the struggle, Brenda's intervention, and the axing of Duke. It was just about the way Washington had figured it. He told them about the panic that overtook him when Proxy called after the killing of Duke and of his need to escape. Washington's jaw moved in rhythm to the nod of his head. Chinsky didn't know if the detective understood or was just encouraging him to keep on talking. He told them about finding Duke's motel key, going there, finding the equipment and the handwritten notes, about the explosion caused by Brenda and his decision to talk to Charlie and Proxy. Brady was sent to pick up Charlie. He told them about the toughs, the beating, and the note, gone with his money.

"You remember the number?" Washington asked. They were the first words he had spoken to Chinsky in an hour.

"It was the Westin Hotel. I called, figuring I might get through. No one answered. I checked the registration. No Spangler."

"How'd you know which room to call?"

"There was an extension on the note. 1028, 1870, or 1078, I can't remember. Anyway, it was a wild guess that he had anything to do with it."

"Son," Washington said patronizingly, "this whole business is putting together wild guesses. What about some of the other numbers—on the other sheets of paper?"

"One was mine, another was Brenda's. I didn't try either of them."

Brady brought Charlie in. Charlie's customary reverence for the doctor evaporated when he saw the battered man sitting by the desk.

"Holy shit, mon, who skinned you? I almost didn't recognize you."

Chinsky just nodded.

"I told you to stay, to call a cab. In Haiti, we say

you play with zombies." Charlie laughed at his little joke. "You find zombies out there?" He was instantly contrite, fearful that he had offended his doctor.

"No zombies, Charlie, just a bunch of punks. They almost killed me. I don't know what they were after."

"They don't need to be after anything. They don't need no reason. I told you not to go out. They beat up on people who don't live here."

"So I learned."

"Take him," Washington said, motioning to Charlie but talking to Brady, "into the conference room and check out the story."

"Your story is checking out pretty well, Doctor," the detective said, turning back to Chinsky. "Hope, for your sake, it continues to. Could make the difference between first degree and self-defense."

"It should. It's the truth."

"Yeah," the detective said noncommittally. "Let's finish up. You really onto a cure for AIDS?"

"Not me, Rathbone. I think he was, but I have no idea what he used. The only lead I haven't followed is that phone call from Proxy."

"Gotta tell ya, Doc," the policeman said, "I got mixed feelings about a cure. If nothing else, the fear of dying's slowed down heroin traffic." He shrugged. "On the other hand, junkies are going crazy with crack and that cheap Colombian coke. Maybe the only ones who get hurt if you don't find a cure are the innocents. That's the way it is, isn't it?"

Chinsky had nothing to add.

The detective's unlikely lapse into reflection was

over as quickly as it had come. "Where's the girl, the reporter?"

"She went to interview Snell at his house."

"Where's he live?"

"In Bloomfield Hills, I think."

"She's a good interviewer. Does her homework. At least she won't get into trouble there."

The desk phone rang and Washington picked it up.

"Washington?" the switchboard operator asked.

"Right."

"I have a patch in for you from your office."

■

Brenda gagged as she recalled the sight of the maid lying on the kitchen floor, blood oozing through a hollow eye. It was taking forever for Sergeant Washington to answer. She wasn't sure she could stand it much longer.

"Washington," he said without inflection. She could picture his stoic face waiting for input.

"This is Brenda Byrne. I'm at Bradley Snell's house," she explained. "I came here to do an interview, but he's dead." It sounded dumb, but those were the facts, "So is another man and a woman." She was on the edge of hysteria. "They shot the woman's eye out." Somehow the vacant eye appalled her more than the bloody slime that sprayed the walls of the study.

"Calm down, Miss Byrne. Anyone there with you?" Washington recognized signs signaling imminent loss of control. He spoke in a strong, yet reassuring, tone.

Brenda had difficulty focusing on the question. He

repeated it, this time with more insistence. "Yes," she said. "The cab driver who drove me here is looking around the building." She noticed her hand trembling and thought it strange.

"I want you both to go sit in the cab and wait for me. I'll be there in twenty minutes. I'll call the Bloomfield police. They'll be there in a couple of minutes. Don't touch anything. Don't go looking for anybody. Just sit in the cab. Understand?" The drill instructor's voice replaced the patient tone of the previous moment. Now that he knew someone was with her, he was less concerned about her acting rashly.

"Yes. I'll find him, and we'll wait for you in the cab."

"Don't bother finding him. Just wait in the cab. He'll find you. You understand?"

"Yes," she said.

"I'm going to hang up now. Remember, I'll be there in twenty minutes." The phone connection clicked closed.

Brenda took a deep breath, shut her eyes and let her head sag back on her shoulders. The moment of quiet helped her regain control. She still had work to do. She dialed another number.

"Yo!" the voice on the other end answered in a parody of Stallone.

"Billy, this is Brenda. Get some paper, I want to dictate a story to you." The words were said without inflection or emotion.

"Hey, Brenda, I'm the ace reporter. I don't—"

"Goddamn it, Billy, don't give me any shit right

now. I've got a story, and I'm in no condition to write it. So will you just shut up and do what I tell you? Get some paper or get your recorder, just tape what I tell you." The force of her words was enough to cut off any argument.

"Okay, kid, okay." Billy got the signal. "Tell me what's happening and I'll put it together."

She described the events and the scene with closed eyes. The images in her brain were vivid enough to allow her to paint word pictures with tight detail. Through it all, she tried to be antiseptic, clinical; it was the only way she knew of getting through it. Then, to give perspective, she told him about Chinsky and the cure. After he had heard her out, Billy put her on hold and called for a photographer. Five seconds later, he was back. He then started to take her over it again.

"Whew." He whistled. "This is something. If this is on the level, you may have a Pulitzer. You're not putting old Billy on, are you?"

"No, Billy." She sighed. "This is on the level."

"Oh, Brenda, baby, I love you! This is going to be some story. Just tell me two things. You have backup on the facts of this cure, don't you?"

"I have backup, sort of. Chinsky has patient records showing clinical improvement in the subjects, but he doesn't have the formula for the cure. That's the piece we're trying to get. The important thing, though, is that there's a way to beat AIDS. We can win this one for the Gipper."

"The patient records, you've seen them?"

"Yes. I have copies at my place."

"Okay. One last thing. About the dead men, are you certain of their identity?"

Brenda knew the problem. The paper didn't want to print an obituary, only to find that the death, like that of Mark Twain, was exaggerated. "Only of one," she said. "Snell. I don't know who the other one is."

"Could it have been a murder-suicide or a murder in self-defense?"

"No way. Both of them were gunned down. You'd have to see it to understand." The memory of the blood set her stomach churning again. She needed to get off the line and out of there. Billy started to take her through the details again. She stopped him short.

"Billy, I've given you enough of the story to get a scoop. Get it out and then get down here. The police will want to grill me and I'm not sure I'm up to it. I need help."

"Okay, kid, just relax. Ernie and I will be over there in a few minutes. Just hold together, you hear?"

"I hear. And Billy, make sure my byline is on that story. You hear?"

James was standing in back of her as she hung up the phone. From his expression, she could tell that his search of the outside had not turned up anything significant. His tough bravado was gone. He stood there with his hat in hand, fingers fidgeting over its brim. He was clearly uncomfortable. Ignoring him, she dialed her apartment. Certainly Luke would be there by now. After ten rings she hung up. Where was he? Bloody images filled her mind and she shuddered. She had to find him.

James was making faces.

"I've called the cops and the paper," she said. "Let's get out of here." A look of relief came over the cabbie's face. Both Washington and Billy would be pissed, but that was their problem. Hers was to get to Chinsky and make sure he was safe.

■

The first cars called by Sergeant Calvin Washington arrived in twelve minutes—one and a half minutes after the reporter left. Washington, with Chinsky in tow, made it twenty-seven minutes later, almost a record from downtown.

There was nothing subtle about his arrival. The flashing red, white, and blue lights of his entourage marked the Snell house as a place for a crowd to gather. Within minutes, he had surveyed the situation and issued orders to organize the investigation. Chinsky, without a word, stayed at his elbow. They made a circuit of the property without spotting Brenda. As she predicted, Washington was pissed at her absence. Chinsky was concerned.

Yellow ribbons marked the property as off-limits. Portable spotlights made the grounds as bright as a nighttime football field. Technicians arrived and swarmed over the house and grounds like locusts, devouring anything of significance.

Billy arrived just as Washington was completing his first quick inspection of the carnage.

"What're you doing here?" Washington barked at Billy. "Where's that girl reporter of yours who called me?" It was the second question to which he really wanted an answer.

"I thought she was here," Billy answered. "She called me and told me the outline of what happened. I was supposed to meet her here. She told me she called you. You don't think whoever did this took her, do you?"

"Don't know what to think," was Washington's curt answer. Then to his partner he said, "Brady, get this son of a bitch out of here."

"Hold on, Cal," Billy protested. "I've got a right to be here. The public's got a right to know and my reporter gave you the call. Now she may be in trouble. Don't pull this crap on me."

"Sue me," Washington said. He motioned to Brady again. "Get him out of here."

Brady started working Billy out of the house. "Look, Cal," Billy said, giving it one last shot, "Brenda gave me the whole story over the phone and I'm printing it. We can work together on this, and I can tell you what she told me, or you can read it in the morning edition. What do you want to do?"

His point caught Washington's attention. "What'd she tell you?" the detective said, motioning Brady to stop ushering Billy to the door.

"Can Ernie start taking some pictures while we talk?" Washington's eyes grew round in outrage at the suggestion. Before he could erupt, Billy interrupted him. "I need the pictures, and you know Ernie; he stays out of the way. If I know he's taking pictures, I can concentrate on telling you what she said, instead of worrying about getting material. Come on, Cal, you know I need the pictures. Besides, I can help you on this."

Washington, who had a strong suspicion that reporters were close to leeches on the evolutionary scale, was inclined to book Billy as a material witness, but thought better of the impulse.

"Let him go, Brady. Okay, Billy, what'd she tell you?" Washington moved in front of the reporter and stood an intimidating six inches from his face. Billy retreated a step to get his space back.

"She told me Snell, another guy, and a maid had been shot to death. She gave a pretty graphic and gory description of all three. It seems she heard the shots, at least two of them, while she was knocking on the door. Whoever did the shooting made a quick exit, probably through the back door, since she was at the front. She finally got in through the kitchen door; it was open. A cab driver was with her. They looked around the place, and, except for the bodies, it was empty."

"What kind of cab?" Washington asked.

"She didn't say, but we usually use Metropolitan."

Without shifting his stare from Billy, Washington said, "Brady, check out Metropolitan and the other cab companies. Find out who picked up a fare for this location, then put out an alert for the cab."

"Right," acknowledged Brady, as he moved to carry out the instruction.

Instinctively, Washington looked for Chinsky. He was out of sight. "Shit!" he said, then turning back to Billy, put Chinsky out of his mind. "Keep going," he told the reporter.

"Snell worked for Croft. You know Snell, he was the president. Brenda didn't know the other guy. You have their names?" Billy asked, hopeful of enhancing the story.

"Know them both," Washington said, not giving the reporter any information.

"Brenda is more involved in this than I knew. She knew the researcher, Dr. Chinsky. It seems he's onto a cure for AIDS."

The rest of it tracked Chinsky's story.

"She doesn't know who's behind this, but she's convinced it's not Chinsky. The whole reason she was here, tonight, was to see if she could get Snell to implicate himself."

Washington waited. Had Billy finished telling what he knew, or was he holding back to protect the girl? "That it?"

"That's it."

"Your girl's an accessory to murder, Billy. She better get herself a good lawyer."

"No way. You know better than that. She was on a story and has privilege to protect her sources." Washington ignored the protest.

"What else she say?"

"That's pretty much it. We're running what we know in this morning's edition. I expected to meet her here to get the rest of it."

Washington turned to Brady, who had returned. "Get an all-points on that girl reporter. Pick her up on sight. Don't think she's dangerous. Where's Chinsky?"

Brady didn't know. He hadn't seen him for the last five minutes or so.

"Check the area. Find him."

Brady nodded, then said, "Mrs. Snell has returned. She's in the living room. I've got the medical examiner with her, trying to keep her calm. She's in bad shape. You'd better talk to her."

Washington knew it was necessary, but wished he could avoid it. "Stay here," he said to Billy, as he turned and walked toward the living room.

CHAPTER
26

TWO MORE, Chinsky and the reporter. Then it would be finished, the slop cleaned up, and he could leave.

It was messier than he liked. Not exactly true. He had enjoyed the messy parts. More accurately, it was less discreet than the boss liked.

He would miss Golden. The emotion he felt, if it could be called that, was akin to the loss of a favorite jacket: used, worn out, discarded. In the act of discard there's a moment of remembrance—how well it fit, how elegant it looked, how comfortable it felt. But the sadness of the loss is quickly put out of mind with the anticipation of the replacement. It was a part of life. Business.

Now to find Dr. Chinsky and Ms. Byrne. The problem was where to look for them. If they had gone underground he might not be able to find them. That would be unfortunate, but unavoidable. His safety mattered more than risking capture while chasing an elusive target. He had the records, the formula for the cure, and Snell's tapes. Without them Chinsky would be an irritation, but not a threat to the boss. He would give himself until dawn. If the job were not finished by then, he would take what he had and leave. Most likely, though, they were not in hiding—

not both of them. From Proxy's disjointed story, Spangler assumed it was Chinsky who killed Duke. It took strength to drive an ax through a neck like the Dutchman's. The girl was the key. If he were in hiding, she would know where he was. Maybe he was with her. In either case, the place to start was with her.

Spangler turned the wheel sharply and made an eighty-degree turn into a gas station. The open air pay phone was on the opposite side of the lot. He parked his car out of the glow of the overhead light and walked ten feet to the familiar blue phone station. He let the phone ring a dozen times. Then, to make sure he had not misdialed, he called again. Still no answer. Fine, he would wait for her there.

■

"I'm not sure we should leave." James was having second thoughts.

"Neither am I, but I can't stay." It hadn't ended with Van Allen. And, if it were still going on, Luke was in danger. He was out there, somewhere. Where was he? He said he was going to visit the patient, Charlie, then try to get hold of Proxy. Had he? Was he on his way back to her apartment? Was he still with them? Had he gone someplace else?

God, how her arm hurt. She had avoided the painkiller to keep alert. Now she was paying the price.

"Lady, I been thinking," he started. "This is a mistake."

"James," she interrupted brusquely, "I'm in the middle of the biggest story of the year. I don't need

this from you right now. So just do what I tell you."
There was more bluff than reality to what she said. In
fact, her dominant emotion at the moment was fear.
Not for herself, for Luke. There was nothing more she
could do with the story; it was in Billy's hands. Maybe
there was something she could do for Luke. If only
she didn't hurt so much. She thought of the painkillers left on Snell's driveway. Oh, hell, I need one now,
she thought. But first, Luke. "James," she said, "head
south. I'll tell you when to turn."

■

The detective had just sent a hysterical Mrs. Snell
to the comfort of a neighbor. He stood in the plush,
all-white living room. Nothing more he could do.
Dealing with the aftermath of murder was a shit job,
he told himself for the thousandth time. Brady added
to Washington's foul mood when he told him Chinsky, along with the Snells' Lincoln, was gone.

"We have people at Chinsky's?"

"Affirmative. It's sealed, and we have a scout car
on thirty-minute rounds."

"Alert them, and put a couple outside the girl's
house. As soon as she gets there, I want to know
about it. I don't care where I am." Washington sat for
a moment thinking, his jaw undulating. "There's
something wrong with this case," he said. Before they
had picked him up, Chinsky was the odds-on favorite
suspect. "Everybody's story ties in to Chinsky's.
There's no way he could be tagged with the three in
here. We had him while it was going on. Besides, if
you believe Chinsky, there's no motive. As soon as

that goddamned newspaper goes to press, all hell's gonna break loose. Politicos gonna be all over our asses, asking for confirmation. We need Chinsky or that girl, someone to give us answers. I don't want to be sitting here looking like a shithead when the captain calls."

"Did you talk to Billy about killing the story?"

"Yeah. No deal. Take someone bigger than me to squelch it."

Brady didn't have Washington's political sensitivity, but he got to the heart of the matter. "If Chinsky's not behind this, who is?"

Washington shook his head. "Back to square one. Before we had a suspect and a weak motive. Now we have neither. Five dead people, and except for Chinsky's cockamamy story, we have no idea what the hell is going on."

"That's what they pay us to find out," Brady said sardonically.

Washington didn't appreciate the dry humor. "Get the order out on the girl," he said brusquely.

■

The moment he saw the pockmarked bodies, Chinsky knew they were dead. There was still blood on his cuff from trying to find a pulse where none existed. The EMS people had made their check ten minutes earlier, but as a doctor he had an obligation to find life and save it if he could. The isolation of research had dulled the insensitivity to mutilated humans learned in medical school and residency. The pulverized face of Snell and the blond man had flipped his stomach. The surgical penetration of the bullets in the black woman had flipped it back.

Washington had identified the blonde as Ben Proxy. Proxy, his last contact. Proxy, his savior. The man who had the answers. If so, he took them with him. Christ, why didn't I listen to him when he called? He tried to tell me.

And where was Brenda? Why had she run? The thoughts ran together in his head. Snell and Proxy were massacred. Brenda is out there alone. Van Allen is dead. He had assumed Snell, if anyone, had hired the killer. Snell is dead. Proxy said he had the records. Proxy is dead. Where is she? They had tried to kill him once. And her. Would they try again? She would go to her place. Were they waiting for her? Or to his place. Where will she run? Why is she running? She must be in shock. The wound. The trauma of these gruesome deaths. She needed help. His help.

He gunned the Lincoln; the speedometer edged over seventy. His apartment was closer, but to go there would take him away from hers. She could be at either place. If she were in shock, he needed his kit. Was it possible to get into his apartment? Who knew? He was in enough trouble with the police, a little more wouldn't matter in the long run. At Big Beaver Road he took a left and headed east toward his apartment.

■

Spangler got to Brenda's apartment before the police.

A quick case of the building told him it was clear.

Silently he worked his way up the service stairwell and found her apartment. Without a sound he eased the lock open and cracked the door. Inside was nothing but darkness. Using a narrow-beam penlight he moved from room to room, checking corners and blind spots as he went. The apartment was empty.

Sooner or later someone was going to show up: the reporter, Chinsky, or the police. If he was looking for the girl, good bet the police were too. He left the lights off and watched through a partially opened venetian blind. It didn't take long for his guess to materialize. He saw the plainclothesmen park and set up their surveillance. One unmarked car pulled around the back of the building, while the other took up station a quarter block from the front entrance. In a moment, they would be at the door to check if the girl was home. If they had a warrant, the door would come down. It would be better if they found the flat empty.

He eased his way out the back door and took up a position where he could see the corridor yet not be seen. In less than five minutes the rear stairwell door opened. One of the men from the street slipped in. The policeman said something into his walkie-talkie, then waited. In a moment, there was a dull crackle from the receiver. The policeman acknowledged the message, then backed away from the apartment door. Five feet from the door, the plainclothesman drew his weapon and assumed a two-handed firing stance.

Spangler knew the routine. The cop on the front door hammered to see if anyone was home. Anyone trying to bolt through the back would run into this guy. A minute passed. The receiver crackled again. The next move would tell the story.

The plainclothesman slowly moved away from the apartment toward the door through which he had entered. They didn't have a warrant.

Spangler smiled a thin smile. He would get a crack at the girl before they would.

■

Chinsky drove around the block twice, noting the cars parked near the entrances to his building. Nothing moved. He did a figure eight and brought the Lincoln to the underground garage from the opposite direction. Parking the car, he moved in the direction opposite the elevators. Then he sat, waiting to see if anything moved.

Nothing did.

Carefully, staying in the shadows next to the wall of the underground, he made his way back to the elevator. The pass card opened the door to the elevator and he stood on the side of the door until he was sure the car was empty. Satisfied that it was, he slid in and pushed the button for the floor above his. His luck held, no one was in the hall. He walked down one flight of stairs to his floor. Cautiously, he pried the stairwell door open a crack, then more. Again, there was no one in the corridor.

The doors to his apartment were posted with official-looking notices cautioning that the property was sealed by order of the police department. Two bands of yellow tape were stretched from jamb to jamb. Along the side of the door closest to the lock a fluorescent orange-red plastic sticker printed in bold white letters formed the official seal.

SEAL

DO NOT BREAK

The seal had been neatly sliced, as if by a razor. Unless you looked, the cut was hard to see. Someone had entered the apartment. Not the police. They were the ones who posted the seal, they could seal it again. Indecision gripped him. Was someone still in there? Turn. Run. Get away, reason screamed. If someone were in there, he was a link to the cure. Rathbone was dead. Van Allen was dead. Proxy was dead. Snell was dead. All the links in the chain were broken. Too many people had died searching for this cure.

He tried his key in the kitchen door.

It worked. He opened the door cautiously, praying it wouldn't squeak, or let in too much light, giving him away to whoever was in there. If he still was.

The kitchen was dark, no light reflected from the other rooms. He could feel his heart pounding, It was too loud. It would give him away. His breath was becoming heavy, labored. With his mouth open wide to minimize the sound of rushing oxygen, he drew long, slow drafts of air to regain his composure. He had control of his nerves. There was no one here. He must have left. This room, at least, seemed safe enough. Was he in another room? Silently, he edged his way into the dining room. The furniture was still pushed against the wall and the wire noose dangled from the outlet. Nothing had been disturbed from the eerie morning episode. Had it only been this morning? Feeling his way with each step on the carpet, he crept into the living room. It, too, was in disarray. Was the body still there? Involuntarily, he shuddered.

The moonlight was strong enough to cast shadows. The slow progress in the dark had dilated his irises, so the light bathed everything in soft moon glow. The body was gone. Its former location was outlined by tape. The ugly brown bloodstain fanned out from the neck area. Chinsky stepped over the area marked by the tape as if the body were still there. Something ran through his mind about stepping on graves.

■

Spangler gave the policeman enough time to get to the bottom of the building before he entered the stairwell. It was only three flights to the roof. The door was secured by a fire latch. He pushed it open and put a wood scrap between the door and the jamb to prevent it from closing. Slowly, he edged around the perimeter of the roof, careful to stay back far enough to avoid creating a silhouette against the royal blue of the night sky. The officer he had observed in the hallway got into a car parked to one side of the rear entry. Iron fire escapes flanked each side of the building. These were what he was looking for. While the police came up the stairs and elevator—if they came up—he would go down one of these. His escape route secure, Spangler went back down the stairs to Brenda's apartment.

There was nothing left to do but wait.

∎

The bedroom door was ajar. Although now certain that he was alone, Chinsky moved to it with the same silent caution. It was darker in here; less light flowed through the cloaked window. The red signal light on the answering machine blinked eerily, like a neon sign outside the window of a cheap hotel room. The bed and propped-up mirror were as he had left them. Gently, he closed the bedroom door and checked the drapes to make sure they were completely shut. Then he switched on the small bedside lamp. Even at fifty watts, the light was more than his eyes could take. He blinked once, then again. As he did so a slight figure curled in the far corner of the room lifted her red head.

"Brenda?"

"Luke?"

In three steps he was at her side. "It's okay, it's me," he said, holding her down.

"Thank God it's you," she said in a drowsy voice. "I must have fallen asleep. I'm so tired. What time is it? How long have I been here?"

"It's eleven-thirty."

"My arm hurt. I came here to get some painkillers. There were some in your bag." Until then he hadn't noticed his black emergency kit sitting on the bed. "They must have knocked me out."

"What did you take?" he asked, alarmed.

"Propoxyphene, the same as your prescription."

His relief showed on his face. It also explained her drowsiness, especially if she had taken them on an empty stomach. "How did you know which pills to take?"

He could see these were hard questions for her, but he needed the answers to make sure she had not done herself harm.

"You said there were some in your bag and these were the same color as mine," she answered with difficulty.

"How long since you ate?"

She screwed up her face, fighting to remember the answer to the simple question. "This morning, I think."

"How many did you take?"

Again, the answer required concentration. "Two, I think. That's what you said, right?"

"Right. But the ones in my bag are 65 milligrams, twice as strong as those I prescribed. No wonder they knocked you out." Intently, he checked the dilation of her eyes. She was going to be all right. "How's the arm?"

"It feels good. Doesn't bother me at all."

"No wonder," he said again. "You'll be okay. Let's walk you around a little bit." He helped her to her feet. "How do you feel?"

"A little dizzy."

"I'll bet. Let's move around a little." He walked her a few feet in each direction. "You could use something to eat, some milk. I'll get you some." He sat her down on the bed. When he returned, she had slumped over again. He helped her drink the milk and got her on her feet again. Best to keep her talking.

"How did you get in here?"

"I used your card. I gave it to the cab driver, he drove into the garage." Her response was slightly faster, more alert than before. "I don't think anybody saw me. When I got up here, I saw the seal but came in anyway."

"You cut it?"

"Un-huh.

"Luke," she said tentatively, "I did something you need to know about. I'm sorry, but I had to do it."

"Whatever it was, it's okay. Believe me, it's okay. Anything's okay so long as you are."

"I told the newspaper about the cure. About your suspicions. About everything. They're going to print it."

"I know. It's okay. I was with Washington when you called. Your partner, Billy, was at Snell's when we arrived. He told Washington everything you told him. I had already told them."

"What happened to your face? My God, are you all right?"

Using few words, he told her.

"Does it hurt?"

"It did at the time. The biggest blow was to my ego. Nobody ever hit me before."

"Don't feel bad, I've never been shot before, either." She started crying.

"Is the pain coming back?" If it were, it would be a good sign. But it was too soon for the analgesic to wear off.

"No." She shook her head emphatically. "It was horrible. The dead woman. Mr. Snell. The other man. His face—his beard was all bloody. It made me think of you. I was so scared for you." Her body convulsed with the memory. He sat her on the bed. What words could he say to get it out of her mind, to comfort her? There were none. So he said what was on his mind.

"The man was Ben Proxy. The one who said he had the records."

"Oh, no," she said. The swiftness of her response told him she was coming out of the mild overdose.

"He was my last link to the cure," Chinsky said dejectedly.

"What now?" she asked after a while.

"Probably best to check in with Washington. He's probably got the whole force looking for us. I left him without official permission."

"Call him," she said.

He reached for the phone on the bedside table. The message light was still blinking. Reflexively, he pressed the playback button.

"Dr. Chinsky," said the voice from the dead, *"this is Ben Proxy. I tried to talk to you earlier, but you hung up. I went to your apartment this morning and saw the body. I don't know who it was, but I understand why you couldn't—wouldn't—talk. I just wanted you to know that I really have Dr. Rathbone's records. Please trust me,"* the voice pleaded. *"I've left them with my friend Horst. You can trust him too. It's very important that you get the records."* The anxious emotion in the voice demanded belief. *"Please call him. He'll deliver them to you. His number is 555-3000, extension 1087. Please, Dr. Chinsky, this is important. Tomorrow, after*

you have the records, you can call me. Please, Dr. Chin-sky." He left his own number and hung up. Chinsky, dazed, pressed the SAVE button.

"Oh, my God!" Brenda said. "It must have been the last thing he did before he went to Snell's." The memory of the bloody blond face made her shudder again. She closed her eyes to blink it away. "Thank God for that," she said regaining her composure. "The records are safe. Poor Proxy did that for us."

Chinsky sat staring at the phone, not saying anything. He half believed the voice. He was now certain that Proxy's voice was the same one that had called him at Croft. Proxy was the elusive Knowles. Knowles had taken and returned the records. Proxy had taken and returned the records. And he had held some back. Now he was offering them up. Almost. It was another trap. He had been through so many, like a rat escaping the lethal snap of the steel spring. *"Trust me,"* Proxy had pleaded. *"Please,"* he had implored. The man was lying. If he were lying, why was he dead, shotgunned in the face? Brenda was staring at him, waiting for a response. *Poor Proxy did that for us*, she had said.

"Not quite," he said flatly. "The note with Spangler's number on it was stolen when I was mugged. I couldn't remember the room number until Proxy said it. The phone number is the Westin Hotel. The one the killer, Duke, wrote down. He wrote Spangler's name too. Horst's room at the Westin is the same as Spangler's." He looked at her, pained, knowing he must play the last act to this tragedy. "Horst is Spangler," he said. "Proxy is connected to Spangler, who is connected to Duke. Proxy and Duke are dead." He didn't want to say it. He didn't want it to be true, but he knew it was. "Spangler must have killed Proxy and Snell. And he has the records."

■

A uniformed policeman, new to the force, interrupted Washington in mid-sentence. The detective turned on him with a cool stare. "Boy," he said, "don't ever interrupt me when I'm talking to someone."

"Sorry, Sergeant," the rookie said apologetically, "they said to get you right away. There's a patch on your car phone. A doctor named Chinsky."

Washington made an abrupt about-face and moved to his car.

"This is Washington," he said, keying in the hands-free speaker.

"I'm at my apartment," said a voice he recognized as Chinsky's. "Brenda Byrne is with me." Washington gave the nearby Brady a look that said, How the hell did they get in there without my knowing it? Brady shrugged his shoulders. Chinsky, unaware of the byplay, continued. "When I got here, I checked my answering machine." He told Washington about most of Proxy's call.

"And?" the detective asked.

"And I think he's telling the truth. I recognized Proxy's voice. He's the same man who called himself Knowles, the security guard who said he took the records. I think Proxy gave Horst the records before he went to Snell's."

"So call this Horst," Washington said impatiently.

"I think I know who Horst is. I'm not sure I want to call him."

"Why not?"

"I told you about the notes I took from Van Allen, the ones from his motel room. The ones the muggers stole. I couldn't remember Spangler's extension at the Westin at first, but it was the same one Proxy gave me."

"You sure?"

"Positive."

"What was it?"

The speaker was silent for a moment.

"I want to be there when you go in. I'll meet you at the Westin."

"Goddamn it, Chinsky!" Washington exploded. "This is police business. You do what you're told." Putting his hand over the mike, he turned to Brady. "You put people on Chinsky's place?"

"Affirmative," Brady answered.

"Chew some ass. Somehow both Chinsky and the girl slipped in without their seeing. Then get them upstairs to grab him." Removing his hand from the mike he said, "Chinsky, you stay there. Somebody'll pick you up."

"No, I'm going to the Westin. I called you because I thought you should be there. But I'm going whether you're there or not."

"Chinsky, goddamn it, stay where you are. This is police work. Stay out of it."

"Bull. I want those records. I'm going to get them.

You can help by being there with a warrant that will get me into that room."

"Can't get a warrant in half an hour."

"Then get something, I'm heading downtown."

"Back off, Chinsky. Bust down a door and I'll book you on a B & E, in addition to second-degree murder. Got it? Now, shut your mouth and listen. Before I can even apply for a warrant I need two things I don't have. Want a warrant? Want the records? Cooperate. Understood?" The longer he kept them on the line, the better chance his men would have of stopping him.

"What do you need?" The question sliced with an edge of hostility.

"A place, and a reasonable cause to believe the object is at that place."

"I already gave you that."

"Did you? What's the room number?

"You'll get that when I see you at the Westin."

"Shit. Chinsky, I'll have your ass for this."

"Fine. But when you go in for Spangler, I go in for the records. What else do you need?"

Washington shook his head. The normal rhythm of his jaw was frozen by the pressure of his clenched teeth. "For probable cause," he said with more than a little venom, "I need either a copy of that tape or an affidavit from you affirming that you listened to a voice you recognized as Proxy's, giving you information concerning priceless stolen records."

"I'll bring the tape with me."

"I need it now."

"No way. I can't get it to you. Besides, it has the room number on it. I'll give it to you at the Westin."

"Shit," the detective said again. "Okay. You win. My men are on the way up to your apartment. They'll take you downtown."

"If they try to take the tape I'll magnetize it," Chinsky warned.

Washington kicked the side of the patrol car. Goddamned civilians. "Chinsky," he said evenly when he regained his composure, "Blank that tape and I'll book you for destroying evidence in a capital crime. Think about that."

"I've thought about it. Your men make one move to the tape and it goes. Believe me on this one, Washington."

"Okay, Chinsky. Okay. I believe you. You win. Let's do it your way. I've got no more time to argue with you. I'm gonna have Brady draft a warrant and take it over to recorder's court. I've got a few details to work out, since Detroit's not in my jurisdiction," he said sarcastically. "But don't you worry your civilian head about that little technicality. By the time Brady gets to the judge, you'll be downtown. Bring the tape. Meet you there and we'll pick up on this, understood?"

"Understood," said Chinsky with a tad more deference.

"One last thing." The detective paused to add emphasis. When he spoke it was with slow, measured words. "Now, listen hard. You may be absolutely right about those records. They may be there. They may tie everything in a neat little bundle. They may be the key to this case." A pause. "But if you fuck up the way we get our hands on them, we won't be able to use them in court and your little friend may just walk away. So when you decide you're gonna jump in and get ahead of us, just pull back." Another pause. "Got that?"

"I'll wait for you when I get there," was Chinsky's only acknowledgment of the dressing-down.

■

Spangler moved the furniture around so he had an equally good line of fire to either entrance. He had no intention of shooting, but it was smart to be prepared. With the police outside he would forgo the shotgun and rely on the 9mm Intratec. The eight-inch silencer made it a bulky but quiet weapon. The size of the gun was enough to frighten most people into submission, as it had Murcheson. And he intended to frighten the redhead. She would talk, one way or another. Before the night was out he would have Chinsky.

He pulled a chair to the streetside window and adjusted the blind so he could look out. The dull red glow of a cigarette signaled that the plainclothesmen were still in their car. Traffic on the street was minimal. He could wait. Eventually, she would return.

Eventually. Did he have that long? The empty time preyed on his nerves, giving him time to think. Was the wait worth the risk? The risk, when you added it up, was quite small. There was absolutely nothing to tie him to Duke, Murcheson, Snell, or Proxy. Indeed, as far as he could tell, there was no one alive—other than the boss—who knew he was in Detroit. Even if there were, tracking him would be difficult. His trail was littered with aliases and fake ID's. As he had been in the shadow of Snell's house, he was invisible. Even better, if the police were looking for anyone, it would be Chinsky. If there were a risk, it would be caused by relaxed vigilance, letting the cops out there make a move without his knowledge. He shuddered involuntarily. As small as the risk was, the consequence of failure loomed high. He would not allow himself to be taken. He would not be caged, confined like an animal. Death was better. How long could he stay alert? Two, three hours? *No girl in two hours and I'll leave. The boss will be pissed, but he'll have to understand. Anyway, I've got the tapes and the records. They can't do anything without that stuff.* Why not leave now? He would if the cops outside made some sudden, unexpected move. That would be enough of a threat. Until then—or for two hours—he would wait for the girl. Then he would leave. It was a good compromise.

CHAPTER
27

THE CHROME GLASS cylinder of the Westin flanked by its shorter acolytes stood like a priest overseeing a concrete flock. Lacelike ivy cascaded down the cement chancel rails flanking the high altar of commerce that was Renaissance. Chinsky, his plainclothes escort riding shotgun, negotiated the Lincoln up the four-lane entry, through the two story ivy-covered cement surrounding the complex. A sharp left brought him to the covered circular drive of the skyscraper hotel. Two DPD scout cars with lights flashing blocked the entry to the hotel. No sooner had he stopped than a police officer dressed in flak jacket and riot helmet jerked the door open.

"You Dr. Chinsky?" he asked without ceremony.

"Yes. Is Sergeant Washington here?"

"He asked us to detain you until he arrived." The officer moved lower so he could see into the car. "Are you Miss Byrne?"

"I'm Ms. Byrne," Brenda said.

Murphy, the plainclothesman, flashed his badge and received a nod of acknowledgment in return.

"How long do you think it will be before Washington gets here?" Chinsky asked.

"He didn't say."

Four minutes later a plain olive-drab Chevy outfitted with a portable rotating beacon screeched to a stop at the entrance. Washington pelted out. After a brief word with the paramilitary policeman who had quizzed Chinsky, he started toward the Lincoln.

Once there, Washington leaned over and looked into the car. "He give you any trouble, Murphy?" the detective asked, ignoring Chinsky.

"None at all, Cal," Murphy replied. "Drives a little fast, though."

Finally, Washington looked at Chinsky. "Ought to cuff you," he said.

"What for?" Chinsky asked irreverently. "You're here. I'm here. Now, let's get the job done. Did you get a warrant?" Then as an afterthought, "Do you need one?"

Washington gave a derisive snort. "Yeah, I need one. Let's cut the bullshit, Chinsky. What's the room number?"

"I go in with you."

The policeman shook his head in disgust. "Okay. You go in with us. You keep out of the way. Now, the room number?"

"Ten eighty-seven."

Washington yanked the car door open. "Let's go," he said.

Chinsky needed no prompting. Brenda was close on his heels. Only Murphy sat back and watched. Obviously, he had no need to be part of the action.

Before they made it to the rotating door, a well-dressed executive-type stopped them. "I'm the assistant manager here. Can you tell me what's going on?"

"You in charge?" asked Washington.

"Yes, what's the problem? None of these people"—
he gestured to the SWAT team—"will answer my
questions. I have guests here—"

Washington stopped him. "Let's go somewhere we
can talk. Got an office?" the detective asked.

"Yes," the manager said, startled by his brusque
manner.

"Got a fax machine?"

"Not in my office, but my secretary has one."

"Good," the rubber-jawed detective said. "Let's
get to it."

∎

The mobile phone rang in the car.

"Yo!" Brady answered.

"Washington. We're all set. How about you?"

"I talked to DeLove about fifteen minutes ago. He
wasn't too happy about this. Said it better be good.
I'm parked outside his place now."

Judge Edmond DeLove lived in the fashionable
Boston Circle section, just off Woodward. He had
been on the bench of the recorder's court for fourteen years. Before that he ran a successful law practice, specializing in criminal law. Business was brisk.
His four years as assistant United States attorney and
seven in essentially the same position at the state
level gave him an insider's view of the system. On his
initial appointment to the court he had been deemed
"eminently qualified" by the State Bar of Michigan.
It also helped that for eight years running prior to his

appointment he had been the principal fund-raiser for the Wayne County Democratic Party.

"Nothing ventured, nothing gained," said Washington. "You hang up and try this fax thing. Here's the number. I'll call you when I get it." Then, acknowledging the fallibility of technology, he said, "If nothing comes through in five minutes I'll call you back."

The portable fax was the department's newest toy. At budget time there had been a heated argument about the purchase of this machine. Street cops said it was a useless piece of paraphernalia, something to create that most hated of all activities, more paperwork. The street cops wanted the money for bulletproof vests, or corsets, as they were called by the men who wore them. The department accountants, supported by the inside technical staff, said the machines would save money. The original request had been for six machines as a test of their feasibility. The budget compromise was that three were purchased, two of them portable—for field use.

Washington, along with Brady and most of the officers in the major crimes division, was ambivalent. He could see both sides. There were times when he would trade all of the office equipment, all of the computers, all of the copy machines and anything else he could think of, for a corset. At other times, like tonight, he could see the value of the gadgetry.

On a couple of occasions Brady had used the portable phone attached to the fax for stakeouts. It worked pretty well. But he had never used the part of the unit that sent facsimile documents over the airwaves.

He didn't even understand how a portable phone worked without wires, let alone flying documents. But slowly, he was coming into the age of electronics.

The illumination of the map light was just sufficient for Brady to make out the "Procedure for Sending a Facsimile" from the slim manual. He pressed the buttons in sequence and dialed the number. The machine purred and began to consume the affidavit. Washington called. They had it. Brady watched the paper edge out of the machine as the return message came through. It was a perfect copy of the document he had just sent. There was only one technical change that he could see. It was signed by Chinsky.

■

"What's this shit?" Judge DeLove asked. "You want me to authorize a search warrant in the middle of the night on the basis of a photocopy?"

"Actually, your Honor," explained Brady, "it's a facsimile copy. I have the original typed affidavit right here." He showed him the unsigned document. "The only difference between the two is the signature and you can see that the machine date-stamped the copy along the top line." It was true. In little dot-matrix print they could see the identifier of the Westin Hotel along with the date and time.

"Where's the true signed copy?"

"It's with Sergeant Washington at the Westin, your Honor. Dr. Chinsky is there too."

"Is this thing admissible?"

"I believe so, sir. We can produce the original."

"I never authorized anything based on a fax before."

"You can see that Sergeant Washington has signed it and certifies that the signature shown is a true copy of the original signature in his possession."

"That does a hell of a lot of good. Who's going to swear that Washington's signature is true? You see what I mean?"

"Yes, your Honor. I guess you'll just have to take our word for it."

"Shit. This ain't even your jurisdiction. You two hightailed it out to the fancy suburbs—"

Brady interrupted. He had heard the lecture before. Those who could get out, did, abandoning the city, leaving it to rot. If they had any conscience, they would stay behind and help rebuild from the ashes of the '67 riots.

"Yes, sir. But let me point out that the request for search is being made by Sergeant Carmichael, who has jurisdiction."

"Is somebody going to vouch for his signature too?"

"No, sir. You're just going to have to trust us. We have no reason to be anything but straight."

"You can bet on that. If there's anything hokey here, your ass will fry, suburbs or not," he said, signing the warrant.

■

The machine in the manager's secretary's office buzzed, and paper inched down the roll. Washington ripped it off, checked the signature, and handed it to the manager. "Get your keys," he ordered.

■

His legs were cramped—no, more like asleep— from sitting in one position too long. Slowly he stretched them, then stood. His legs had to be ready, couldn't let them get numb. Holding the side of the chair for balance, he shook each leg until feeling returned. It had been an hour and a quarter.

That was the trouble with waiting, your senses dulled. It was one thing for a leg or arm to fall asleep. Another if it were his brain. He walked to the kitchen and poured a glass of water. He popped two 10-mg. amphetamine tablets into his mouth and washed them down. That would hold him. He refilled the glass with water and took it back to his chair. In half an hour his mouth would be dry and he would need to pee—the pills always had that effect on him—but he would be alert.

He settled back again to wait for the girl.

■

The group filled the elevator. Washington had sent teams up both stairwells to cover those routes. Besides Chinsky, the manager, and Byrne, he had Carmichael with his SWAT team.

The manager was incensed. More than a few residents had seen the display of force. He had just gotten occupancy back up to a decent level. He could count on a dozen premature check-outs tomorrow, and if this hit the paper, a 10 percent decline in business for the next few weeks. Thank God for convention traffic. Maybe he would take that job in Columbus, Ohio.

The SWAT team was out of the elevator first. They fanned in both directions searching for alcoves into which to duck. It would be hard to distinguish between these highly trained policemen and a crack military combat team. Outwardly, the only difference was the color of the uniform: black instead of terrain colored. Inwardly, there was no difference at all. The training, attitudes, and lack of emotion were the same. As they moved down the corridor, their eyes flicked, focused, flicked again. Their semi-automatic Colt AR 15A2's focused, flicked, and focused as efficiently as their eyes. At the slightest pulse of danger, or even movement, they were prepared to shoot. But not before they had evaluated the threat and concluded that firing was the appropriate response. The public might want to be protected by these new gladiators, but was reluctant to become their inadvertent victims. So the gladiators trained. Thousands of hours on urban simulation ranges had honed their responses so that they could make instant discriminations between real threats and mere distractions.

Carmichael, in the middle of the loose formation, got a high sign from the point and waved Washington and his entourage out of the elevator. Washington shepherded his group forward, holding them behind the area of potential action. He then signaled Carmichael, who, in turn, gave a sign to the point. The officer, careful not to expose himself to potential gunfire from the doorway, knocked on the door and announced, "Police. Open up." One or two other doors in the hallway opened, but 1087 stayed closed.

Washington, protecting his body with the adjacent wall, slid the plastic key into the electronic slot, then removed it. He eased the L-shaped handle down, and as it reached the end of its arc a SWAT officer gave the door a powerful kick above the keyslot.

The door bounced open without resistance. The chain lock was not fastened; the lights were out. Team members flowed into the small suite, fanning their semiautomatic Colt carbines in wide sweeps. The third man in flicked the light switch. The small sitting room, bedroom, and bath were all empty.

■

Cranshaw hated surveillance duty. It was dull, and to make matters worse, his feet or arms were always falling asleep. He wondered if he had circulatory problems. Maybe he should see a doctor. Chances were he wouldn't; he hated doctors more than he hated surveillance. He pulled out another cigarette and lit it. He knew it was bad procedure to light up in a dark car, but what the hell, he wasn't going to go without a smoke. The only thing that made surveillance bearable was a good partner, someone who could keep up a conversation. Someone who could talk about hunting or sports. The only thing Malek liked to talk about were his kids. Cranshaw didn't have any kids, and he didn't give a damn about Malek's. He wished he had a different partner.

"You shouldn't smoke," Malek said. "Every time you take a drag this whole car lights up. Besides, it's bad for your lungs. It's bad for my lungs. I shouldn't have to eat your smoke."

"So roll down the window," Cranshaw answered. That was another thing; Malek was a whiner. He was always complaining about something. Might as well make the best of it, he thought. "What's up with this broad we're looking for?" he asked, changing the subject.

"You know as much as I do. She's involved with that Rathbone murder out at Croft. Washington wants her, that's enough for me."

A car approached them from behind, and Cranshaw snuffed out his cigarette. It drove by without stopping. That pissed him off. He had wasted another good cigarette. It was another reason he hated this duty. Still, it was better than being a traffic cop.

The radio crackled. "Four sixteen, this is Brady. Any action?"

Cranshaw picked up the handset. "This is four sixteen. Negative. All quiet."

The detective's voice came over the air again. "If anyone enters the building, Washington wants to know about it. Confirm?"

"Confirm," said a bored Cranshaw.

"Five fifty-three, do you monitor? Acknowledge," Brady said.

"Confirm," responded Officer Robinson, from the car on the other side of the building. "Nothing's happening here. A quiet night in Georgia." The last words were sung, rather than spoken.

"That Robinson's a cocky bastard," Cranshaw said

to Malek. "Listen to that quiet night in Georgia bullshit. These kids think they know it all."

"He's okay," said Malek. "And smart. We'll probably both be working for him someday."

Cranshaw grunted. It was going to be a long night.

■

One brown cardboard file box was by the side of
the bed next to two packed, expensive-looking leather
suitcases. Another was in the closet. The file in the
closet had three cassette tapes, some loose papers and
a dozen file folders in it. Washington hefted the one
from behind the bed onto the table next to the window and flipped off the cardboard lid. "Are these
what you're looking for?" he asked, motioning Chinsky over.

The box, seam split down one corner, was filled
with files. Folders were segregated by color: red, blue,
green, yellow, and the plain manila variety. At random, Chinsky pulled a blue file. The top document
looked like a patient chart similar to those at the
clinic. "These are Croft records," Chinsky said off-
handedly. There was no name at the top of the form,
just a familiar six-digit number pattern. It looked re-
markably similar to the numbers on the patient
charts in Brenda's apartment. The rest of the file was
other charts, medication orders, a history, and the
medical record of a patient. He pulled another blue
file. As suspected, there was a similarity in the first
four numbers. He quickly pulled out a red file. No
good. He tried a green. The first four digits were
2212, the same code as the series of patients whose

disease was in remission. "This is it!" he said, unable to control his excitement. He wasn't alone; Brenda, standing next to him, let out a little yelp, then gave him a squeeze.

"Not quite." he corrected himself. "These are only the patient records. I need the notes, the treatment protocols." He pulled a manila folder out of the box. The data here was different, inexpertly typed and handwritten notes. Each was dated. This file was from six months ago. He pulled out the folder nearest the front of the box. The date on the top paper was August tenth, little more than a week old—just before Rathbone's death.

"He knew he had it," the researcher said, quickly scanning the paper, flipping through the pages. "It's an offshoot of some tests on various doses of sulfamethoxazole trimethoprim combinations used in treating certain cancers." He was talking to the room. Although everyone heard, no one understood. "We market the tablets as Bactaxy." Chinsky read a few more pages silently. No one else in the room made a noise. "Here it is," he said, excitement in his voice. "He started a series of trials with virus victims using a glycoprotein derivative paired with vaccinia. Jesus," the researcher said with reverence and awe. "Who would have thought of it, except him? The man was a genius. Glycoprotein isn't even an approved substance, it's experimental." Chinsky turned to Washington. "I need these records. I need to study them." The tone was imperative.

Washington, as usual, was unimpressed. He had his own agenda, and it was not likely to be altered for a mere civilian. Chinsky had identified the records as Croft property. The contents of the file boxes was now evidence, properly attained evidence. There was no way he was going to taint the validity of his catch by letting this smartalec doctor have his way.

"You can look at them at our offices. That's where they'll be," said Washington.

"No. I need to look at them now. I need to compare, to match them with the other data I have."

"No go, Doctor. This is evidence. This is the stuff we came here for. Remember the affidavit you signed? That was the basis for the search warrant."

"I didn't mean for you to confiscate them," Chinsky said with irritation. "What good are they locked up in your vault?"

"They're evidence for a murder trial. Unless you've forgotten, five people are dead, one by your hand. Want to look at them? Do your looking at headquarters."

"What do you lose if I take them for one day?" Chinsky asked reasonably.

"For one thing, you take them, I lose my ability to verify that the records presented in evidence are the same records found here."

"Appoint me as an expert witness and charge me with inspecting, analyzing, and verifying the records. I'll testify to the fact that records taken from here are the same as those I'll return to you. Look, Washington," Chinsky said in a judicious tone, "I've been through hell to get a look at these files. I've been harassed, beaten, and almost killed. My girlfriend"— Brenda gave him a surprised, perhaps disapproving, look—"has a hole in her arm that she got as an admission ticket to that box. I need a look at those records to prove that it's all been worth it. Maybe there's nothing there. Maybe it's a gold mine. I need to get into the records and compare them with the stuff I already have to find out just what it is we've got. Give me that much. Hell, I brought you here."

Washington looked at Chinsky appraisingly, his rubber jaw moving. "Chinsky, I can say this for you. You're good. You know how to jerk tears. But sorry. Before I can release this to you or anyone, I got procedure. Need to tag and catalog the documents. It'll take time. Besides, what's your hurry?"

"For one thing," Chinsky said, in a not unkind parody of Washington, "five people are dead, one by my hand. Their deaths are linked to these records. I don't want to take the chance that something will happen before I get a look at them. Anything important enough to kill five people for is too important to treat casually. Especially if it's what I think it is, the formula for the AIDS cure. I need to verify the notes, and if it is the cure, have copies made of the formula. Christ, Washington, this is what all this has been about. Don't lose it now. For a second thing, you don't know it's evidence until I say it's evidence. All you have right now is a couple of file boxes. I'm the only one who can pull it together for you. If you want to nail this guy, you need me." Washington's eyes hardened at the implied threat, but Chinsky was quick to catch it. "But," the doctor said apologetically, "right now I need you more than you need me. Give me some time, a day, to check out the boxes. I need to know." Chinsky closed his eyes, straining to find words to turn the tide. All that came out was a forced, "Please?"

Brady walked in the door, signed warrant in hand.

"Chinsky," Washington said, "you're a persistent son of a bitch. Have to admit I'm not one of your fans. But so far, 'cept for taking a high-handed road with procedure, you been pretty straight." The detective's jaw made little movements as he searched for words. "And you make good arguments." The detective paused again, collecting his thoughts, trying to find a solution that would satisfy both of them.

"What do you think?" he asked Brady.

Brady, who didn't have a hint of what they were talking about, shrugged.

Washington wasn't really looking for a response; he just needed time to weigh his options. If there was something here, it would go to his credit for helping find it. Good publicity never hurt. His risk was that the doctor would screw up the chain of evidence. That he could not allow.

"Chinsky," he continued, "I'm not as sure as you that these papers are any formula. If they are, I'm not sure I'm anxious to make life easier for the dopers on the street." He held up a stern hand to silence Chinsky's objection. "On the other hand, you may be right. And I can't play God. The job"—a smile stopped the moving jaw—"doesn't pay enough for me to be God, barely enough for me to be a dick. Besides, without you, we wouldn't have the evidence. I owe you that. So, here's my offer." He looked at his watch. "It's quarter of two. You can take the records tonight. Brady here goes along to keep them in his custody while you review them. Tomorrow morning, nine o'clock sharp, he brings them to headquarters for tagging and copying—you can come with him if you want. After that, we'll copy them and you can have a set. Take it or leave it. I've still got a killer to catch."

Brady closed his eyes and shook his head—another all-nighter.

Chinsky said, "I'll take it."

"Good," said Washington. "Where'll you be?"

"At my place," said Brenda, unused to remaining quiet for so long.

■

In the euphoria of the moment, none of the occupants of Detective Brady's car noticed the two men sitting in the unlighted car across from Brenda's apartment. The men in the car, however, noticed them.

"That's the reporter," Malek whispered to Cranshaw.

"Yeah, but she's with Brady," said Cranshaw, as Brady got out of the car. This was not how it was supposed to be. "Why the hell are we sitting out here watching for her, when we've already got a tag on her?"

Malek motioned to Cranshaw. "Get Washington," he said.

"What the hell are we going to tell him?" Cranshaw objected. "That we're watching Brady take her up to her apartment?"

"I don't care how dipsy it sounds, he wants to be called. Get him."

"Shit, man, you get him. I think he's already got this covered with somebody else. They just forgot to pull us off."

As they argued, Brenda, the detective, and Chinsky —hefting the two cardboard boxes—filed into the building.

■

The amphetamines worked their effect. He was alert, and his body was forcing the moisture out of his body.

A dry-lipped Spangler, coming out of the bathroom, missed their arrival.

He checked the police car. It was still there, complacent, unsuspecting, typical of police. He sneered, imagining how they would squirm tomorrow or the next day when they found out he had been there, under their noses, and outfoxed them. He sat down again, the 9mm autopistol on his lap. The cold steel of the barrel forced erotic images into his mind. He wished the girl would hurry up and get home. He still had Chinsky to take care of. Maybe he would get lucky and they would show up here together.

■

Brenda searched through her purse for the key. "I'm hurrying," she said apologetically. "I know those things are heavy, but I can never find my keys. That's the problem with a purse, nothing stays put."

"Don't worry," Chinsky said. "I'm tough."

"Speak for yourself." Brady laughed. His claim to a bad back left Chinsky lugging the load, one box stacked on another. The weight of the paper-filled boxes was arm wrenching. Brady, empty handed, made the boxes seem heavier by saying insensitively, "I just want to get my shoes off and settle down with that drink you promised."

"I found them," Brenda announced and slid the key into the lock.

■

The sound of metal against metal caught Spangler's ear. The low rumble of voices on the other side of the door told him it was not the police. It also told him that if it was the girl, she was not alone. He flicked the safety off with his thumb, checked to see that the weapon was set to single shot, then raised his long pistol to a firing position.

■

"This is Washington," the sergeant said into the radio microphone. "What's up?"

"We just saw a woman we believe to be Brenda Byrne enter the building. She was accompanied by a male and Brady. Can you clarify the situation for us?" Malek's voice crackled over the airwaves.

Washington pressed the transmit button on the microphone. "Affirmative. Brady is securing evidence. Any sign of any other activity?"

"Negative. This is peaceable lane. They roll up the streets at ten."

"Okay. I thought she might get a visitor, but I

guess I was wrong. I'm going to pull one car off. Malek, you go in and tell Brady to call me. I'm still at the Westin."

"Roger," Malek said and switched off.

"I'll tell him," said Cranshaw. "You wait here."

■

As the key released the latch, Brenda pushed the door open. Chinsky, arms slung low holding the two fileboxes, walked through the entry. As he did, Brenda's good arm snaked around the door jamb and her fingers flicked the light switch.

The sunglasses helped but couldn't compensate entirely for the sudden light that filled the room when the girl threw the switch. It was a bad moment, but it would be over quickly. He squinted his eyes, cutting off light, giving his pupils time to contract. The squinting momentarily blurred his vision, but he could see the bulk of a body in the doorway. He aimed for its center.

■

As the room brightened, Chinsky, peering over the box top, saw an unfamiliar man sitting in the window chair looking back at him. The man's hands held a long, black pistol.

It was enough for Chinsky. He had been here before, and he was a fast learner. All he said was "Oh, shit!" It was enough to cause both Brenda and Brady to pop their heads over his shoulders, searching for a peek at the expletive's cause. Realizing his error, he tried to shout them off, but it was too late. Brady's

momentum had pushed Chinsky through the door
and nudged him forward enough to knock him off
balance.

■

"They're in the apartment." Malek radioed the
other car, as he saw the lights go on. "Washington
said he's going to pull one of us."

"Roger," the rear guard acknowledged. "We monitored your last with Washington. Sitting tight."
Malek hung the handset on its hook. He wondered
how much longer they would be out here.

■

Spangler saw Chinsky lunge toward him. His eyes,
recovering rapidly, recognized that the bulk in front
of him could not be the girl. Chinsky's expletive confirmed the instinct. Whoever it was, was coming forward, instead—as he intended—of being frozen with
fright. He had no way of knowing that Chinsky's
movement was the result of Brady's inadvertent push.
Things were moving too rapidly. The light would
alert the stakeout cops. They'd be up here in a minute. Too soon. Time to act. Time to get out. He
squeezed the trigger of the Intratec and it spit out a
9mm round. At this range it was what he called a
stopper.

■

The stopper caught Chinsky squarely in the middle
of the box. The force of the slug was enough to stand
him up and stop his fall forward. Then, connecting

the meaning of the *phffft* noise and the sudden arrest of his momentum, he realized that he had been shot at, and that the box of paper had taken the bullet. "He's got a gun," he shouted. His feet churned as he reinitiated his forward movement, intent on rushing the gunman. A second round hit the stack of paper, then a third. On impact, each slowed him and straightened him up, but his supercharged body overcame the resistance and moved relentlessly toward the window. The six giant steps between him and the killer seemed to take an interminable time. It would be but a second before the pistol would be raised or lowered, its bullets tasting flesh instead of paper. His flesh. He had to get to the gun before that happened.

■

Too late, Spangler recognized that his rounds were being absorbed by the boxes. He would have had time to release another shot at Chinsky's head or legs. He raised the long pistol to land a round in the charging head and squeezed the trigger.

The long barrel was working its way up. The oval of the bore was becoming round. When it was a perfect circle it would be focused between his eyes. Chinsky, in anticipation of the red spit that would flare from the borehole, ducked his head behind the box. The slug grazed the top of his head, shaving hair and perhaps a single layer of skin. Chinsky gave a final pump to his legs and slammed into the gunman with the full momentum of his one hundred and eighty pounds, plus the weight of the boxes of paper. The top box dislodged the gun from Spangler's hand, while the force of the juggernaut bowled the gunman and a delicate, chintz-covered chair over backward.

Chinsky, lying atop the boxes, pinned him to the floor.

Across the room, Brady pushed through the door reaching for his service revolver. Seeing Chinsky ram the gunman, he pointed the barrel toward the ceiling and squeezed off a round. "Police," he shouted. "Stay where you are. Don't move."

Chinsky froze.

■

The crack of Detective Brady's shot landed on ears trained to recognize the sound of a gun discharging. Malek pushed the car door open. Cranshaw, on his way to see Brady, was already at the building entrance. He jerked the front entry door open. Malek turned back to the car and grabbed the handset. "Five fifty-three, this is Malek. There was a shot in the suspect's building. We're going in. Relay to Washington and cover the rear. Confirm."

As soon as he released the push-to-talk button on the handset, Robinson's voice came over the speaker.

"Confirm. You're covered."

■

As he hit the wall, Spangler's right hand groped for the shotgun lying next to the chair. Even though he was pinned by the weight of Chinsky's body, he was mobile enough for his fingers to curl around the double barrel of the weapon and draw it to him. Brady's shot, rather than deterring him, clarified the

situation. It was imperative that he return the fire,
then move. He would not be trapped here. He would
not submit to capture and its corollary, confinement.
Dying was preferable to captivity. But dying was foolish when escape was possible. Move! he commanded
himself. Now!

Muscles straining, he swung the butt of the shotgun in a long arc, which he assumed to be in the path
of Chinsky's head. He was nearly correct. The stock
caught Chinsky on the shoulder with enough force to
knock him back. Like a cat recovering from a fall,
Spangler was out from under Chinsky and on his
haunches. He swung the barrel of the shotgun toward
Brady.

■

Brady moved to get a clear shot at the assailant,
but Chinsky was blocking his way. The killer was fast.
Faster than Chinsky. Faster than Brady. The policeman saw the shotgun hit Chinsky, then the catlike
move that brought the killer to his toes. But Brady, a
desk-jockey, was not quick or callous enough to take
what a street cop would have called immediate protective action. His gun was aimed at Spangler's head,
but the bullets were stayed in the chamber. The instant of indecision proved costly.

■

Spangler's eyes locked onto Brady's. Less than fifteen feet separated them. His shotgun was aimed at
the policeman's midsection. He knew that a pull of
the trigger would splatter his guts over the room. Just

as certainly, the policeman would pull the trigger before the pellets reached him, and his round would take a piece out of Spangler's head. They were at a standoff. The moment seemed eternal. His left hand, hidden from the policeman's view, latched on to Chinsky's hair. A hostage, he reasoned, was at this point as good as a kill.

■

Cranshaw took the stairs two and three at a time. Still, he moved with enough caution to avoid a blindside trap. In less than a minute he was on Brenda's floor. Cautiously, he cracked the stairwell door and peeked out to gauge the situation. He saw the redhead still standing in the doorway, her back to him. Whatever was going on in there, she was no more than an observer, but an observer who blocked his access to the action. He was on her in a step. Grabbing her arm, he jerked her out of the doorway and to the floor. It was not a gentle maneuver.

■

Brenda's movement distracted both Spangler and Brady. But Spangler was more experienced. He shifted his aim slightly to focus on the threat he perceived at the door. The blast from the right barrel of his shotgun sent pellets flying into the hallway. In the same instant, he jerked Chinsky's head up and ducked behind it for protection. Brady never got a shot off. Pellets on the periphery of the blast pattern tore into the right side of his body and he went down like a rag doll.

Cranshaw, sticking close to the floor, thrust his gun in the direction of the shotgun, but held his fire when he saw the gunman's hostage.

Spangler had no such inhibition. He had one objective: escape.

As the gunman fired, Chinsky's arm came up under the shotgun and deflected the blast into the ceiling. In the same movement, he jerked his head free of the killer, leaving a handful of hair behind.

Cranshaw, more experienced than Brady, took advantage of the momentary opening and squeezed off three quick rounds into Spangler's exposed trunk. Spangler straightened like a puppet whose strings had been jerked, then folded as the last shot hit his midriff. The shotgun flew from his hands as his eyes, marveling at the unexpected outcome, grew wide. No words came from his open mouth as he crumpled to the floor.

It was the end of the fight.

As the thick, sulfur-laden air quieted, Chinsky, Brenda, and Cranshaw all experienced the same relief as the tension flowed out of their bodies. Chinsky rushed to Brady. There was lots of blood, but little damage. "You're going to be okay," Chinsky told him.

"Sure," Brady said. "But Washington's going to be pissed. He does the work and I grab the headlines."

"Yeah," Chinsky said, "I know what you mean."

STEPHEN COONTS

❝...A fast-paced graphic thriller...
THE MINOTAUR is red-hot.❞
—Washington Post Book World

☐ 20742-8 **THE MINOTAUR** $5.95

❝COONTS SCORES AGAIN...
AN EXCITING, RAPID READ AND
EXCELLENT ADVENTURE.❞
—Denver Post

☐ 20447-X **FINAL FLIGHT** $5.95